Biography of an Idea

Biography of an Idea

John Maynard Keynes and The General Theory
of Employment, Interest and Money

DAVID FELIX

Transaction Publishers
New Brunswick (U.S.A.) and London (U.K.)

Copyright © 1995 by Transaction Publishers, New Brunswick, New Jersey 08903

This book is printed on acid-free paper that meets the American National Standard for Permanence of Paper for Printed Library Materials.

Library of Congress Catalog Number: 93-39855
ISBN: 1-56000-149-6
Printed in the United States of America

Library of Congress Cataloging-in-Publication Data

Felix, David, 1921–
    Biography of an idea : John Maynard Keynes and The general theory of employment, interest and money / David Felix.
        p. cm.
    Includes bibliographical references and index.
    ISBN 1-56000-149-6
    1. Keynes, John Maynard, 1883–1946.   2. Keynes, John Maynard, 1883–1946. General theory of employment, interest, and money.   3. Economists—Great Britain—Biography.   4. Economics—History—20th century. 5. Economic history—20th century. I. Title.
HB103.K47F44   1994
330.15'6—dc20   93-39855
                                                                        CIP

For Georgette

Contents

Preface

Making their ultimate statement with *The General Theory,* the life and works of John Maynard Keynes constitute an eloquent argument to the effect that, as Clemenceau might have said, economics is too important a business to be left to economists. Keynes was the greatest economist of the twentieth century, but practiced politics and policy-making along with the economics. He entitled one of his volumes of collected essays *Essays in Persuasion.* Although he complained of being relegated to Cassandra's role, no numerator of advice accepted could keep up with the always expanding denominator of Keynesian advice. He was a persuader of world-historical importance.

This book proposes to rescue Keynes from the economists for everyman. It also means to suggest how economics can be inserted into twentieth-century historiography, where it has been too often absent or misunderstood. Ignorance of economics has dulled the meaning of much of the century's history. The inability of historians to view the Great Depression clearly, for example, cripples their account of the total history in which it is embedded. Part of the problem lies in the fact that the economists themselves have failed to produce a sufficiently capacious interpretation. This suggests a difficulty greater than any historian can resolve. In the same sense I would argue that both professions missed much of the meaning of the economic dislocations caused by World War I and the peace arrangements, these latter including German reparations and interallied war debts. That failure has contributed to a failure to comprehend much of interwar history: the dysfunctions in the international economy, the rise of fascism and Nazism and their destruction of constitutional government in Italy and Germany, and the role of the United States in all this. In 1919, exceptionally, Keynes himself began to instruct all who would be instructed on these issues in the acutely comprehensible English of his *Economic Consequences of the Peace.*

If this writer scolds his fellow historians, he can offend economists all the more by intruding upon their territory. As one economist put it to me, he had spent years learning his business: how could I claim to think along with him on the difficult and pervasively mathematical questions of his profession? Yet economics is everyman's business. Every one of us, buying and selling, making economic judgments daily, is a practicing economist. Furthermore, every large economic issue is interpenetrated with noneconomic materials, which must be understood along with the economics. No economic model reproduces the economy accurately because it leaves out the noneconomic factors that are continually conditioning, jostling, and sometimes shattering it. The economist must learn from the historians and the members of the other disciplines as they must learn from him. This suggests that those belonging to any of the relevant disciplines—social scientists, historians, philosophers—can contribute to the comprehension of the great economic issues.

This book has been driven by the irritable desire to understand *what* has happened to us in the twentieth century. Why did a generation have to endure the Great Depression with its discouragement to the point of hopelessness and its war-generating conflicts? Why should so many people desiring nothing so much as to work be unemployed? Keynes's *General Theory* promised the best answers, but it has remained as impenetrable in the popularizing interpretations as it did of itself. One halted helplessly before such mysteries as "liquidity preference" or the "IS-LM diagram" (which is not in it but has been accepted as a key to it) unless, as the instructors bade, one made the leap of faith with them.

The fundamental economic questions nevertheless require no specialized economist's knowledge and technical skill despite the mathematical language of the profession today. While nonmathematical in its reasoning, *The General Theory* is an extremely difficult technical treatise that hurls back the untrained reader. Indeed professional economists of the intellectual caliber of a Frank H. Knight of the Chicago school have complained of its resistance to their best will to understand. Few economists have read it through; I ask how many understand it. Politicians and policymakers have uncomprehendingly carried out its ideas. We live ignorantly in a Keynesian world.

A number of economists, in person or through correspondence, were helpful in guiding me during the earlier stages of my research and writing. I would like to thank Richard D. Bartel, Alan S. Blinder, Walter Block, Paul Davidson, the late Dudley Dillard, Richard Jackman, Hyman P.

Minsky, Donald E. Moggridge, John Muellbauer, Guy Routh, Paul A. Samuelson, Gordon Tulloch, and Stanislaw Wellisz. I specify "the earlier stages" to emphasize their innocence of any responsibility for interpretations that they may define as crimes or at least misdemeanors committed upon the body of economic science. As in the case of my last book, George J. Lankevich, my colleague and friend, enduringly read all of the manuscript as it emerged and contributed an exacting historian's and editor's judgment. Georgette Byk Felix, wife and editor, was essential as both.

These institutions were major resources in my research: the New York Public Library, the libraries of the City University of New York and Columbia University, and, in England, the Public Record Office, the Beaverbrook Library, and the library of the London School of Economics. The prime source, it should be mentioned here, was the Royal Economic Society's splendid, thirty-volume edition of Keynes's *Collected Writings,* permission to quote from it having been granted by Macmillan Ltd. I am also grateful for financial assistance in the form of grants from the City University of New York and a senior fellowship award from the National Endowment for the Humanities.

I am grateful to the Royal Economic Society for permission to use extracts and reproduce two diagrams from *The Collected Writings of John Maynard Keynes.* Reproductions of the two diagrams and others conceived by me are by Lynn E. Yost, Editorial Design Consultant.

Introduction: The Idea as Hero

The point of the book—this joint enterprise of writer and reader—is to arrive at an understanding of the *idea* of which it is the life story. Bearer of the idea is *The General Theory of Employment, Interest and Money*. Saying this is not to specify the exact relationship of book and idea. *The General Theory*'s overt purpose had been to construct the model of Keynes's General Theory, his pure abstraction of the essential workings of the modern, free-enterprise economy. We are not, however, to assume that the abstraction is the idea. Just as Keynes was more than an economist, *The General Theory* is more than an economic model; and philosophy, social philosophy, politics and political science, and supportive obiter dicta from history enter vitally into the economics.

To arrive at Keynes's idea one begins with the man. John Maynard Keynes was the son of John Neville Keynes, a Cambridge University economist and logician. Suggestions of the ultimate John Maynard appear very early, thus the child absorbing some sense of the matter at issue as his father and a fellow scholar discussed revisions in John Neville's classic treatise on logic. As an Etonian the boy plunged interestedly into his studies, demonstrating his skills in a range of subjects from mathematics to Latin poetry, while impressing even unstudious scions of the aristocracy and becoming a leader as well as the top student of his class. Beginning at Eton, John Maynard, like his father (who became the chief administrator of the university), had enough time to join too many committees and do most of their work. At Cambridge the undergraduate Keynes was a competent mathematician and the prolific author of many papers for the Conversazione Society, a philosophizing, terribly elite secret society. Also, in an afterthought, he became an impressive (to the great Alfred Marshall) one-semester graduate student of economics. He temporarily escaped the constrictions of Cambridge to spend twenty months as a bored but impressively competent junior civil servant in the India Office; he was actually expending most of his en-

1

ergy writing a dissertation on a problem situated in logic and epistemology. And then, not illogically, he returned to Cambridge as a lecturer in economics. In this provisional professional definition of himself young Keynes began as an obedient follower of Marshallian economics, adeptly applying neoclassical theory as given, but his functional pattern remained open-ended. He was moving in a straight line toward his vision of wisdom, which he confidently thought he had glimpsed early on, and power, which he would hold only in moderate magnitude but see himself possessing retroactively and greatly.

Keynes had given himself the task of achieving two disparate goals; wisdom and power are never easily compatible. Inevitably associated with this task were considerable inner tension and compulsive work. When he had first tasted economics, and before veering into the India Office, young Keynes found it, as he wrote a friend, "increasingly satisfactory" and himself "rather good at it" but imagined using it "to manage a railway or organize a trust."[1] He did become chairman of a large insurance company, but wisely limited his management to its investments, while, at the same time, managing his own investments well enough to become wealthy. He had much more on his mind, however, than wielding power and making money for use as an instrument of power. After his return to Cambridge he self-appreciatively told another friend, "Really the most substantial joys I get are from the perception of logical arguments."[2] He paid variously for his presumption. If he was immodestly satisfied with the fruits of his intellection, he was always frustrated in his quest for unqualified power. He could only lay claim to it in a posthumous future. Yet, as the reiterations of this book's chapter headings emphasize, Keynes's genius expressed itself precisely in the conflict or dialectic of idea and act, theory and policy.

Shifting from one foot to the other, Keynes, dexterously for the most part, lived a double or doubled life. If he theorized for his dissertation on India Office time, he used his practical experience there in his early writings, including his first published book, *Indian Currency and Finance* (1913). His early lectures at Cambridge, drawing upon a quickly achieved intimacy with the financial marketplace, concentrated on the pragmatics of applied economics. His scintillating ability created for him an opportunity for war service in an important ad hoc Treasury position as manager of the funds doled out by England to her needier allies. After World War I his comprehension of the political economy of war and peace gave him prophetic vision and set him resoundingly against the government's policy. The book he wrote attacking that policy helped raise him to a position of notorious impotence. He further secured that position on other issues of the interwar period by being similarly and repetitively wrong in effect because right in fact and logic. One will observe him complaining of his Cassandra role and stylishly thrashing the effective policymakers of those years. He would amplify his arguments with the money his other skills gained for him, thus becoming master of *The Nation,* the Liberal journal of opinion, and a leading ideologue of the party; and he would also see the Liberals vanish as a political force.

At the time, Keynes, the man of politics and policy, mostly failed; no matter. He would try to make sense of the monetary economics of the 1920s with an ambitious two-volume treatise; its theory failed, as his friends, and very soon he himself, admitted. No matter. He would, with total success, encompass the grand economic and political issues of the interwar world in his *General Theory.* Overcoming his fastidiousness, Keynes had finally learned to play politics. *The General Theory* was a theory excogitated for specific policy purposes, a political act genially integrated into the politics of its time. In the discussion of it here I find that Keynes necessarily bent theory to fit policy. Yet it was great policy. It remains great and applicable, if appropriately adapted, today. Overrunning the bounds of economics, *The General Theory* as idea triumphs.

Notes

1. Letter to Lytton Strachey, 15 November 1905, quoted in Robert Skidelsky, *John Maynard Keynes,* Vol. 1: *Hopes Betrayed 1883–1920* (New York, 1986), 165.
2. Letter to B. W. Swithinbank, 13 May 1908, quoted in Roy Harrod, *The Life of John Maynard Keynes* (London, 1951), 20.

1

The Theorist as a Young Man

The various fields of competence and interests that made John Maynard Keynes the unique economist that he was developed early. They included a sense of how to attract and command people; and literature, mathematics, pure philosophy, formal logic, argumentation, history, politics—and economics. The economics came early as something in the air at home but late as a discipline. While it would establish order among these scattered elements, his other interests retained their importance for him; and his social philosophy, as his greatest work would show, gave ultimate direction to the economics and everything else. Keynes was still a boy when he began assembling and shaping the parts, the noneconomic ones first, of *The General Theory of Employment, Interest and Money*.[1]

Keynes's parents, and everything about and around them, were very nearly perfect. They had the eminently suitable number of three children. John Maynard, born on 5 June 1883, was the eldest, followed in less than two years by Margaret, and after another two years by Geoffrey. Maynard followed his father into mathematics, logic, and economics. Margaret, who would marry a future Nobel laureate in physiology, became an active social worker following her mother's example. Geoffrey, somewhat distant from parental concerns, became a distinguished surgeon and, in his medical capacity, a vice marshal in the Royal Air Force during World War II. Like Maynard, he developed into a bibliophile and author, publishing critically recognized editions and bibliographies of the works of William Blake. John Neville Keynes (1852–1949), as lecturer at Cambridge University, wrote *Studies and Exercises in Formal Logic* and *The Scope and Method of Political Economy*, first published in 1884 and 1891, respectively, both reprinted several times as standard treatises on the subjects, impeccable guides to impeccable reasoning in general and in economics. Roy Harrod, John Maynard's first biographer, has recommended "diligent study of the logical writings" of father and son "to explain characteristic tendencies (even perversities!) in the economic writings of Maynard."[2] From 1910 to 1925 John Neville was registrary, chief administrator, of Cambridge University.

Honoring John Neville's ninetieth birthday and his parents' diamond wedding anniversary, John Maynard could celebrate his father: "He was one of the best administrators there ever was, and...this university was a better place, in my judgment, than it has ever been before or since." Lovingly, literarily, and patronizingly, John Maynard painted John Neville: "Elegant, mid-Victorian, highbrow, reading Swinburne, Meredith, Ibsen, buying William Morris wallpaper, whiskers, modest and industrious, but rather rich, rather pleasure-loving, rather extravagant within carefully set limits...loved entertaining, wine, games, novels, theater, travel, but...the withdrawal, gradual, very gradual, to his dear wife and the bosom of his family."[3] Permitting this rather rich ease, John Neville as a young don enjoyed a combined earned and unearned annual income of £1,000, of which he could save £400.[4]

Florence Ada (1861–1958) was the perfect wife for John Neville, if he, perhaps, was not quite so perfect for her. The daughter of a scholarly Congregationalist divine who wrote a popular biography of John Bunyan, she was one of the first students at the women's college of Newnham, at Cambridge. As her children grew she began to operate efficiently and charitably outside the home. In 1895 she became secretary of the Charity Organization Society and went on, beyond that, to help establish an employment agency for juveniles and a residence for tuberculosis sufferers. In 1911 she was the first woman elected to the Cambridge Council and, in 1932, the first to become mayor. While John Neville was withdrawing from the world, she was going further afield in it, helping to found the National Union of Women Workers, which she chaired, while also becoming president of the National Council of Women.[5]

As a child John Maynard alternated in closeness to either parent. As a university student, civil servant, and young don he consulted closely with his father, but presently found his mother a more responsive correspondent on the great issues of the times.[6] Maynard grew up in the solid, undistinguished comfort of a substantial Victorian home at 6 Harvey Road, one of a number of similar residences freshly built in Cambridge for young dons like John Neville. Maynard, all his life, could build his confidence upon the security provided there. Like his brother and sister, he never stopped coming to share the family roast on Sunday.

In that cultivated academic home the very young Maynard was sensitized early to the form and content of disciplined thought. In the early 1890s, as he remembered years later, Neville was revising *Formal Logic* for its second edition and discussing the changes over weekly lunch with W. E. Johnson, the Cambridge logician and economist.[7] The first book the younger Keynes wrote was the *Treatise on Probability*, an exercise in logic.[8] Other guests in the Keynes home included the philosopher Henry Sidgwick, then a leader in Cambridge's life of the mind, and, of course, several economists, Alfred Marshall particularly. Maynard was "ready from an early age to join in learned discussions."[9]

Intermittently handicapped by vulnerable health, Maynard became a star student. At Eton from the ages of fourteen to nineteen, with his father functioning as trainer by mail, he won heaps of prizes in subjects ranging from mathematics to classics, and graduated first in his class.[10] He worked compulsively but easily and found time to join committees and, like his father, do "all the work" on them, as he boastfully complained to John Neville.[11] The exemplar of the scholarship boy, Maynard could still gain the respect of the nonscholarship and nonintellectual aristocratic and well-to-do boys, and become a member of Eton's most exclusive social club. Yet he had been independent-minded enough to resist the jingoist spirit during the Boer War without, however, being pro-Boer. In the school's homoerotic ambiance Maynard launched himself into homosexual relationships that would dominate his emotional life for more than a score of years.[12]

At Cambridge University, which Maynard naturally entered, the Eton pattern of work and play continued on the level appropriate to his approach to majority.[13] He concentrated on mathematics, but found it confining and insufficiently promising: he was realizing, while pleasantly discovering new areas to explore, that his talent for it was more limited than his ambition. Upon graduation he could win a respectable, but disappointing, twelfth place on the list of first-class honors, precisely as he had predicted. Developing his varied skills, he had joined various discussion groups and wrote many papers for them; he also joined the university's debating society, the Cambridge Union, where he rose to the positions of secretary and president. His predecessor as president was Edwin Montagu, scion of a prosperous and political Jewish family, who "became Keynes's first and most important political patron."[14] A cool and crushingly logical debater, Maynard had won Montagu's attention with his maiden speech. In due time Maynard also became president of the university's Liberal Club. This might have suggested politics as a career, and, in 1904, he was sufficiently interested in the subject to write a ninety-nine-page prize essay on the politics of Edmund Burke. He would enter active political campaigning in the elections of January 1906 and January and December 1910, speaking for Edwin Montagu, among others. During the first election of 1910 Maynard wrote a friend, "Life without a howling audience to address every evening will seem very dull." The next year he joined fifty Liberal members of Parliament touring Ireland, and having "mixed with politicians at close quarters," told another friend that he found them "awful.... Their stupidity is inhuman."[15] Such fastidiousness—and arrogance—severely limited his capacity for politics as politicians played it. The Burke essay remained the best indicator of what he could bring to it.

At the university in early 1903, meanwhile, after a preliminary inspection the past December, Maynard's person had so presented itself that, exceptionally for a first-year man, he was inducted into the Cambridge Conversazione Society, *the* Society for short. Its members were known, reflecting its mock-religious character, as the Apostles.[16] The Society became the center of Maynard's social and private life for the next half-dozen years. The order of business was the discussion of a paper by one of the members, often enough the prolific Maynard, on Saturday evenings. Subject matter was ethical and metaphysical speculation about the state of their souls and feelings. Lively relations did not end with graduation; risen to the rank of Angels, senior members, some of them becoming dons *in situ* and others no further distant than in London, continued to attend meetings and present papers. The Society had a distinguished membership that began with Alfred Tennyson and, more recently, included Bertrand Russell and Russell's erstwhile collaborator, A. N. Whitehead, the novelist E. M. Forster, and the Soviet spies Guy Burgess and Anthony Blunt. In Maynard's time the secretary was Lytton Strachey, the future popular biographer. Pursuant to his own inclinations, Lytton was convinced, on the basis of a purposeful study of its history, that many of the earlier members had been repressed homosexuals, and campaigned for greater sexual frankness and freedom. He found an able deputy in Maynard, who became his best friend and occasional lover.

Many of the Apostles, Maynard markedly, were profoundly affected by the publication, in the fall of 1903, of *Principia Ethica* by the Angel and resident saint G. E. Moore. While carrying out a revolution against late nineteenth-century idealism in the name of empiricism, the book expressed itself in neo-Platonic abstractions purer even than those of idealism. Moore's powerful sincerity, derived from his lost post-Puritan faith, gave him the "accents of infallibility," Maynard remembered instructively.[17] As digestible as strawberries and cream, Moore's philosophy replaced religion and resolved the Apostles' ethical problems. While still an undergraduate and developing his own accents of infallibility, Maynard began to erect upon the *Principia Ethica*'s base the most important theorizing of his life.

Upon obtaining his degree in June 1905 Maynard was uncharacteristically uncertain about what to do next. One course would be to take another examination and so improve his less than extraordinary record; the field would be either moral science or economics. And so he discovered economics as an undefined possibility and, as it turned out, enlightenment. Before the end of June he was "working assiduously," his father noted, "at Marshall's *Principles of Economics*."[18] Almost immediately Maynard told Lytton that he found Stanley Jevons "exciting," indeed "thrilling," reading. In the fall Maynard attended Marshall's lectures and wrote papers under his supervision, whereupon the great man began insistently to urge him to turn "professional economist."[19] At the time Maynard was reluctant to stay in Cambridge, interpreting such a fate as burial, and, encouraged by Lytton, who had reestablished himself in London, decided to take the civil service examination. He spent the first half of 1906 cramming efficiently, but that did not prevent his campaigning for Edwin Montagu in the winter and taking a month's Continental holiday in the spring. Maynard won second place among 104 applicants. This meant, however, that he had missed the first-choice Treasury post and had to settle for the India Office. Doubtless feeling that this was not definitive, he kept other possibilities in mind. After taking the examination he had gone on another holiday and commenced working on probability, a subject suggested by Moore's *Principia,* for a fellowship dissertation. The tie to Cambridge had reasserted itself.[20]

From 1906 to 1914, while defining himself publicly as a brilliant civil servant, don, and applied economist, Maynard was privately a serious theorist of logic and epistemology. The dissertation would be expanded into a sizable book, a virtuoso performance, to be published after the wartime interruption.

Maynard was an India Office clerk for twenty months.[21] The work almost immediately bored him, although he found secondary gratifications, while his ability to write pellucid, practical memoranda and complete his assignments swiftly won his superiors' appreciation and respect. He also had plenty of time to pursue his dissertation, which provided him with the intellectual challenge a subordinate role in a government office could not. The sum of these effects meant reentry into Cambridge in the best possible way. Although, consistent with his dissertation topic and his training in mathematics, he spoke of logic and statistical theory as his fields of interest, he would find it practical to fold them into economics, which providentially produced a demand for his services. In June 1908, on Marshall's initiative, Maynard was invited back to Cambridge as an economics lecturer on the basis of his eight weeks of study and the few research papers he had written. The appointment brushed past the fact that Maynard's dissertation had failed, in March of that year, to win a fellowship attaching him to King's College, but the reports on it suggested that he would succeed, as indeed he did, on the second submission the following March, when already installed as lecturer.

In London, meanwhile, Maynard, following Lytton, had become a member of the Bloomsbury group, which went back to 1905.[22] Bloomsbury is a characterless, formerly fashionable region of London near the British Museum. The four Stephen siblings, who had settled there in the fall of 1904, were the nucleus of the group; the world beyond knows two of them as the painter Vanessa Bell and the novelist Virginia Woolf. Aesthetic and literary in culture on the model of Vanessa and Virginia, Bloomsbury became a force for enlightenment and liberation in life and, specifically, sexuality. Maynard, yearning toward the aesthetic, had found another extended family to warm a needy heart and deepen his ambition, originally imperceptible, to improve the world. A two-year affair with the painter Duncan Grant, which began at the end of his India Office period and thereafter became a lifelong friendship, further strengthened the familial fabric.

Delayed by an attack of influenza, Maynard settled into rooms in King's College in late November 1908 and began lecturing in January. He was already launched as a writer on economics and related fields, having in 1908 placed an article in a statistical journal and two notes in the *Economic Journal*. In December, while preparing his lectures, he wrote the major article, "Recent Economic Events in India," which appeared in the *Economic Journal* in March 1909.[23] Despite his thin formal background in economics he was an immediate, absolute success as an economics lecturer as well as a writer.[24]

Maynard moved into his new life with a characteristically rich burst of experimental ideas rising out of his established competences and his confident ambition. By early 1909, according to newly discovered material, he had dashed off outlines of eight papers, two monographs, two treatises, and two textbooks. (The discovery also turned up outlines of six book projects, to be addressed here later, from the 1920s and 1930s.) Subjects of the papers included such technical matters as the Indian gold standard reserve and index numbers, but extended to a speculation on "The 'Long Run' in Economics." While one of the monographs also addressed index numbers, the other, entitled "The Theory of Crises and Commercial Fluctuations," signaled another long-run Keynesian preoccupation. The treatises were "The Principles of Probability" and "Methods of Statistics," and the textbooks, "The Principles of Money" and "Mathematical Organon of Economics."[25] If Keynes never wrote any of these, he pursued and, indeed, went beyond their suggestions variously in his published work.

At Cambridge Maynard advanced on plural lines. Within a year his father was recording that "there wasn't even standing room" at Maynard's lectures on the Stock Exchange and the Money Market.[26] In the years 1909–14 young Keynes taught ten different courses, most of them in monetary economics but also the Principles of Economics, this last the responsibility of Arthur C. Pigou—"the Prof."—department head as Marshall's successor. While experimenting with radical formulations in probability and occasionally peering beyond the horizon of conventional economics, Keynes taught economics according to Marshall. In October 1909, less than a year after settling in Cambridge, he organized the Political Economy Club for the abler students. Operating on the model of his various discussion groups; it would provide another channel for the expression of his ideas and the expansion of his influence. His original appointment, which had been informal and temporary, was transformed into an official five-year appointment by December 1910 and further solidified into a permanent position as college lecturer in economics in June 1911. Later in October 1911, Marshall, still a force in retirement, worked Keynes's selection as editor of the *Economic Journal*, which became another element in the young don's burgeoning influence. Although a supervisory board was created in view of his Wunderkind character, he was so secure and decisive in editorial judgment, reading one hundred articles yearly, that he commanded the publication absolutely from the beginning. (This conscientious editorial work helped make up for his limited studies in economics.) In 1913 he became secretary of the Royal Economic Society as well. Continuing his earlier pattern he accepted various committee responsibilities. In 1909, calling upon his practical financial ability, he had become an inspector of accounts at King's College. By 1912, with the provost's support, he was leading a rebellion of the junior fellows against the college's rachitic financial administration. The rebellion worked modest reforms, but positioned Keynes, in that slow-moving institution, for the posts of second bursar in 1919 and first bursar by 1924. With the first appointment he began to achieve a much greater return on the college's capital. If he had easily established himself as the complete don, he was simultaneously bursting beyond that character.

Keynes was as combative as an ambitious knight in all areas open to his increasing expertise. His first item for the *Economic Journal*, following interests developed in a prize essay and his probability dissertation, argued that the Board of Trade was wrong in putting English real wages above Irish real wages. He had deftly switched Irish for English figures as the base of 100, and the figures, assisted by the fact that English rents were indexed at twice those in Ireland, had obediently switched with his mathematical operation. Accused by a statistician of neglecting to change the weights of food and other prices along with the base, he ignored the charge and countered that the man was using arbitrary reasoning. Later, in his career-long campaign for better statistics, he successfully recommended his opponent for appointment as university lecturer in statistics at Cambridge.[27] In 1909, questioning the figures given, Keynes wrote an article and four letters-to-the-editor defending the Indian administration and free trade against protectionist arguments that England was investing too much abroad and specifically in India.[28]

In 1910–11 he debated with Karl Pearson, Britain's leading statistician, who had supported a subordinate's finding that parental alcoholism had no perceptible effect on children. It was a poorly designed study offending common sense as well as the impulsion to reform, but it permitted him to express doubts that could severely limit the use of valid statistical methods.[29] Energetically right or wrong, he soon developed a publicly visible persona.

As his articles and published letters indicated, Keynes was serving the India Office even better since he had left it—and was receiving appropriate compensation.[30] A book review in the *Economic Journal* permitted him to defend the government of India's financial policy against demands for change.[31] Drawing upon Lionel Abrahams, the India Office financial secretary, Keynes gave a series of lectures on Indian finance at the London School of Economics and then at Cambridge. Pursuing these ideas further, he presented a paper on the subject to the Royal Economic Society in May 1911,[32] and further through 1912 into early 1913, to complete his first published book, *Indian Currency and Finance*.[33] In it he described and found secure and eminently practical what he called India's gold *exchange* standard, which operated with currency supported by sterling credits and avoided the general use of gold coins and thus their loss into hoards. Keynes's book redounded to the benefit of the India Office and his career, but the benefit did not stop there. In late 1912 the London *Times,* after carrying articles that criticized the Indian financial administration and responding to suggestions of at least two financial scandals, successfully called for the creation of a commission, early in 1913, to study Indian currency and finance. Keynes's expert knowledge and his agreement with the India Office made him an ideal candidate for the secretary's post. Upon reading the proofs of the book, however, his former superiors recommended that he be elevated to the Royal Commission on Indian Finance and Currency itself.[34]

An aggressive examiner of interested witnesses as commissioner, young Keynes unabashedly reiterated two major theses, the excellence of the present system and, in accord with Financial Secretary Abrahams, the need to improve it with an Indian state bank as its capstone.[35] Exploiting his skills as a memoranda writer, Keynes wrote an annex to the commission's report, on which he had also labored, containing his plan for the bank. Published on 2 March 1914, the report, incidentally helping disperse the scandalous rumors, roundly defended the Indian financial administration. The commission was too divided within itself to recommend creation of the bank, an approximation of which, however, came to pass in 1935.[36] During the drafting of the report toward the end of 1913 Keynes expended perhaps too much of his physical and nervous energy on a minor point of currency issue, bolted for the French Riviera to enjoy a holiday, and suffered a serious case of diphtheria.[37] Meanwhile his book, a masterly exercise in applied economics, had won Alfred Marshall's praise and general respect upon publication on 9 June 1913. It was only natural that he would offer his services to the government when World War I broke out.

Invited to express an expert opinion on Britain's finances at that critical moment, Keynes launched himself toward war service in the Treasury on 2 August 1914, two days before England entered the war.[38] His response was a 5,000-word memorandum recommending that Britain continue to make gold payments, that is, remain on the gold standard. This was in the face of huge obligations, some £350 million in bills of exchange outstanding, and contrary to the advice of the leading bankers. Together with the opinion of Walter Cunliffe, governor of the Bank of England, Keynes's memorandum persuaded Chancellor of the Exchequer Lloyd George.[39] While the banks were short of funds, it was because foreign debtors were temporarily unable to remit payments. It was thus a problem in financial bookkeeping rather than a true financial crisis. The British government could resolve it by printing special Treasury notes and providing financial backing to the embarrassed banks. The services of the ad hoc expert, however, were not required for anything more at the time. Keynes proceeded to demonstrate his continuing usefulness by showering the government and the public with apposite memoranda and articles.[40] On 6 January 1915, he got his Treasury post. Actually he was brought in as assistant to an adviser who was losing Lloyd George's confidence, but, with unerring intuition, he dropped the man and made himself useful elsewhere with his marvelous memoranda and keen committee work.

It remains a question whether remaining on the gold standard made much difference. Great Britain did so with more and more difficulty, as war expenditures caused a true and intensifying crisis, until 1917, and with American aid until 1919. When the aid stopped, Britain dropped away painlessly. In a memorandum of 1939 Keynes argued that the decision to stay with the gold standard prevented worse damage by maintaining the nation's credit, although he had expressed doubts about gold in an *Economic Journal* article of December 1914.[41] Assisting his gold-standard rationale, Keynes, who had a political sense of their effectiveness in the circumstances, used ad hominem arguments that were doubtless as sincere as they were irrelevant and unjust. In an earlier *Economic Journal* article, in September 1914 and in private statements, he asserted that the bankers were cowardly and without a plan of action.[42] A leading banker, pointing to the real threat of bankruptcy and referring to a plan actually submitted, got him to make a partial retraction, at least, in the December article. Keynes excused himself: "But my disappointment...was that of an admirer, my complaints those of a true lover."[43] In his lifetime this was a rare, indeed singular, expression of warmth for banks and bankers.

Keynes very quickly made himself an expert on interallied finance, which was crucial, since Britain was subsidizing its poorer allies. He never got close to Lloyd George, but Lloyd George was moving on to other posts, beginning with the Munitions Ministry in May 1915, and Keynes became a trusted adviser and permanent friend of the new chancellor, Reginald McKenna. He would later gain the trust, if not the friendship, of McKenna's successor. By February 1916, responsible for all questions of external finance, Keynes became head of the new A Division, carved out of the Treasury's No. 1 Division, and eventually comprised a staff of seventeen, not including clerks and messengers. His work also led to his first experience with the United States, when he assisted a special envoy in clearing channels for financial aid—and alienated the Americans with his rudeness.[44] He would learn to charm them when he got over his shock at Britain's humiliating decline in power and wealth relative to America. His only serious problem was the effect of overwork on his indifferent health. After an emergency appendicitis operation in mid-1915 he nearly died of pneumonia, which affected his heart, and in the winter of 1916-17 he endured "three bad attacks" of influenza.[45]

Another problem was conscience complicated by Bloomsbury. While his social activities were simultaneously expanding beyond it into the upper reaches of position and power, Maynard's life was more tightly interwoven into the group with time and his round-the-week London existence. One expression of his developing Bloomsbury character was his establishment, in 1916, at 46 Gordon Square, Bloomsbury's master mansion and original residence of the Stephens. Pacifist and even defeatist, Lytton Strachey aggressively representing its distaste for combat, the group imposed its conscience upon Maynard's and made him suffer for his distinguished war work. He was particularly vulnerable because he richly enjoyed employing his superb skills on a national—indeed international—scale, while at the same time he had to experience and agonize over the deaths of friends. In October 1914 he got back a letter written to a student friend with "Killed" scrawled across the envelope. He wrote Duncan Grant, who was a conscientious objector, "It makes me bitterly miserable and long that the war should stop on almost any terms. I can't bear that he died."[46] In April 1915 he wrote Duncan of the death of the poet Rupert Brooke, "I find myself crying for him."[47] The crying was as true of Maynard as his cool intellection—and affected it visibly.

Of course the Treasury had won an exemption for Maynard, but, reacting to the battlefield slaughter, he made a demonstration of refusing to register and told a conscription tribunal that he had a "conscientious objection" not to military service but to surrendering his "liberty and judgment" in regard to it.[48] His argument was a too clever effort to find an excluded middle: the law provided for conscientious objection to military service, not, as he demanded, for the individual's liberum veto. The tribunal paid no regard to his logic and exempted him on the basis of the Treasury's request. In 1918, after a change in the legal provisions, individuals were required to register personally; he obediently complied, requesting war-work exemption.[49] Meanwhile, as he reported impressionistically, "I spend half of my time in the boring business of testifying to the sincerity, virtue and truthfulness of my [conscientious objector] friends."[50]

Such feelings and a fastidious resistance to war hatred strengthened Maynard's desire to see a negotiated peace and his efforts to move government policy toward it. Disguised as "Politicus" and less than correctly in his position, he published a letter and an article demanding it.[51] Officially, as adviser to Chancellor of the Exchequer McKenna, he provided the exquisitely reasoned memoranda opposing conscription and related measures of all-out war. In fact, universal military service was not made law until May 1916. While the Keynes-McKenna policy might prevent the war effort from maiming necessary general production, it also tended to reduce the nation's ultimate effectiveness at the front.[52] Within limits, it also enraged Lloyd George, organizer of that ultimate war effort. In February 1917, as prime minister, he rejected the Treasury's recommendation of Keynes for the order of Companion of the Bath, but did not object to his promotion to head of the A Division, nor did Lloyd George resist the Treasury's renewal of the CB recommendation three months later.[53] As for the hope of a negotiated peace, it made sense only if, contrary to reality, public opinion in the combatant nations were not demanding absolute victory. Maynard's humane presumptions had got out of bounds.

Keynes retained his sensible half-heartedness to confront the problems of a victorious peace. His A Division had been made responsible for Treasury policy on the indemnity (to be euphemistically translated as "reparations") and he precisely projected how much could be demanded in given instances "without... or with crushing Germany."[54] In view of the vengeful ambiance and the general ignorance of economics, the Treasury opted for the greater figure, but the ambiance dictated more than that. Lloyd George, accepting the verdict of politics, took the indemnity problem away from the Treasury and gave it to his politically minded Committee of the Indemnity. Preparing for the Paris Peace Conference, the committee recommended an indemnity a *dozen* times greater than the Treasury's crushing figure. As the department's chief representative in Paris, Keynes, straining against all the destructive forces loosed by war and peace, made himself ill impotently fighting for more reasonable peace terms. He was also seeking to allay his guilt for having been, as he put it, "an accomplice in all this wickedness and folly."[55]

Three weeks before the Versailles Peace Treaty was signed, on 7 June 1919, Keynes left Paris and his official responsibilities. Out of his pain and his old memoranda he set himself to writing *The Economic Consequences of the Peace,* published before the end of 1919, to correct some of the damage done and, inevitably, to reestablish his career and his life on a new basis. That it meant accusations of Germanophilia and disloyalty he insouciantly accepted as a reasonable price. (Contrariwise, it won Bloomsbury's forgiveness for his war service.) The book would also express his economic thinking to date and provide a base for newer thoughts about a world economy that was becoming less and less tractable to the economics he had taught and practiced.

Notes

1. The major source on Keynes and *The General Theory* is *The Collected Writings of John Maynard Keynes*, 30 vols. (hereafter *CW*), managing eds. Sir Austin Robinson and Donald E. Moggridge (London, 1971–89). Useful biographies are: Roy Harrod, *The Life of John Maynard Keynes* (hereafter, *The Life*) (London, 1951); D. E. Moggridge, *John Maynard Keynes* (New York: Modern Masters, 1976; revised ed., 1980) and *Maynard Keynes: An Economist's Biography* (hereafter *MK*) (London and New York, 1992); Charles H. Hession, *John Maynard Keynes: A Personal Biography*...(New York, 1984); and Robert Skidelsky, *John Maynard Keynes*, Vol. 1: *Hopes Betrayed 1883–1920* (New York, 1986) and Vol. 2: *The Economist as Saviour 1920–1937* (London, 1992) (hereafter *JMK*, 1, 2). See also obituary article, E. A. G. Robinson, "John Maynard Keynes 1883–1946," *Economic Journal* 57 (March 1947).
2. Harrod, *The Life*, 8.
3. Quoted in Hession, *John Maynard Keynes*, 4–5.
4. Skidelsky, *JMK*, 1: 55.
5. Ibid., 18–19, 57–58.
6. As shown by the correspondence in the *CW*. Keynes "was becoming less dependent on his father, more on his mother," Skidelsky, *JMK*, 1: 268.
7. Harrod, *The Life*, 7–8.
8. It was not his first *published* book, although he began working on it seriously in 1906. Two others appeared first.
9. According to Geoffrey Keynes, quoted in Skidelsky, *JMK*, 1: 69.
10. On Maynard at Eton, see Skidelsky, *JMK*, 1: 74–105; Harrod, *The Life*, 13–54; Moggridge, *MK*, 32–51.
11. Letter dated 9 February 1902, quoted in Skidelsky, *JMK*, 1: 96.
12. Ibid., 87–88. Harrod did not mention homosexuality in *The Life*.
13. On Maynard as undergraduate at Cambridge, see Skidelsky, *JMK*, 1: 106–32; Harrod, *The Life*, 55–103; Moggridge, *MK*, 52–81.
14. Skidelsky, *JMK*, 1: 114.
15. Letters to Lytton Strachey and Duncan Grant (to be introduced below) of 14 January 1910 and 3 October 1911, quoted in Harrod, *The Life*, 154, 157.
16. On Keynes and the Apostles, see Skidelsky, *JMK*, 1: 115–25; Harrod, *The Life*, 69–81; and Michael Holroyd, *Lytton Strachey: A Critical Biography*, vol. 1 (New York, 1968), 157–239 passim. On the Apostles, see (with caution) Richard Deacon, *The Cambridge Apostles* (New York, 1985).
17. Keynes, "My Early Beliefs," *CW*, 10: 438.
18. Quoted from his father's diary, in Harrod, *The Life*, n. 106.
19. Letters to Lytton Strachey, 8 July 1905, quoted in ibid., 106–7; and 23 November 1905, quoted in Skidelsky, *JMK*, 1: 166.
20. On the next period of Keynes's life until World War I, see Skidelsky, *JMK*, 1: 161–288; Harrod, *The Life*, 104–94; Moggridge, *MK*, 82–232.
21. On Keynes and the India Office, see *CW*, 15 (*Activities 1906–1914: India and Cambridge*) passim; Anand Chandavakar, *Keynes and India* (London, 1989); Skidelsky, *JMK*, 1: 175–87; Harrod, *The Life*, 122–31.
22. On Keynes in Bloomsbury, see Skidelsky, *JMK*, 1: 242–62 (including his affair with Grant); Harrod, *The Life*, 172–94; Moggridge, *MK*, 213–32.

23. *CW,* 11: 1–22.
24. Editorial note in *CW,* 15: 16–17; Skidelsky, *JMK,* 1: 211–14; Harrod, *The Life,* 133, 142-47.
25. R. M. O'Donnell, "The Unwritten Books and Papers of J. M. Keynes," *History of Political Economy* 24 (Winter 1992): 767–817; table, 769.
26. Quoted in an editorial note in *CW,* 15: 30. On Keynes's early Cambridge teaching, see Skidelsky, *JMK,* 1: 206-32; Harrod, *The Life,* 142-71.
27. On Keynes's item and related material, see *CW,* 11: 178-82; Skidelsky, *JMK,* 1: 432.
28. For Keynes's letters, other documents, and editorial note on the issue, see *CW,* 15: 18-28.
29. For Keynes's various comments, see ibid., 11: 189–216.
30. See Skidelsky, *JMK,* 1: 272–83; Harrod, *The Life,* 163-70.
31. Review of *The Rupee Problem,* issue of September 1910, *CW,* 11: 23–26.
32. Editorial note and the paper, "Recent Developments of the Indian Currency Question," in ibid., 15: 65–66; 66-85.
33. Ibid., 1.
34. Relevant documents and editorial notes, ibid., 15: 90–96.
35. Relevant documents, editorial notes, commission minutes, ibid., 97–128.
36. Keynes's annex, itself published on 6 October 1913, ibid., 151–211.
37. Editorial notes and documents, ibid., 220-71.
38. Details on the crisis, editorial notes, ibid., 16: 3–4, 6-7, 15, 16, 20. R. S. Sayers, *The Bank of England 1891–1944,* 3 vols. (London, 1976), 1: 66–109; 3 (Appendices): 31–45. E. V. Morgan, *Studies in British Financial Policy, 1914–25* (London, 1952), 3–32.
39. Keynes's persuasions, according to the diary of Basil Blackett, the Treasury official who had asked his counsel, quoted in Harrod, *The Life,* 197; see also note on Cunliffe's influence by the economic historian Sir John Clapham, published in Sayers, *The Bank of England,* 3: 36.
40. Reprinted, summarized, or noted in *CW,* 16: 16–57; ibid., 11: 238–71, 299–328, 278-98 (articles in the September and December *Economic Journal,* November *Quarterly Journal of Economics*).
41. Memorandum (excerpted), "Notes on Exchange Control," 24 September 1939, ibid., 11: 210-12; article (mentioned above, n. 40) with reference to gold, ibid., 11: 319–20.
42. Article cited also in n. 40 above; reference to bankers' cowardice, ibid., 11: 239, 252, 253; letter to J. N. Keynes, 6 August 1914, ibid., 16: 15 ("The bankers completely lost their heads"); letter to Alfred Marshall, 10 October 1914, ibid., 16: 30 (of the two leading bankers: "The one was cowardly and the other selfish").
43. Ibid., 11: 327-28; quotation, p. 328.
44. Skidelsky, *JMK,* 1: 342. Keynes's Treasury friend, Basil Blackett, on duty in Washington, reported that he was "[r]ude, dogmatic, and disobliging."
45. Harrod, *The Life,* 202; Skidelsky, *JMK,* 1: 336 ("three bad attacks").
46. Quoted in Skidelsky, *JMK,* 1: 296.
47. Quoted in Harrod, *The Life,* 201.
48. From Keynes's draft declaration, *CW,* 16: 178.
49. Editorial note, ibid., 179.
50. Letter to Dennis Robertson, 18 June 1916, quoted in editorial note in ibid., 177-78.

51. Ibid., 157-61, 179-84.
52. For example, memorandum, "The Freight Question," 18 December 1915, and draft Treasury report and appendix, "Part IV. The Financial Problem," 4 February 1916, ibid., 150-56, 162-77. See also Skidelsky, *JMK*, 1: 305-15.
53. Keynes to Florence Ada Keynes, 11 February 1917, *CW*, 16: 222-23; letter to both parents, May 1913, quoted in an editorial note in ibid., 223.
54. "Notes on an Indemnity," 31 October 1918, ibid., 338-43; quotations, 341-42.
55. Letter to Florence Ada Keynes, 14 May 1919, ibid., 458.

2

Early Theorizing

In the tolerantly self-critical paper, "My Early Beliefs," read to the Memoir Club of his Bloomsbury friends in 1938, the author of *The General Theory of Employment, Interest and Money* and survivor of a recent severe heart attack reflected on the book that had started his serious theorizing.[1] Moore's *Principia Ethica* "dominated, and perhaps still dominates, everything else." Looking back, Keynes insisted, "It was a purer, sweeter air by far than Freud cum Marx. It is still my religion under the surface." He was not using the word lightly; Mooreism was so satisfactory because it was indeed a religion. In the barer light of maturity he refused to give it up although he had soon become aware of "the thinness and superficiality, as well as the falsity, of our view of man's heart." He and his Apostolic friends had been "water-spiders, gracefully skimming, as light and reasonable as air, the surface of the stream without any contact at all with the eddies and currents underneath."

"Now what we got from Moore was by no means entirely what he offered us," Keynes explained. "We accepted Moore's religion, so to speak, and discarded his morals." Moore had commanded that responsible persons act in a manner to produce the maximum amount of eventual good. The Apostles, however, saw no need to inquire into the eventual effect of present action. This permitted them to repudiate, as the Keynes of 1938 put it, "personal liability...to obey general rules.... We repudiated entirely customary morals, conventions, and traditional wisdom. We were, that is to say, in the strict sense of the term, immoralists. Before heaven we claimed the right to be our own judge[s] in our own case." With these amendments the quinquagenarian Keynes could insist, "I see no reason to shift from the fundamental intuitions of *Principia Ethica*."[2]

The amendments, however, were modest, when one takes into consideration everything said in the memoir and everything Keynes did in his life from Moore to memoir. In it Keynes also asserted specifically that "not the slightest notice" was taken of chapter 5 of the *Principia Ethica*.[3] Yet he had written an Apostolic paper under that chapter's title, "Ethics in Relation to Conduct," which indicated the direction of his best thought, beginning with his exploration of probability, for most of the next decade of his life.[4] This has led R. M. O'Donnell, the most thorough student of that thought, in his *Keynes: Philosophy, Economics and Politics,* to call the memoir "possibly the most deceptive document in Keynes's oeuvre, flawed by error and vagueness, internal inconsistency and hyperbole."[5] O'Donnell is correct but hyperbolic about the paper's deceptiveness. Keynes was characterizing his friends and himself as *principled* immoralists, with a clear sense of Apostolic duty to others as well as themselves. When the Apostles accepted Moore's religion, Keynes meant "one's attitude toward oneself and the *ultimate,*" while "morals" merely meant "one's attitude toward the outside world and the *intermediate*" (italics added).[6] His friends and his own presumptions about espying the ultimate were laughable, Keynes easily granted, but their concern was a concern for the good. The young Keynes himself had thought he could find a better way to that good than Moore had plotted.

The better way—Keynes's way—would be given by the proper study of probability, hence the *Treatise on Probability*. This was to reject Moore's practical counsel. Clinging to his indefinable good, he had desperately concluded that the existing rules of morality were the best available standard for determining if one was, in fact, doing good. Keynes had not been able to accept so conventional a standard, indeed one that compromised itself by maintaining or tolerating evils that had to be overthrown. Instead, he reasoned that probability, in the special sense used by some philosophers (although not by Moore), was a better guide. Yet Moore's raising of the problem of probability "was, indeed, an important contributory cause to my spending all the leisure of many years on the study of that subject."[7] Furthermore, probability, as Keynes would come to see it, suggested the importance and pervasiveness of uncertainty in the economy, a major thesis of *The General Theory*.

A reading of some two dozen Keynes papers or fragments from the period 1904-10, among other writings, gives a clear view of the intellectual origins of the treatise. This has been undertaken by, among others, O'Donnell and, in the Keynes biographies cited here, Robert Skidelsky and Donald Moggridge, who have their disagreements among themselves, but who agree approximately on probability itself. The most important paper is "Ethics in Relation to Conduct," mentioned above, which took exception to Moore's demand for rigorous, indeed impossible, proof that a given act would have good effects into the vaguely extensible future. Keynes countered, "It is not obvious that any such proof is required before we are able to make judgments of probable rightness."[8]

Keynes was proposing that one could act with good conscience in the pursuit of the *immediate* good, which could be determined by rational thought. Moore's mistake was to base his reasoning on the frequency theory of probability, which claimed, Keynes argued, certain knowledge that a given event would happen more or less often than another. Keynes insisted that such certainty of knowledge was unattainable; hence, one had to reassess the ethics, the essential goodness or not, of a given action. Probability was more modest in its claims. It meant simply "I have more evidence in favor of A than in favor of B." In other words, "A statement of probability always has reference to the available evidence and cannot be refuted or confirmed by subsequent events."[9] With this Alexandria stroke Keynes cut the knot connecting action to rules of conduct.

Free to act, the individual, however, was not liberated from the moral imperatives of good and rational action. The guide to this was no longer established behavior, but lay in the sense of probability itself, understood not as mathematical frequency, but as a study of belief and partial belief within the frame of philosophy and, more narrowly, logic. With these precisions Keynes set out to build the base and lineaments of probability, thus his *Treatise on Probability*.

Keynes's other papers of the 1904-10 period deserve another glance because of their other indications of his style of thinking and their contribution to its future development. A simple list suggests his easy capture of ideas for theorizing, his catholicity of interests, and his confidence—arrogance even—that he had something significant to say: "The Political Doctrines of Edmund Burke," "Truth," "Toleration," "A Theory of Beauty," "Science and Art," "Egoism," an untitled article on the principle of "organic unity," and "Modern Civilization."[10] On 5 September

1905, before settling down to Marshallian economics, he constructed a "Scheme for an Essay on the Principles of Probability," which comprehended the application of probability to metaphysics, economics, and statistics, and investigated the application of mathematical methods to the moral sciences.[11] With this scheme, shifting from exploration to concentration on a delimited topic, his creative intent had become precise while remaining ambitious.

Moving on to probability young Keynes permitted himself to speculate on the grandiose. In an ultimate embrace of Mooreism, he made detailed notes, dated July–September 1905 and entitled "Miscellanea Ethica," for "[m]y scheme of a complete ethical treatise." For a part of it, the "notion of the good...Moore himself might be employed...to write it under direction." Keynes the bibliophile proposed in a final thought: "The whole would be printed in Baskerville type and published in 150 volumes."[12] He would not continue in this boundless sense, although, as O'Donnell has noted, he would, beginning with probability and ending with economics, establish claims for general theories subsuming other theories hitherto accorded primacy.[13]

This was as far as Keynes would go as philosopher. He was drawing upon Moore's philosophy to undertake the study of probability as an exercise in the logic (and perforce) epistemology of knowing. Building upon the Mooreian ethical concern about good and evil, he never looked back further to inquire into them. He thought he knew them well enough to proceed onward into action engaging with the problems of society. Moggridge has emphasized the explicit statement of the *Treatise on Probability*: "To believe one thing in preference to another...must have reference to action."[14] Moggridge interpreted: "Connected with the doctrines of [the *Treatise on*] *Probability*...was a role for the professional moral scientist/economist that Keynes was about to become."[15] Implicitly and powerfully connected with this complex of belief and action were what Harrod has called the "presuppositions of Harvey Road" embodying "the stable values of the civilization in which [Maynard] was bred."[16] Thus, young Keynes's investigations into philosophy went no further than accepting the reinforcement of a social philosophy, itself content to have solved the deeper, purely philosophical problems. From this Keynes had, as we have seen, moved on to the methodological problems of probability, thus action toward the good as a priori known. Moggridge has further related Keynes's action upon the world to the process of persuasion,[17] a striking characteristic of the man. This was the Keynes urgently impressing his knowledge of the good upon others for their good, articulated by himself in his title, *Essays in Persuasion* (1931).

Keynes's active concern for the good had also led him to politics, a theoretical expression of which was his essay on Burke. The essay did not deny the Mooreian influence; rather it achieved a compromise between the two, which the resilient Burke, if not the infallibilist Moore, would have approved. Young Keynes commended Burke's moderation, even his "extreme timidity in introducing present evils for the sake of future benefits." In this, Maynard was leaning on the thinking that would correct Moore in the sense of restricting one's judgments modestly to the probabilist present. Burke also needed correction. In a more democratic age Maynard resisted his post-French Revolution fear of the plebs and blank opposition to the redistribution of wealth. Politic but cautious, he interposed the benefit of the doubt: "Democracy is still on its trial, but so far it has not disgraced itself."[18] The thought, combined with Maynard's political action supporting the Liberals in defending free trade, constructing a welfare state, and reducing the power of the House of Lords, would provide a comfortable personal context for his progression into economics.

The prewar economics lecturer Keynes, trusting in laissez-faire, was a straightforward follower of Marshallian neoclassical economics, as his early lectures show.[19] In "Principles of Economics" he applied the law of supply and demand, as refined by marginalists and Marshall, to every element in the economy. Thus, "The value of money depends, like anything else, upon the interaction of supply and demand, and can be treated, therefore, as a special case of the general theory of value." (One might note his concern for the special/general categorization.) He defended the quantity theory of money against "unreasoning attacks" with precise definitions; "In this form the Q. T. of M. is *absolutely valid*." In "Theory of Money," however, his view extended beyond the constraints of pure theory and he approvingly quoted a nineteenth-century economist: "'There are few practical problems that do not present other aspects than the purely economical—political, moral, educational, artistic aspects—and these may involve consequences so weighty as to turn the scale against purely economic solutions.'"[20] Reflecting his own interest in politics and the range of social experience, this suggested an escape from the dictates of economic theory that he was not yet taking, at least not in his lectures.

Arthur Pigou and three other colleagues, however, "were at this time developing Marshall's ideas in interesting ways while Keynes was not."[21] Keynes stopped short with the pure economics, while Marshall, Pigou, and other colleagues in agreement, proposed to make economics an instrument of social reform. Yet the free-trader and elitist Keynes was willing to enter into thought experiments with new ideas, thus the message of the lively Cambridge University Fabian Society. In February 1911, he spoke, along with Sidney Webb, the leading Fabian, in support of a motion at the Cambridge Union: "That the progressive reorganization of Society along the lines of Collectivist Socialism is both inevitable and desirable." Perhaps he enjoyed demonstrating his persuasions in the cause of an absurd and detestable social arrangement. In 1913 he nevertheless found lunch with the coequal Fabian leader Beatrice Webb a "deep spiritual experience," while between the encounters with the Webbs he told his father he was "in favor of the confiscation of wealth."[22] But these were isolated episodes in the life of Keynes's mind, an *interested* mind that had to investigate all possible paths to understanding. While he would associate his ultimate thinking with "democratic socialism" he found anything *collectivist* repellent, and, in the last analysis, rejected both Fabian and Marxian socialism as antiquated and boring. In the *Economic Journal* of September 1913, he reviewed *Gold, Prices, and Wages* by John A. Hobson, the theorist of underconsumption (and an important influence on the thought of Lenin) and found it so wrongheaded that he refused to review any more of his books.[23]

Meanwhile, proceeding with his probability, Keynes attacked the subject of index numbers in a prize essay of 1909, a long and impressive one.[24] Supported by artful equations, he was arguing that mathematics, specifically probability (in the sense of frequency) as a branch of it, could not produce a satisfactory index number. That led him to call into question the standards set for such numbers by Francis Y. Edgeworth, professor of economics at Oxford, one of his dissertation referees, and, incidentally, Keynes's predecessor as editor of the *Economic Journal* (as well as an agreeable joint editor with him informally during World War I and formally beginning in 1919).[25] In a memorandum, the sense of which was adopted by the authoritative British Association, Edgeworth, following Stanley Jevons, had said it would be sufficient to take an unweighted geometrical mean of a random sample of prices to arrive at trustworthy figures. Keynes was struck by the word "unweighted." He laid down his judgment: "Professor Edgeworth's preoccupation with that branch of probabilities, which is the same analytically as the typical game of chance, has led him, I believe, to look at this problem in an erroneous manner."[26] Keynes was constructing his *Treatise on Probability* on the distinction between the Jevons-Edgeworth mathematicians' probability and the logicians' probability as belief or partial belief.

In the essay, confronting the laws of frequency, Keynes raised up "the method of approximation, [which] simply omits the less important and less manageable items, and attempts to substitute for them others supposed to be representative of them or which enter largely into their composition."[27] He had, however, provided no replacement for the mathematics he was casting out—except disguised, blurry mathematics. He would be obliged to *count* the items in his index of "approximations" and estimate their *representative* character by *proportion,* thus fractional numbers. Yet the essay was not as bad as its logic. Keynes had roamed the increasingly important field of index numbers widely and discussed its problems in easy prose and adept mathematics. He deserved his prize, although the essay would have been improved if his conclusion had been reversed.

The essay provided important materials for Keynes's probability studies. Its Appendix B used sophisticated mathematical reasoning to deal with problems in the theory of averages.[28] Keynes revised it into the article "The Principal Averages and the Laws of Error Which Lead to Them," published in the Royal Statistical Society's journal.[29] To discover the laws of error, the article proposed, "it is necessary...to introduce the fundamental symbol of probability." He immediately introduced the symbol A/H,[30] which he dropped into lower case and elaborately refined as probability relation in the treatise itself. Essay, article, and dissertation used mathematics to attack what Keynes regarded as its excessive use. The essay had put forward "approximations" to challenge index numbers as overly precise. The *Treatise on Probability,* as expanded from the dissertation, would limit the value of probability in the sense of frequency to subordinate it to probability as belief, this latter a question of the credibility of propositions and situated by Keynes in the field of logic. Probabilistic belief, as he would develop it, covered the gamut from conclusive belief through various descending degrees of partial belief to no belief.

Among Keynes's many projects of the prewar years the writing and rewriting of the treatise was the most important, receiving his most concentrated thinking and longest thoughts. A substantial amount of the book was set in type by August 1914, but his wartime and immediate postwar activities delayed its publication until August 1921. Whatever changes were made in 1920–21, it remains the expression of the young prewar Keynes just emerging from his twenties but already at the topmost level of his powers of intellection.

The *Treatise on Probability,* extending to almost five hundred pages, was the first systematic work in English on the logical foundations of probability in fifty-five years, Keynes could assert, although one comparable work in another language did appear.[31] He created his own symbolic logic around the probability relation a/h, which joined with other symbols to form dense thickets of equations in ten of the thirty-three chapters. The index numbers essay had spoken of A as "conclusion" and H as "evidence"; in lowercase the treatise called a alternately "conclusion" and "proposition," and h "evidence" and "premise," an indication of Keynes's sometimes casual way with key words. The relation or fraction a/h was equated to P for probability. If a given evidence/premise h completely justified the conclusion/proposition $a,$ then P would equal 1, thus the relation of certainty; if h was valueless, then P would equal 0, the relation of "impossibility." Between the extremes of 1 and 0 was the range of probability known as partial belief.[32]

Keynes firmly placed his probability in the frame of logic, but its character as a study of degrees of belief or knowledge stirred up a cluster of problems in epistemology. One that should be mentioned, Keynes providing no means for a solution, however, is his interchangeable use of "belief" and "knowledge," although the first can be based on faith or similarly incommunicable intuition. While noting the epistemological lacuna, one should, however, let him develop his argument. He introduced it with a measure of clarity: "Part of our knowledge we obtain direct; and part by argument. The Theory of Probability is concerned with that part which we obtain by argument, and it treats of the different degrees in which the results so obtained are conclusive or inconclusive." He went on to say that in "most branches of academic logic," geometry for example, arguments claim to be conclusive, but many disciplines and areas of life must operate with beliefs that are rational but inconclusive.[33] Probability-as-belief, which Aristotle, Leibniz, and Locke propounded, was a second way of believing or knowing. Thus, Keynes et al. had interposed a radical scission between knowing conclusively and knowing insecurely. One should note that with these distinguished exceptions Western thinkers have been content to use the same rules for the entire range of knowing; the minority of intellects agreeing with Keynes have not *conclusively* shown the need to change those rules. In an epistemological exercise, however, he did go on to illustrate the scission with the case of inductive reasoning.

Later in the treatise, Keynes proposed, "If for instance, we base upon the data, that this and that and those swans are white, the conclusion that *all* swans are white, we are endeavoring to establish a universal induction." He introduced a second kind of inductive reasoning: "But if we base upon the data that this and those swans are white and that swan is black, the conclusion that *most* swans are white . . . then we are establishing an inductive correlation."[34] But by definition induction consists of generalizing to discover or create a law out of a series of instances, any future unit of the series having the capability of differing from the preceding ten or ten trillion. Keynes had tried to make off with a characteristic of *de*duction, its perfect completeness if correct, for his *induc*tion. In this he is attempting the capital crime in logic of the *petitio principii,* implanting his conclusion in his premises. His second example gives the lie to the first: a black swan can always appear and so annihilate the claimed universality of the universal induction. The term is an oxymoron and only emphasizes another failure of Keynes's epistemology.

One question that has aroused continuing conflict among Keynes's interpreters is whether his probability relation is subjective or objective. At the very beginning of the treatise, while granting the presence of the subjective element, Keynes insisted: "But in a sense important to logic, probability is not subjective. It is not…subject to human caprice.… Once the facts are given…what is probable or improbable…has been fixed objectively, and is independent of our opinion."[35] In one of a number of examples of concurrence, Bradley W. Bateman, an American economist-philosopher, similarly insisted that the "actual existence of the logical relationship"—thus Keynes's *a/h* relation—remained constant, however differently different individuals saw it.[36] But neither Keynes early nor Bateman late could show how an individual could penetrate to a total and accurate sense of that relation, granted its objective character. They had to admit that whatever anyone reported about it was mediated by the person's unique subjectivity. Keynes admitted it himself: "What we know and what probability we can attribute to our rational beliefs is...subjective in the sense of being relative to the individual." In another passage he simply used the phrase "subjective probability."[37] With the operative logic of the book resting heavily on it, furthermore, Keynes made a better case for the *subjective* character of his probability.

Another problem was the matter of definition. Following Moore, who refused to define such ultimate propositions as the "good," Keynes insisted, "A *definition* of probability is not possible.... We cannot analyze the probability relation in terms of simpler ideas." He argued, "In any case desire to reduce the indefinables of logic can be carried too far."[38] He did not explain why. At this point the effort to understand must be given up.

Related to the definitional problem was the division of knowledge into direct, which was necessarily indefinable, and indirect, constructed on these ultimately simple essences. Thus, Keynes tentatively suggested, "About our own existence, our own sense-data, some logical ideas, and some logical relations, it is usually agreed that we have direct knowledge." But then, "Of the law of gravity, of the appearance of the other side of the moon, of the cure for phthisis...it is usually agreed that we do *not* have direct knowledge." Up to now he had been assuming that direct knowledge was conclusive, but he also had to grant that there "do *seem* to be degrees of knowledge" in cases of direct knowledge because of what he now saw as the "difficulty of distinguishing direct from indirect." Then there was "a confusion between *probable* knowledge and *vague* knowledge." Disarmingly he let confusion reign: "At any rate I do not know how to deal with it."[39]

Then there was the problem of polarity. On closer view one sees that "certainty" and "impossibility," as Keynes called his two extremes, do not represent true poles in relation to one another: impossibility expresses as much certainty as does certainty. This was recognized by Richard B. Braithwaite, a student friend of Keynes who had risen to Cambridge University philosopher, in his "Editorial Foreword" to the *Collected Writings* volume reprinting the treatise. He silently translated Keynes's "impossibility" into "certainty of falsehood."[40] The repetition of the word "certainty" only emphasizes the problem. Keynes had posited a logical gamut from 1 to 0, but he could move no further away from 1 than 1/2, the point where degrees of negative certainty would begin to accrete. This is not an effort to solve Keynes's (and Braithwaite's) problem, but to suggest its inherent difficulty, if not insolubility.

Keynes illustrated probability with a diagram as a grand abstraction of the general meaning he was trying to express. Part of that meaning was the element of the incomparable and immeasurable, a thesis, one may recall, he used in the case of index numbers, and which, accompanied also by the unpredictable, he would bring into *The General Theory* (which also has one grandly abstract diagram representing, in its case, half of its general meaning). Here is the treatise's diagram (figure 2.1) with its range, as Keynes had posited and reading from left to right, from the impossibility of 0 to the certainty of 1.

The line running from 0 through A to 1, thus 0-A-I, represents the dimension of measurability and comparability, with A being a "numerically measurable probability intermediate between 0 and 1," while the rest of the diagram represents nonmeasurable probabilities, some of them comparable, some not. In other words the 0-A-I line and only that line illustrates conclusive knowledge, ordinary knowledge as it is conventionally accepted; Keynes's probability as partial belief takes up all the rest of the diagram. In this latter area, given points, V, Z, U, and so on, can be comparable with each other but the comparability is not expressed in figures—not measurable. Keynes does not explain, but let us try to follow his logic, stipulating noncomprehension, in the hope of eventual enlightenment.

FIGURE 2.1
Keynes's Probability

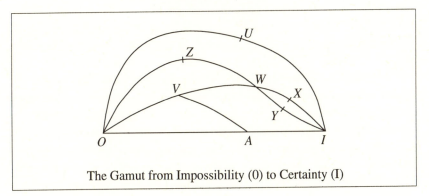

The Gamut from Impossibility (0) to Certainty (I)

Keynes proposed, "Some probabilities are not comparable in respect of more or less, because there exists more than one path, so to speak, between proof and disproof, between certainty and impossibility." These incomparable probabilities are diagrammed as the lines looping upward from impossibility before descending at the other extreme upon certainty. Thus, reading from left to right, the points V, Z, U, W, Y, X on those lines are all "non-numerical probabilities," which are or are not comparable to each other, comparability being permitted between those points on the same line and those located on lines that intersect each other. Thus, V is comparable to W and X because they are all on one line and also comparable to A because of V's location on another line leading to A. Similarly, X and Y are both comparable to and greater than W and V, which are either on the same line or a line intersecting that line, but not comparable to each other because they are not on the same or intersecting lines.[41]

How can we apply this to our thinking about some points, such as V, Z, and U, positioned similarly on a graph with its vertical and horizontal grid lines permitting comparison and measurement? Keynes did not explain. His multiple lines suggest multiple series requiring multiple proofs and disproofs, all existence fragmented into different thought systems unable to communicate with each other. Keynes had locked himself into one and rendered himself incommunicado.

Probability-as-belief was one of the two major strands of the treatise's argument. The other was Keynes's thesis of probability-as-frequency as a special case of belief. Actually he devoted much more space to frequency. Speaking loosely, given the ambiguities, the difference is overwhelming—some ten or twenty times as much sheer wordage expended on probability-as-frequency as on probability-as-belief. The ambiguities include the equations and the many chapters and passages devoted to frequency although Keynes would have himself discussing belief.

Probability-as-frequency, emerging with the help of Galileo, was consciously developed as a branch of mathematics by a line of distinguished mathematicians beginning in the seventeenth century. Jakob Bernoulli (1654–1705) discovered the Law of Large Numbers, which proposed that many repetitions reduce error. Further developing the Law of Large Numbers, Siméon Denis Poisson (1781–1840) insisted that a single observation was of no interest while the "*stabilization of relative frequen-*

cies can be observed as the number of observations increases more and more."[42] Keynes's contemporary, Richard von Mises (1883–1953), continued to clarify and advance the Law of Large Numbers and probability generally. Keynes did not list any of the Mises writings in the treatise's bibliography, although Mises published important articles in 1918 and 1919, the second leading to his classic study of 1928, translated as *Probability, Statistics and Truth*.[43] The Mises articles and books treated probability (i.e., frequency) theory "as a scientific theory in mathematical form like mechanics or thermodynamics. Its subjects are *mass phenomena* or *repeatable events*, as they appear in games of chance, in insurance problems, in heredity theory, and in the ever growing domain of applications in physics."[44] It is this conception of probability-as-frequency that Keynes tried to command with his probability-as-belief.

Early in the treatise Keynes launched one argument against the reasoning of the insurance broker at Lloyd's of London as a classic example of financial operations based on frequency: "I doubt whether in extreme cases the process of thought through which [the broker] goes before naming a premium is wholly rational and determinate." Keynes did not quite explain, but completed his argument in the treatise's concluding chapter. The best that frequency theory could do was to "assert a characteristic of a *series* of propositions, rather than of a particular proposition."[45] He was accurately defining the *raison d'être* of all frequency calculations; they count the frequency, the series. The continued economic existence of insurance brokers is proof that they understand and obey the laws of frequency. (Keynes would become chairman of one large insurance company and a director of another, more modest firm, both prosperous.) If we pause we can appreciate the outrageousness of his logic: he was demanding that the practitioners and theorists of frequency predict the next accident, the next flip of the coin—the individual instance. Keynes had given an opponent an impossible task to perform and condemned him for failing.

The pairing of probability-and-belief and probability-as-frequency is the most important expression of Keynes's failure in epistemology. This was pointed out by Frank Ramsey, a brilliant young don who was a mathematician and philosopher—and a young friend of Keynes. Indeed Keynes had helped secure a fellowship at King's for him.[46] In a 1926 essay, which was published in 1931, Ramsey found it "likely that the two schools are really discussing different things, and that the word 'probability' is used by logicians in one sense and statisticians in another."[47] Max Black, author of the entry "Probability" in the *Encyclopedia of Philosophy* agreed with Ramsey: "There seem to be no compelling reasons for recognizing radically different senses of probability." In the case of frequency, Black reasoned, we are dealing with the number of times anything objective occurs out of all possible times; the second sense has to do with the accuracy of propositions describing given parts of reality. "Probability" is a homonym, the result of an odd accident of linguistic history (a chance the possibility of which a frequency theorist might find it challenging to estimate), which had inserted two different and unrelated conceptions into the same verbal expression. The treatise, while providing more than one distinction without a difference, is constructed upon the failure to distinguish a fatally absolute difference.

Keynes's probability can nevertheless claim dominance over frequency in one sense, already granted, that knowing is more fundamental than counting. The epistemologist can ask the Lloyd's broker how he knows that the insured ship had really sunk. Did he dream it? Did he dream the existence as well as the question of the epistemologist? Is he certain he is an insurance broker? In epistemology these are all reasonable questions: the knowing always mediates the counting in the mind. But the dominance of knowing extends not only over frequency, but over physics experiments, theories of aesthetics, tales by gossips, reports of meteorologists, computer printouts, congresses of theologians, dentists' bills, information relayed by satellite, the baying of dogs at the moon, prayers—all experience. The *pairing* of probability-as-belief and probability-as-frequency was the primal error.

The reviews of the *Treatise on Probability* were well mixed. O'Donnell has reprinted excerpts of eight "favorable," six "unfavorable," and three "others."[48] The Apostolic Bertrand Russell damned the book with overrich but vanishing praise. He began by calling it "undoubtedly the most important work on probability that has appeared in a very long time," but arrived circuitously at a negative judgment. He questioned Keynes's thesis of nommeasurable probabilities and thought that Keynes had failed to refute a fundamental criticism made by his colleague, A. N. Whitehead, as dissertation examiner: Keynes's "objections are not addressed to the principle but consist in showing the technical difficulties which, one feels, might be overcome with ingenuity and skill."[49] The members of the probabilist school of logicians, according to O'Donnell, received the treatise respectfully at the time without, however, necessarily sharing Keynes's unique vision. He had to add, "[I]ts current status is relatively low," but he could qualify that "it is not without its firm advocates."[50] Author of the most detailed study of Keynes's probability theory to date, O'Donnell has defended it with loyal thoroughness, but his introduction specifies: "My general silence on evaluation should be taken neither as implying complete assent nor as indicating wholesale disapproval." In his summation he adjudicated: "We should be wary, then, of dismissing Keynes's philosophical thought as outmoded simply because *some* of his basic positions cannot be sustained."[51]

The treatise, violating all the major rules therein laid down, was an act of rebellion against John Neville's *Formal Logic,* which had announced: "[I]t is essential that logic should recognize an objective reference in every judgment, that is, a reference outside the state of mind which constitutes the judgment itself." John Maynard's intuition recognized no such foreign power. Furthermore, his probability, which was sometimes belief, sometimes frequency, and sometimes both, attacked "the foundation of all reasoning," breaking all "Three Fundamental Laws of Thought" as listed by John Neville: identity, contradiction, and the law of the excluded middle.[52]

The best judgment on the treatise was perhaps made by John Maynard Keynes himself. In 1926, writing to his German translator, he confessed, "[A]s time goes on I myself feel that there is a great deal in the book which is unsatisfactory, and, indeed, I felt this even when I was writing it."[53] The final chapter, headed "Outline of a Constructive Theory," failed to produce that theory.[54] The writer seemed demoralized, his writing expressing mental exhaustion more than anything else. Keynes, as he tended to be at such moments, was disarming: "In writing a book of this kind the author must, if he is to put his point of view clearly, pretend sometimes to a little more conviction than he feels. He must give his argument a chance, so to speak, nor to be too ready to depress his vitality with a wet cloud of doubt." He begged his reader to excuse him "if I have pressed on a little faster than the difficulties were overcome, and with decidedly more confidence than I have always felt."[55] The reader was left to wonder what lay back in the preceding thirty-two chapters, which merited only partial belief.

In the final paragraph of a little more than a page in length, Keynes, while making gestures of resistance and withholding his universal induction, surrendered to the theorists of frequency. He was willing to contemplate their vision of the universe, with "those peculiar characteristics of atomism and limited variety which appear more and more clearly as the ultimate result to which material science is tending." He remarked that the frequency theorists "have been often and justly derided for arguing if nature were an urn containing black and white balls in fixed proportions." Keynes wrote that the astronomer and statistician Jacques Quetelet (1796–1874) "once declared in so many words: 'l'urne que nous interrogeons, c'est la nature'.... [I]t may turn out to be true—reversing Quetelet's expression—that 'la nature que nous interrogeons, c'est une urne.'"[56] Keynes's reversal of the metaphor expresses Quetelet's sense better than Quetelet did himself. It was a gracefully, skillfully accepted defeat.

Whatever failures of the second order compounded in it, the treatise developed Keynes's skills as logician and enriched his scholarly credentials. More important, the work tempered, as it demonstrated, his steely will. Over nearly two decades, including the long interruption of the war and the peace conference, that will would persist in driving an idea through any resistance and beyond any limits. It was that undeterred will, Keynes's faltering only momentary and emphasizing it by contrast, that gave him the advantage over mere intellectual genius— contributed the necessary force to his theorizing.

Notes

1. *CW,* 10: 433–50.
2. Ibid., 435, 442, 449, 450, 436, 446.
3. Ibid., 436.
4. Moggridge has argued that the date given by Skidelsky and O'Donnell for the essay, 23 January 1904, was too early by two to three years, but there is no dispute about the essay's importance. See *MK,* Appendix 1, 131–36.
5. R. M. O'Donnell, *Keynes: Philosophy, Economics and Politics* (New York, 1989), 148.
6. *CW,* 10: 436.
7. Ibid., 445.
8. Quoted in Skidelsky, *JMK,* 1: 153.
9. Quoted in ibid.
10. O'Donnell, *Keynes: Philosophy,* 385.
11. Ibid., 13.
12. Quoted (and discussed) in Skidelsky, *JMK,* 1: 147–48.
13. O'Donnell, *Keynes: Philosophy,* 173.
14. *CW,* 8: 339.

15. Moggridge, *MK,* 164–65.
16. Harrod, *The Life,* 183, 1.
17. Moggridge, *MK,* 164.
18. Quoted in Skidelsky, *JMK,* 1: 155, 156. For the entire discussion, see ibid., 154–57. See also Moggridge, *MK,* 124–27.
19. Notes of the early lectures, *CW,* 12: 690–783.
20. Ibid., 693, 695, 725.
21. Skidelsky, *JMK,* 1: 221.
22. Quotations and account, ibid., 241.
23. Keynes's review, *CW,* 11: 388–94; his refusal, Skidelsky, *JMK,* 1: 218.
24. "The Method of Index Numbers with Special Reference to the Measurement of General Exchange Value," winner of Cambridge University Adam Smith Prize of £60, *CW,* 11: 49–156.
25. See his warm obituary notice (*Economic Journal,* March 1926), ibid., 10: 251–66. "The appreciation was reciprocal. Edgeworth could not say too much in praise of Keynes." Harrod, *The Life,* 373.
26. *CW,* 11:90.
27. Ibid., 100.
28. Ibid., 136–56.
29. February 1911, ibid., 159–73.
30. Ibid., 160.
31. Ibid., 8: xv, 473.
32. Ibid., 145.
33. Ibid., 3.
34. Ibid., 244–45.
35. Ibid., 3–4.
36. Bradley W. Bateman, "Keynes's Changing Conception of Probability," *Economics and Philosophy* 3 (April 1987): 100–101. Bateman was building upon the work of, inter alia, Henry E. Kyburg, Jr., *Epistemology and Inference* (Minneapolis, 1983) and Ian Hacking, *The Emergence of Probability* (Cambridge, 1975).
37. *CW,* 8: 19, 312.
38. Ibid., 8, 9.
39. Ibid., 14, 17.
40. Ibid., xvii.
41. Keynes's explication, ibid., 38–43; quotations, pp. 42, 38, 42.
42. Hilda Geiringer, "Probability: Objective Theory," *Dictionary of the History of Ideas* 3: 611–23; quotation, p. 615.
43. Richard von Mises, *Probability, Statistics and Truth* (New York, 1981; 1st English ed., 1957).
44. As summarized by Hilda Geiringer, "Probability: Objective Theory," 3: 615–18.
45. *CW,* 8: 23, 444.
46. Harrod, *The Life,* 320.
47. Frank P. Ramsey, "Truth and Probability," in *The Foundations of Mathematics and Other Logical Essays,* ed. R. B. Braithwaite (London, 1931), 157.
48. O'Donnell, *Keynes: Philosophy,* 25–27.
49. Bertrand Russell, *Mathematical Gazette* 11 (July 1922): 119–25; quotations, 119, 124.
50. O'Donnell, *Keynes: Philosophy,* 331.
51. Ibid., 5, 334. Other recent studies of Keynes's probability include: Anna M. Carabelli, *On Keynes's Method* (London, 1988), which began, like O'Donnell's

work, as a Cambridge University dissertation, indeed under Moggridge's supervision. It avoided direct criticism, restricting its demands on Keynes by proposing that his probability related to uncertainty and not truth (pp. 21–22). Athol Fitzgibbons, *Keynes's Vision: A New Political Economy* (Oxford, 1988), saw "the logical theory of probability" as a "challenge to the primacy of the scientific method" (pp. 14–15). Also: Moggridge, ed., *Perspectives in the History of Economic Thought*, Vol. 4: *Keynes, Macroeconomics and Method* (Aldershot, England, 1990) and Bateman and John B. Davis, eds., *Keynes and Philosophy: Essays on the Origin of Keynes's Thought* (Aldershot, England, 1991). These latter include articles on such questions as Keynes's thesis of the "weight of argument," the relation of Keynes's theory to policy, and (apparent) changes in his probability theory.

52. John N. Keynes, *Studies and Exercises in Formal Logic* (London, 1906), 2, 450.
53. Letter to F. M. Urban, 15 May 1926, quoted in O'Donnell, *Keynes: Philosophy*, 144.
54. *CW*, 8: 444–68.
55. Ibid., 467.
56. Ibid., 467–68.

3

Keynes Reconstituted:
Thoughts on Policy and Theory

The Economic Consequences of the Peace was a genial exercise in applied economics and a polemical masterpiece generating much of its power through its fusion of political and psychological sense with economics. Its polemics artfully thrashed the conference leaders Woodrow Wilson, Lloyd George, and Georges Clemenceau, whom Keynes, averting his attention from a vengeful public opinion in their countries, made more responsible for the horridness of the peace than they deserved. Still Keynes could correctly point out that the leaders had not only failed to deal with the awesome economic problems that included near-famine, but also made them infinitely worse by the economic terms of the Versailles Treaty imposed on Germany. In charging it with the costs of the war, it gave it an impossible task, thus seriously laming the international political economy and continuing the war's destructive work. If guilt could be more broadly apportioned out than Keynes chose, he was prophetically accurate about the damage done.

Keynes could even foresee the approximate mendacity in the figures for the reparations Germany would have to pay. In 1919 allied public opinion had demanded such vast sums that the leaders avoided naming any figure at all in the treaty itself. *The Economic Consequences* predicted that Germany would later be seriously burdened with a debt of $15 billion (as translated into U.S. currency), although he doubted it could safely produce $10 billion, and unseriously charged with an additional $25 billion.[1] On 5 May 1921, after sterile conferences and more punishment, the London Payments Plan ordered it to pay installments on $12.5 billion immediately and accept responsibility for a secondary, interest-free, thus fictional, debt of $20.5 billion. The installments Ger-

39

many actually began paying amounted to 10 percent of its gross national product (GNP); the plan, however, collapsed by January 1922, when the allies, in the face of a German default, reduced cash reparations for the year to less than a quarter of the payments originally prescribed. Keynes's larger and similarly dire predictions were as accurate.

One could reasonably ask why an efficient Germany could not have paid the 10 percent of its GNP, a severe penalty but not beyond the proportions of the possible. In 1921 it could not solve the short-run problem of producing immediate values with its war-impoverished economy, but recovery would make no difference. The only way it could earn the income was to sell more to its major trading partners than it bought from them, but the United States and the allies were those trading partners. Naturally they would not permit it to build up surpluses with them, since that meant trade deficits, with the attendant loss of business and employment, for themselves. Germany had been given an impossible problem to solve and had been driven crazy trying to solve it.[2]

Keynes had been straining against the interlocking forces of hatred and indifference, which denied sense on reparations and Germans generally. In 1919 the hatred was much more prominent, while the indifference, referring to the American attitude, was falsified by the theatrics expressed in Wilson's role at the peace conference. The United States, quickly disillusioned, thereafter preferred to contract its attention within its own borders and forget Europe's problems. If war hatred had proposed huge reparations, indifference to the deeper issues dictated the American insistence on war-debt payment as the discharge of a legal responsibility. Keynes dealt with the United States late in *The Economic Consequences*, almost, seemingly, as an afterthought.[3] Yet he knew that it was the $11 billion in American loans to the allies that had given reparations their too solid reality among the fictions of the peace. This $11 billion called up the comparable $12.5 billion figure of the London Payments Plan. If one could make the American claim vanish, everybody else would have to follow, allies among themselves, and, given time, allies vis-à-vis the former enemy. The United States had to be magnanimous or wise. The solution stopped here.

If the allies persisted with their disastrous policies, "vengeance... will not limp," Keynes predicted. "Nothing can then delay for very long that final civil war between the forces of Reaction and the despairing convulsions of Revolution, before which the horrors of the late German war will fade into nothing, and which will destroy, whoever is victor, the civilization and the progress of our generation."[4] It was an impressionistic scenario for the world's stumbling progress through fascism and Nazism toward World War II.

The weakest part of the book was the "Remedies" of its last chapter.[5] Surely Keynes knew he was forcing reality when, along with reduced reparations, canceled war debts, and a United States-financed international loan, he proposed a "Free Trade Union" of the former enemy territories—a kind of displaced European Economic Community before its time—and, from within it and radiating eastward, a German connection to revive the Soviet Russian economy. He preferred not to see that his schemes would have meant eventual victories of an old Germany and a new Russia encouraged to be unregenerate. If he could achieve nothing much in this sense, he could at least contribute his sane competence and unremitting efforts to reduce even fractionally the new as well as the old evils.

The Economic Consequences served perfectly to establish Keynes in the context of postwar Britain. It made him splendidly notorious, very nearly on the level with such celebrities as the Prince of Wales, Charlie Chaplin, and Queen Marie of Rumania. More than 100,000 copies were sold in a half year, many by way of translations into a dozen languages. It placed him well beyond government, which was clearly too small for his talents. Roy Harrod, noting the accusations of Germanophilia, tried to see him "for many years in the wilderness."[6] This is nonsense. Keynes, continuing to advise prime ministers and chancellors of the exchequer, was invited to join more official committees than he could oblige. Meanwhile he was reconstituting his persona on a higher level of effectiveness.

Keynes directed himself precisely toward money, power, and the Mooreian good. He also sought love, although he may not have known he did until it befell him. His great achievement was to integrate all these objectives, conscious or unconscious, into a remarkably efficient unity, each part enhancing the rest.

A week after he had left Paris and the peace conference, in mid-June 1919, Keynes went up to Cambridge and redefined his relationship with King's College and the university. He told the first he would reduce the number of his pupils, and the second, he would lecture only once a week. He resigned his permanent lectureship the next year. After lecturing during the fall term of 1919 and the winter term of 1920, he skipped the 1921–22 year and, when he resumed, got down to eight heavily attended lectures annually, his improvement on the English academic forty-hour year. To an extent he frustrated his plan to economize on his time at Cambridge. In November 1919 he entered upon his appointment as second bursar at King's. He was still managing the finances of the Royal Economic Society. He was still taking pupils individually, although a reduced number, and actively leading his Political Economy Club, meeting on Monday evenings. He revived the moribund Apostles. He was still editing the *Economic Journal*. In 1920 he was elected a member of the Council of the University Senate, remaining there until 1927. A proper accounting would conclude that he was doing more work than before in college and university, but now he had better control of the Cambridge power levers and more freedom to allocate time for a given activity.[7]

Bloomsbury remained important to Maynard. Its sponsorship of Postimpressionist exhibitions before the war and its many talents were bringing it widening renown and even authority. In May 1918 Lytton Strachey anticipated the success of Maynard's *Economic Consequences* with his best-selling *Eminent Victorians,* the first of his popular, satire-edged biographies. Duncan Grant had his first one-man show in 1920 and Vanessa Bell followed two years later; both painters had arrived. By 1922 Virginia Woolf had published three novels and was firmly established as an important writer. In part, as therapy to help resist the madness always threatening Virginia, Leonard had started their Hogarth Press, which became a modest commercial success while publishing her novels and other worthy books, including an occasional work of Maynard's and Sigmund Freud's collected works as translated by James Strachey, a brother of Lytton's. At 46 Gordon Square Maynard found himself surrounded by other members of the group, most of them Stracheys, at numbers 41 and 42, and 47, 50, and 51. But he was moving beyond Bloomsbury by way of love, money, and his other activities.

In 1918 Maynard had enjoyed the dancing of Lydia Lopokova, a principal dancer in the Ballets Russes company of Sergei Diaghilev, and enjoyably made her acquaintance. In 1921 the company and Lydia returned for a dance series that began well but, despite a great personal success for Lydia, lost its allure for London. Maynard, who had had a heterosexual affair during the war but had recently entered into a mild relationship with a younger don, attended Lydia's performances regularly and "conspicuously in the thinly occupied stalls."[8] Their affair evidently began before the end of 1921,[9] and immediately became a serious liaison despite the counsel of Vanessa, who took Maynard's mock-desperate cries for help seriously.[10] Bloomsbury found it peculiarly inconvenient, but it began at a peculiarly appropriate moment for both principals.

One of four dancing siblings from St. Petersburg, Lydia had led an adventurous life that included two periods in the United States, one enduring seven years, as an actress as well as dancer, in entertainments less distinguished than the ballet.[11] She had a talent for comic parts expressing a sense of humor that carried over intriguingly into her personal life. She was also intelligent although not at all intellectual. About thirty at the time, she found herself without a home in the theater, despite her recognized talent, since the Diaghilev company was in the process of foundering. For her, Maynard seductively joined two necessary characters, adorer of the ballet and her person, and masterful man of a distinction as much recognized as hers.

Perhaps the impress of the family mores of Harvey Road had at last taken effect upon Maynard. Bloomsbury was too extended a family and his homosexual affairs had paled. He had a deep need for the emotional support and adoration Lydia promised to lavish on him in return for his equal support and adoration. In sum she provided an entrancing way of slipping into the conventional mode suitable for the career he was reconstructing.

Taking over Lydia's finances and life, Maynard moved her into Gordon Square, indeed into the rooms at number 50, which Vanessa had temporarily vacated for a period of painting in Paris. That did not disturb her, but Lydia's presence did, as it disturbed most of Bloomsbury. Vanessa's sister articulated it precisely two years later: "You can't argue solidly when Lydia's there." Virginia complained seriously but laughed at all parties: "Bloomsbury steals off to its den, leaving Maynard with Lydia on his knee, a sublime but heartrending spectacle."[12]

Maynard and Lydia did not marry until 4 August 1925, but it was the law's delay, not theirs, since she had a husband of sorts whose existence posed a difficult legal problem. The new couple's relationship was solid from the beginning, as documented in their almost daily letters to each other. The letters expressed its originality as well as solidity. It had established itself by way of slow immersion, Maynard keeping to the pattern he had begun as early as 1910 and usually spending five days of the week as a Cambridge bachelor. He spent just two days, Wednesday and Thursday, in London cohabiting with Lydia, hence the many letters. (Of course they spent most, although not all, of the university holiday time together, and Lydia became a round-the-clock nurse as well as wife after his heart attack in 1937.) Content with an associate membership in Bloomsbury, Lydia had her own friends, an active life in London, and an occasional dancing or acting engagement. She found the arrangement so satisfactory that when Maynard, perhaps to comfort her for a passing disappointment, asked her to come to Cambridge, she replied, "[I]t would disturb too much my mode of life, but if you post kisses that would do very well for me."[13] The sexual side of their relationship may have been verbalized more than acted out, but the letters express its charm and ease.[14] Maynard and Lydia lived happily ever after.

Two months after his return from Paris Keynes went straight for the money by way of currency speculation. He was continuing his stock market operations, which had begun modestly in 1905, but expanded considerably during the war. As a connoisseur of jute, spelter (zinc ingots), varieties of wheat, and many scores of other commodities, he would also plunge temerariously into commodity speculation.

In his big biography, *Maynard Keynes,* Donald Moggridge did not mention Keynes's wartime speculation, but the *Collected Writings* volume that he edited provided tables showing that Keynes had securities worth £4,617 (approximately $250,000, present U.S. value) at the end of 1914 and £9,428 by 1918.[15] Clearly there was a conflict of interest, given Keynes's central position in the Treasury as manager of Britain's external war finances. It is true that he would act against his *perceived* interest if it clashed with the nation's good. Thus, in the financial crisis of August 1914 he had opposed the government's guarantee of pre-moratorium bills, a policy which, as he wrote his father, meant "saving you and me several hundred pounds [on loans to discount houses] at the expense of the general taxpayer."[16] In 1931, while counseling the government on leaving the gold standard, he refused to permit his investment group to shift out of sterling; this meant a huge loss of more than £40,000.[17] But in 1914–18 he could not avoid taking advantage of inside information. But he lost all that money in his first postwar currency speculation, and built up his eventual fortune evidently without privileged information.[18]

Keynes's fortune, which remained comparatively modest in the 1920s and fell to less than that at the end of the decade, was essential in financing activities that ranged from politics to philanthropy. He began with a sublime self-confidence that he never lost and mysteriously augmented in disaster. With his great knowledge of their economies and finances he was selling short the currencies of France, Italy, and (after March 1920) Germany, and wagering on the United States, Norway, Denmark, and India. Less than a half year after entering the currency market, by the beginning of 1920, he had profits of £6,154. This led him to organize the Syndicate, the first of four ad hoc investment, more accurately, speculation, groups, bringing in, besides financial persons, relatives and Bloomsbury friends as risk-taking principals and loan sources. (Keynes, however, provided his brokers with an unbusinesslike guarantee against losses suffered by Duncan Grant and privately charged himself with a responsibility for the losses of family and other friends.) The Syndicate had a profit of £7,000 on 14 May 1920, but all of the currencies then acted perversely, rising in the case of weak economies or falling despite the strong economies behind them. It fell into deficit in less than a week, wiping out Keynes and associates. Elevating his confidence to a new level, he proposed to the financier Sir Ernest Cassel that Cassel, sharing the profits as he thought fair, finance a new speculative effort with the astounding sum of £190,000, say £6 million or $24 million in current value. Sir Ernest's confidence in Keynes was not on that level; he *loaned* him a substantial but more realistic £5,000. Also claiming an advance on the income earned by *The Economic Consequences,* certain that his long-run analysis was correct, Keynes plunged again—to see the Syndicate fall into a deficit of £8,587 by 1 August. He refused to lose heart and the currencies began to reflect reality. By the end of 1922 he had cleared all the Syndicate's debts and listed its assets at £21,000.

One important effect of Keynes's self-confidence was his heavy borrowing, frequently at more than half of his own portfolio's value, and one important effect of *that* was his great gains and dizzying losses, particularly during the Depression of the 1930s. The three other investment groups incorporated Keynes's proliferating self-assurance, but their history too closely paralleled the general economic curve—upward to a comfortable level in the middle of the 1920s and then, anticipating the decade's end, disastrous losses. As Moggridge pointed out, Keynes suffered comparatively little from the stock market crash in 1929 because of earlier forced sales of securities to pay off great losses in commodities, particularly rubber, but also corn, cotton, and tin.[19] Between 1919 and 1929, as a result of all this activity, Keynes's net assets had fallen, going from £16,315 to £7,815. In the middle of the decade, however, they had risen nicely to £63,797 in 1924 and held in the £40,000 range over the next three years, providing generous financing for Keynes's other activities.[20]

With the investment companies vanished or quiescent in the 1930s, Keynes independently rebuilt and multiplied his fortune upon his unshaken confidence and newer wisdom. He saw a great opportunity in the United States, with its immensely productive economy and low stock prices. Shifting important investments there, he challenged the Great Depression at its source. In 1930 his assets increased modestly to £12,525, but rose to £55,222 in 1933 and nearly tripled in 1934. The year 1936, the year of *The General Theory* and its somber analysis, was the annus mirabilis of Keynes's speculative operations, his assets reaching £506,522. But the recession of 1937–38 caused a breathtaking drop to £215,244 and £181,547, respectively, in those two years. Once again large losses in commodities—lard and cotton oil—were important factors in the losses. Keynes fought his way back to £411,238, about $20 million in U.S. currency, in 1945, the last full year of his life,[21] and died a reasonably rich man.

This is far from all of Keynes's financial operations. As second and first (from 1924 to his death) bursar he revolutionized the finances of King's College. In 1940, despite his heart attack of 1937, he could not resist entering the Governing Body of Eton, where he also concentrated on investment policy. But this was hobby more than work. Early in the period, deploying his financial skills, he had plucked two opportunities in the insurance business. In September 1919 he was invited to join the board of the substantial National Mutual Life Assurance Society on the understanding that he would succeed the chairman; he did so in May 1921. In December 1923 he became a board member and Finance Committee president of the smaller Provincial Insurance Company. He left the insurance to the actuaries (and *their* probability theory) and led the companies into aggressive investment policy. He cut his style to the measure of his subject, with the greatest caution for King's College (and Eton), and caution on the City's terms (freely translated) for the insurance firms. He had left pure audacity for himself.

At King's College, in 1920, Keynes persuaded the administration to establish the "Chest," a special fund of £30,000 freed from the usual restrictions, upon which he could exercise his skills with less inhibition. With the Chest's index at 100 in 1920, it rose above 200 in the later 1920s, fell to 116 in 1930–31, rose to 738 by 1936–37, and, after a recession decline, achieved 1,124 by 1944–45. This was more than three times better than the college's regular investments, into which Keynes's fund was averaged.[22]

In similar style Keynes moved the insurance firms into aggressive purchases of common stocks. Both saw their portfolios rise, fall, and rise again in the same rhythm, and with moderated extremes, relative to Keynes's. Given the different training of insurance executives, his long experience as investor/speculator meant the addition of valuable expertise in exploiting the funds pouring into them from premiums. National Mutual, however, resisted Keynes's decisions in the depressed 1930s so stubbornly despite its portfolio's improvement that he resigned from it as part of his reduction of burdens after suffering his heart attack.[23] He stayed with Provincial.

How did the speculating relate to Keynes's theorizing? While he made a conscious connection, it remains a questionable one, since neither the speculating nor the theorizing at issue were successful. In the 1920s he had begun on the basis of "credit cycling," as he called it in a note to Richard F. Kahn, his erstwhile pupil and close collaborator.[24] The technique consorted closely with the theorizing of his *Treatise on Money*, written from 1924 and 1930 and developed around the credit (or trade) cycle. The point was to keep a step ahead of the cycle, thus "selling market leaders on a falling market and buying them on a rising one." But the ability to identify falling and rising markets and the market leaders themselves required necromancy more than economic science, and neither he nor five other practitioners of credit cycling demonstrated the "phenomenal skill" it required. Keynes fell back on his "alternative policy," which, as he detailed it in letters to the chairman of Provincial, consisted of carefully selecting a half-dozen companies with superior management and prospects, and persisting with them despite momentary setbacks. Keynes said he could not properly know more than those half-dozen firms.[25] The method would seem to depend on his own talent for personal success, and hence his ability to identify successful firms functioning in an analogous way. This begs the question: Why did he persist in plunging into three very different markets at once and wagering on many multiples of a half-dozen? We have the answer: Keynesian self-confidence.

Reparations and the related economic problems of the peace, causing the dreadful effects Keynes had foreseen, provided a unifying frame of political economy for many of his disparate activities into 1923. Thereafter, these problems continued to be important although receding to become part of the base and background of events.

A series of crises leading to, and following, the short-lived London Payments Plan of May 1921 called for successive commentaries from the expert who had predicted them, and Keynes became a highly paid free-lance journalist. From 1921 he was contributing regularly to the Manchester *Guardian;* after seeing his *Guardian* articles widely and gratuitously quoted in the foreign press, he began to negotiate the sale of simultaneous publication rights to selected newspapers from Argentina to Sweden. If France and the United States refused to be convinced, he was profitably irritating them and winning the rest of the world for his views on reparations and war debts.

In the late summer of 1921, shifting to the popular platform of the *Sunday Times* for the moment, Keynes fired off a volley of five articles on Britain's newly developing depression as related to reparations and war debts.[26] In the second article he pointed out that the need to pay was forcing Germany to compete all the more aggressively in foreign markets, with consequent damage to British exports and employment.[27] In the first article he had already doubted dramatically that the "whips and scorpions of any government recorded in history" would be ferocious enough to extract the demanded reparation sums, and predicted with his usual accuracy that the London Payments Plan would break down by early 1922.[28]

On war debts, addressed in his final article, Keynes could also see what was beyond the view of ordinary journalists. Thus, the war debts, he noted, were piled atop an annual American payments surplus of $2 billion; the situation had remained barely tolerable only because the United States had been lending about the same amount to foreign countries. Debt payments would threaten this fragile arrangement. He advised the Americans to work toward a better international economic balance by buying more and selling less. Keynes was calling attention to a dangerous situation, which, moreover, American economic policy, operating with 30 percent ad valorem tariffs, would make even worse as time went on.[29] The *Sunday Times* articles formed the nucleus of a sequel to *The Economic Consequences,* whose title demanded *A Revision of the Treaty*. Detailed, reviewing the innumerable conferences, failed agreements, and "injurious make-believe," it could not reignite the flare of interest aroused by the earlier book. But it gave longer life to Keynes's arguments and provided a text for collective action.[30]

In 1922 Keynes was engaged in two journalistic projects for the *Guardian,* one reporting for £300 on the Genoa Conference,[31] the major event in the year's economic developments, and the other attempting to alleviate the problems that had led to the conference. Meeting too long, from 10 April to 19 May, the conference was meant to reunite the economy of Europe, fragmented by war and peace, with reparations remaining the central economic issue. Lloyd George, in his last throw as prime minister, hoped somehow to work a reparation solution within a general economic adjustment. But Premier Raymond Poincaré feared a reduction of French claims and forced Britain to exclude reparations from the conference agenda. The war-debt problem remained equally insoluble, with the United States insisting on payment without discussion and refusing to participate in the conference. Genoa was only negative in sense and effect, an anticonference. The one significant act arising from it was the conclusion of the Rapallo Treaty, providing shockingly for cooperation between the outsider powers Weimar Germany and Soviet Russia. When it was signed on Easter Sunday, less than a week after the Genoa meeting had begun, Keynes gave up on the conference, which, he wrote, "is dying very feebly."[32] He had contracted for three weeks and saw no reason to linger with the delegates.[33]

Keynes's other journalistic project combined a number of the major elements of his thought from technical economic proposals to political and social philosophy in an effort to use journalism to break out beyond journalism. The means were the twelve Reconstruction Supplements, totaling 810 large pages, of which he was editor and chief writer, and which were part of the Manchester *Guardian Commercial*. Beginning at the time of the Genoa Conference and continuing into the first week of January 1923, they were meant to provide a helpful survey of Europe's economic problems.[34] With his compulsion toward grand reform, he hoped to use the *Guardian* as a forum to advance correctives of those problems. The subjects included shipping and inland water transport, relations with Russia, national finances, inflation, population and food supply, railways and coal and iron, and European opinion. Keynes wrote thirteen of the articles himself.[35] His collaborators, whom he had confidently contracted to secure wholesale, were some 200 celebrities of his world class, thus past and future government heads like H. H. Asquith (Lloyd George's predecessor), J. Ramsay MacDonald, Joseph Caillaux, and Léon Blum, and irrelevant literary figures like Maxim Gorki and Henri Barbusse, or less celebrated experts in economics like Arthur Pigou. The effort to bring together such diverse personalities in a common enterprise produced extreme diffusion, while many of the essays were harmless staff manufactures distinguished only by the names of the alleged writers.

Keynes's final article, "The Underlying Principles," attempted to lift the supplements to the level of a Bloomsbury utopia. The underlying principles, defined as the "three dogmas of peace" and so removed from rational discussion, were: disarmament, with Great Britain leading the way; English renunciation of force to hold the empire together; and free trade "on the principle of international morals and not merely as a doctrine of economic advantage." The dogmas would have put off any practical-minded person except an enemy of Britain; it is questionable if the usually practical-minded Keynes took them seriously. Indeed, ignoring the morality of it, he would soon reverse himself and attack free trade as harmful to British interests. Now, increasing his wager on the irrational, he granted that such principles or dogmas required a "passionate conviction...a fanatical fervor of conviction." But then his elegiac opening had already undercut it: "Progress is a soiled creed, black with coal dust and gunpowder; but we have not discarded it. We believe and disbelieve, and mingle faith with doubt."[36] Keynes had got back to more truth than consonant with the willed optimism of the supplements or his own utopian vision. The powerful feelings behind that vision would continue to demand expression.

Against the current of events Keynes continued to intervene in the problems of international order and economic sanity. In early August 1922 he gave a talk repeating his attacks on reparations and war debts at a summer meeting of Liberal party members.[37] Toward the end of the month he was at the World Economic Congress in Hamburg, where he pleased his German hosts by telling them much the same thing, although he quite accurately cautioned them that the allies would not make sense on reparations until next year at the earliest.[38]

In November, more actively, Keynes joined an international committee of experts in Berlin to recommend a measure of relief for Germany, unacceptable to France, and new payments drawing upon Germany's gold reserve, unacceptable to it because it was certain to cause immediate financial collapse.[39] On 19 December, back home, Keynes saw Bonar Law, who had succeeded Lloyd George as prime minister in October and, four days later, submitted a similar plan that included a four-year moratorium on German payments.[40] With this Keynes had veered in from the fringe position of observer toward the center of decision-making. His idea was the essence of the official British proposal made to France at a conference on reparations held 2–4 January 1923. Symmetrically, on the day before he saw Bonar Law, Keynes had offered his counsel to Stanley Baldwin, chancellor of the exchequer, who was going to the United States to negotiate terms for Britain's war-debt payments; he told him to resist the American terms.[41] Symmetrically, shunting him back to the powerless fringe, France and the United States rejected Keynes's theses. The United States was so visibly adamant on war debts and its good will so necessary to Britain, other experts and City people advised Baldwin, that he received the onerous terms without great protest and got the cabinet to agree to them in January.[42] Meanwhile, on 11 January, the French (and Belgians) invaded the Ruhr to seize German coal and whatever else they could get their hands on in lieu of the always unavailable German cash. The Ruhr occupation actually harmed the French interest, but France's leaders had to play the self-defeating bully rather than the gulled creditor. Keynes's advice remained too sane for use.

The international economy remained dangerously unbalanced. In Germany passive and active resistance to the occupation troops released an eruption of chaos and furnished additional materials for Adolf Hitler's early operations. As the German inflation turned into hyperinflation, with the mark reaching 4 trillion to the U.S. dollar, Hitler attempted his Beer Hall Putsch on 8–9 November 1923. The effect of it all was a false catharsis, temporarily restorative but noxious in the long run. The French recoiled from their overextended position; the Americans relaxed their isolationist rigidity and cooperated in the Dawes Plan, which prepared the way for loans to Germany to ease the reparation problem. While Britain languished in its depression, Germany and the rest of Europe could enjoy a false-bottomed prosperity.

Keynes had meanwhile found the right path for his own political action. This was by way of the Grasmere group, which met in the Lake

District, where Wordsworth had toiled, and organized itself in the summer of 1921. It would be an ideological vanguard of the Liberal party. The group included a businessman who was mayor of Manchester, a Manchester University professor of history, the historian Philip Guedalla, and William H. Beveridge of the future Beveridge Plan—an unimportant assembly of fine minds and intentions at a remove from the vulgarities of power. The meeting had come upon one idea, the creation of the Liberal Summer Schools, which, beginning in 1922, met alternately at Oxford and Cambridge, to discuss other new ideas expected to arise.[43] Keynes spoke at the first Summer School (on reparations and war debts) and was soon more deeply involved. Providing him with the appropriate instrumentality for his style of political action, the Grasmere group took another initiative in early 1923 and acquired control of the Liberal *Nation and Athenaeum,* the weekly journal of opinion. The original editor, who had steered it too close to Labour in the group's opinion, had obliged it by resigning in December 1922. His successor was expected to be the Manchester professor, but Keynes was in the process of becoming a major contributor of funds to the unprofitable *Nation* and its chairman. He made difficulties and the professor gave up. Keynes worked the selection of Hubert Henderson, a friend and colleague in Cambridge economics, as editor, and brought in Leonard Woolf as literary editor. *The Nation* in hand, he set about to light Liberalism's way toward a renewal of its promise.

At the moment Keynes was trying to move both the British political structure and economic theory toward new objectives that he could not clearly see. He trusted that the new politics and economics would join with each other efficiently.

In the new management's inaugural issue of 5 May 1923, *The Nation* called for a program of "radical social change" in the spirit, Keynes alleged, of the Liberal prewar reforms. Speaking for the party, Keynes would have its "center well to the left." As against this, "socialism" was "merely a word . . . cloak[ing] decently the nakedness of Labour policy." Yet Keynes had only words cloaking his newborn policy. He had to admit that the economic future would take on "new forms not yet shaped.... Here the ideas of all of us are so confused and incomplete.... We have no program to offer ready made.... [W]e aspire to offer a lively spot where...out of controversy and conversation, a comprehensive policy may gradually take shape."[44] Keynes had precisely delimited the Liberal terrain, but had erected nothing visible there unless one saw in the mind's eye, as he did, the flickering image of a Liberal gentleman's brave old world. For practical reasons, surely, it was a very different vision from the utopia he had imagined for his Reconstruction Supplements, but, with his computer intelligence, his genius for simultaneously carrying out innumerable additions, subtractions, multiplications, divisions, squarings, and derivings of the square root, with all his instincts for dealing with individuals and selected groups, Keynes had no sense of everyman's politics. He had written a scenario for the Liberal party to talk itself to death. But then the party was, in fact, dying of its anachronistic principles.

Later Keynesian precisions were more remarkable for their candor than their political effectiveness. At the Liberal Summer School of 1925 in Cambridge Keynes sincerely asked in a talk published by *The Nation,* "Am I a Liberal?" He had to grant that he could not "find a home by the principle of attraction," and had to content himself with "the principle of repulsion." He dismissed the Conservatives as providing "neither intellectual nor spiritual consolation," while Labour was a "class party and the class is not my class." But, "the *positive* argument for being a Liberal is, at present, very weak." He ended by repeating what he had shown to be a real question, "Am I a Liberal?"[45] In another talk and *Nation* article he pronounced: "I have played in my mind with the possibilities of greater social changes than...Mr. Sidney Webb.... The republic of my imagination lies at the extreme left of celestial space." He granted that the Liberal party was finished as a "great party machine." He had to find hope in its nonmaterial presence: "But it may play, nevertheless, the predominant part in molding the future."[46] He may have temporarily believed it.

As chairman of *The Nation,* Keynes showed himself to be a masterful administrator of a failing enterprise. He set down the broad policy lines and confined most of his leadership actions to weekly chats with Hubert Henderson. The first Keynesian issue had carried articles by Virginia Woolf and Lytton Strachey (on Sarah Bernhardt), and contributors would include many Bloomsbury and Cambridge people. There were Clive Bell, E. M. Forster, the philosopher G. Lowes Dickenson, Walter Layton (Cambridge economist, editor of *The Economist,* and a member of the Grasmere group), Osgood Sitwell, Arthur Pigou, Bertrand Russell, and T. S. Eliot, whom Virginia had first recommended for the position that went to Leonard. Keynes wrote a weekly page on finance and investment for a few weeks, and, throughout the journal's life, many articles on any subjects he found important, particularly on issues where economics and politics met. He had reduced the price from 9 to 6 pence to attract a wider readership, but, despite the brilliant talents it commanded, *The Nation*, unable to get a grip on more than the receding hem of reality, never achieved that readership and the influence it might have brought.

Well behind his social and political thought with its utopian speculations, Keynes's economic theorizing remained thoroughly, if flexibly, neoclassical. If, however, one recalls the freestyle intellection of the *Treatise on Probability*, one can see that his mind possessed the potential to radicalize his economics. The wonder is that he moved so slowly in this central area.

Keynes's early questioning of orthodoxy essentially addressed technical weaknesses in the neoclassical mechanism, thus his doubts about the stabilizing value of gold. The pure theory came hard. One of the earliest examples of original economic thinking indicated its limits. He derived one of his first new ideas from the dissertation on industrial fluctuations submitted by Dennis H. Robertson, his student and future collaborator, in 1913. "Your work has suggested to me...a superb theory about fluctuations," Keynes excitedly wrote Robertson, "I haven't nearly enough time to write it down, and am terrified lest I should forget it."[47] A few weeks later he gave a paper with the idea, which, however inspired, was clearly his own. Keynes attributed to bankers great strategic power to affect the economy positively or negatively (hence the close attention, usually negative, he paid them). If they advanced excess funds, they could "establish a scale of investment from which there must necessarily be a reaction" in the form of a slump. At the time Keynes was chiefly concerned to *restrain* investment, quite to the contrary of his future views, in order to prevent eventual depressions.[48] The war interrupted his thinking about investment, saving, and depression, and gave him time to revise it by 180 degrees. But his concern about fluctuations survived and grew.

In terms of pure economics *The Economic Consequences* had been a conservative economic document despite the iconoclasm of some of its obiter dicta. Thus, Keynes impressionistically described the West European economy as possessing an "intensely unusual, unstable, complicated, unreliable temporary nature." This derived from its being based on a "double bluff or deception," which gave the working class "very little of the cake that they and nature and the capitalists were cooperating to produce [while] the capitalist classes were allowed to call the best part of the cake theirs on the tacit underlying condition that they consumed very little of it in practice." Out of this came the double danger that both the workers and the capitalist classes would rebel, each group in its own way demanding to consume more than the economy produced.[49] One expression of the danger was inflation: "There is no subtler, no surer means of overturning the existing basis of society."[50] If this suggested more fragility in the system than most economists would grant, it was part of an argument implying the need for a firmer adherence to the principles of Marshallian economics, thus contradicting the eventual message of *The General Theory*.

Throughout the 1920s, before and after beginning to develop the ambitious theory of the *Treatise on Money* in mid-1924, Keynes expended the greater part of his thought and energy on questions of applied economics, where the theoretical and policy solutions required no more cerebration than the common-sense application of the generally accepted economic verities. It was the case of *The Economic Consequences* all over again, with the clear-sighted Keynes straining to make the practitioners of neoclassical economics *see* the disastrous mistakes they were making in interpreting their own principles. Here he also fired out bursts of radical suggestions about policy and political arrangements overleaping the new treatise and anticipating *The General Theory*, but he lacked sufficient theory to make them last.

In theory and policy Keynes had begun the decade conservatively and modestly. In February 1920 he had counseled Chancellor of the Exchequer Austen Chamberlain to increase "bank rate," the Bank of England lending rate and determinant of the other interest rates, to as much as 10 percent from the current 6 percent to break the inflationary boom.[51] He emphasized his oral advice with a memorandum repeating the figure of 10 percent: "A continuance of inflationism and high prices...will strike at the whole basis of contract, of security, of the capitalistic system generally."[52] With the economists' community agreeing, the Bank of England raised bank rate, but only to 7 percent. It was enough. Unemployment rose from 2.4 percent in 1920 to 14.8 percent in 1921, the figure remaining above 10 percent for the rest of the 1920s— and rising to 22.5 percent during the Great Depression.[53] Britain had entered *her* depression very nearly a decade before. Reacting to the unemployment level, which he had not expected,[54] Keynes readjusted his thinking and presently rated the effectiveness of monetary policy in inverse ratio to the loss of jobs associated with it. Indeed he anticipated other economists in the crucial importance he attributed to unemployment, with particular sensitivity to its political effects.

Keynes's thinking moved carefully away from deflationary solutions and accepted the risk of inflation, as articulated in *A Tract on Monetary Reform*, published as a 205-page book in November 1923.[55] The *Tract* led to more radical expressions in lectures given at Oxford University on 6 November 1924, and repeated with some additions at the University of Berlin in June 1926—the sum published the next month in a similarly entitled pamphlet, *The End of Laissez-Faire*, by the Woolfs' Hogarth Press.[56]

The *Tract* was a scattering of brilliant insights revolving around the rather modest ideal of stabilized prices. This was to be achieved by a managed currency with a flexible exchange rate. It was another effort to imagine a Great Britain freed from obedience to gold and gold standard or, as Keynes modified the sense in midflight, *dollar* standard, since the United States had the gold.[57] Yet he knew well enough, as his discussion indicated, that, given American financial dominance, Britain's currency management could still fail.

Indeed the *Tract* suspended itself between proposals for reform, which it conceded to be of doubtful value, and the neoclassical principles, which it was, at the same time, beginning to question. Thus, Keynes, still calculating in terms of the quantity theory of the Cambridge monetary school, held that changes in money quantity were counterbalanced by price changes, consequently having little economic effect in the long run. But he pointed to its limits in one of his memorable epigrams: "*In the long run* we are all dead." He mocked the professional deformation in his fellows' thinking: "Economists set themselves too easy, too useless a task if in tempestuous seasons they can only tell us that when the storm is long past the ocean is flat again."[58] Contemplating such tempests in the *Tract*, he approached the conception of liquidity preference, an early sensing that the public would hoard money rather than putting it to more productive uses. He arrived at an explicit statement, although he did not use the phrase itself, at a meeting of the Royal Economic Society on 14 April 1924. Working its way through the Cambridge monetary equation, the liquidity preference, if it rose sharply, would cause a correspondingly great fall in prices accompanied by depression and unemployment: "[I]f this is correct it opens up enormous opportunities for far-reaching reforms."[59] Overwhelmed in this way, the quantity theory lost its equilibrium, but he had nothing new to put in its place. That reform in theory would have to await the *Treatise on Money*.

Assuming that the ideal of stable prices was unattainable, the *Tract*, meanwhile, leaned explicitly toward inflation on pragmatic grounds. Keynes was extending ideas already articulated in that direction. A year before it was published he pointed out in a talk to the Institute of Bankers that postwar wages were up 80 percent compared with the 60 percent rise in the cost of living. He concluded, "The only way [wages] will get into gear will be by an increase in the level of prices."[60] In the *Tract* he developed a more general rationale: "[I]t is worse, in an impoverished world, to provoke unemployment than to disappoint the rentier." His reasoning depended on the condition of "rul[ing] out exaggerated inflations such as that of Germany."[61] Yet such inflations were just as real as modest ones. In the British circumstances, however, Keynes the pragmatic applied economist correctly saw where the greater danger actually lay. He would not have to change his thinking on that until 1939—after *The General Theory* and its concentration on unemployment to the exclusion of the inflationary danger.

The great emphasis of the *Tract* was on currency's instability of value, which Keynes saw causing "[u]nemployment, the precarious life of the worker, the disappointment of expectation, the sudden loss of savings."[62] The same motif was carried over into the whole economy by his lecture "The End of Laissez-Faire," its title emphasizing the denouement. With words that sang Keynes composed laissez-faire's elegy: "The orchestra of diverse instruments, the chorus of articulate sound, is receding at last into the distance."[63]

In its final form as a pamphlet, *The End of Laissez-Faire* transcended Keynes's concerns of the 1920s to associate itself by anticipation with *The General Theory*. Keynes explicitly advanced his theoretical operations beyond monetary management: "Most of us in these degenerate days are largely ignorant [of] why we feel such a strong bias in favor of laissez-faire." He insisted, "The world is *not* so governed from above that private and social interest always coincide."[64] He arrived at his positive formulation: social control together with an irreducibly individualistic capitalism. One already operative example of social control, he specified, was the Bank of England. This suggested socialism. Keynes was not afraid of the word and used it explicitly in a 1924 *Nation* article dealing with unemployment policy but projecting its vision further to speculate on the "true socialism of the future" as an "alliance between...the individual and the social" spheres, and in a letter to the *Times* of 25 March 1925: "The Bank of England is a type of that social-ism of the future which is in accord with the British instinct of govern-ment."[65] He also used a variant of the word in the pamphlet, where he pointed to "one of the...unnoticed developments of recent decades... the tendency of big enterprise to socialize itself." Thus, he proposed, "the owners of capital, i. e., the shareholders are almost entirely dissoci-ated from the management," while the managers were more concerned with the "general stability and reputation of the institution...than the maximum of profit." The shareholders had to be content with "conven-tionally adequate dividends," a thesis that would require more argument than he had provided.

In any case all this was a brilliant anticipation of Keynes's own future thinking and James Burnham's *Managerial Revolution* (1941). Keynes, however, was careful to distance *his* socialism from other varieties. While burying laissez-faire, he rejected "Marxian socialism" as "illogical" and "dull," and something he called "doctrinaire State Socialism" as "a dusty survival of a plan to meet the problems of fifty years ago," which might be the stodgy ideology of the Labour party or the "gas-and-water" so-cialism of the Fabians. Once again he speculated on a marriage of capi-talism and socialism, thus "possible improvements in the technique of modern capitalism by way of collective action."[66]

Keynes's socialist expressions had a considerably developed un-published infrastructure. In June 1924, among his six unwritten books of the interwar period, he outlined a "Prolegomena to a New Socialism" as an attempt to balance off capitalism's "pursuit of pleasure" with the Mooreian good of socialist "benevolence." Closely related to this was the next project, "An Examination of Capitalism" in two versions, dated November 1924 and April 1926, speculating on justice in distribu-tion and of which one section was entitled "The Decay of Capitalism." But Keynes was not giving up on capitalism. Again seeking to marry it to socialism, he concluded, "No evil in efficiency when pursued socially."[67]

If his best thinking restlessly scouted the future and undertook aggressions against the period's mental inertia, Keynes's tactical sense had to fight a long defensive battle against reactionary initiatives. The major issue, concentrating too much of the general wrongheadedness in itself, was the return to the gold standard. Having learned to rue his dear-money policy, Keynes now saw an inexorable-seeming movement to perpetuate the consequent deflation indefinitely. In February 1920, the pound was at its lowest point of $3.40, compared with its gold-standard level of $4.86. In the next few years it rose and fell insecurely, but it was at $4.28 in January 1924 and in the second half of the year "began to rise in a sinister manner." One cause of its rise was, perversely, the fact that "a return to the gold standard was definitely in the air."[68] The impalpable nature of the enemy made Keynes's opposition so difficult.

The consensus among knowledgeable people was virtually perfect on the value of gold standard and the imperative of returning to it as soon as feasible.[69] That also comprehended a return to parity, although it was technically possible to reestablish the gold pound on a lower level, as the French would do with the franc later in the decade. But it was accepted that a devalued gold pound would harm Britain's international reputation too much in comparison with such advantages as improved exports. Consistent with the *Tract*'s idea of a managed currency, Keynes was opposed to the gold pound, whether devalued or not, but the assumption of parity simplified, if it did not help, his resistance to the return.

The extent of the consensus was shown by the action in that sense by the country's first Labour government, in power from January to November 1924. In February, Prime Minister J. Ramsay MacDonald reaffirmed its commitment to move toward the gold standard. In May, Chancellor of the Exchequer Philip Snowden incorporated the consensus in a committee under Austen Chamberlain, his Conservative predecessor, to arrange the modalities. Among the members were John Bradbury, principal British member of the Reparation Commission and a former joint permanent secretary of the Treasury, and Arthur Pigou. Keynes had not been named to the Chamberlain-Bradbury Committee, but he was asked his opinion on 11 July 1924. He told its members that they would recommend the return and that they should not because the intensified deflationary effect "would probably prove socially and politically impossible." Aware of the difficulty of precise prophecy, he had weakened his case with such qualifications as "probably."[70] He was, however, supported by another former Treasury chief, his friend Reginald McKenna, now chairman of one of the five major joint stock banks and a banker untypically sensitive to broader economic and political issues. In October, in its draft report, the committee, sufficiently impressed by the Keynes-McKenna testimony, allowed itself to recommend waiting perhaps a year until the pound improved significantly beyond its present level of $4.40, 10 to 12 percent below parity.[71] To informed opinion this was only to postpone the inevitable, which, assisted by politics, came sooner than expected.

The minority Labour government fell on 8 October, before it could deal with the Chamberlain-Bradbury Committee's report; the pound floated higher upon the Conservatives' huge victory in the election at the end of the month. (That victory also drastically reduced Keynes's political base, the Liberals plummeting from 159 to 40 seats in the House of Commons.) By January 1925, the committee, absent Chamberlain as the new foreign secretary and John Bradbury in the chair, was contemplating not the 10 to 12 percent gap but, at $4.74, a teasingly slim one of 2.5 percent. To the consensual economic thought of the time the implications were obvious.

The United States, sitting atop a great gold hoard, gave an additional impulse to the British return to gold, which would help secure that hoard's value. Benjamin Strong, governor of the Federal Reserve Bank of New York, wrote Montagu Norman, governor of the Bank of England, on 4 November 1924, urging that the election results would permit a "strong policy as to...a return to gold payment."[72] In the United States six weeks later Norman heard a stronger argument, the promise of $500 million in credits to assist the move (which Britain never had to use in the end). The Bradbury Committee, similarly, did not need Norman's report of 28 January 1925 on the credits. It had already decided to recommend the return.[73]

Winston Churchill, the new chancellor and without Treasury experience, tested his experts severely in three movements to reach his decision. He first hurled all conceivable arguments against the return in a memorandum known as "Mr. Churchill's Exercise": the gold standard was a fossil that the United States wanted more than England—let it offer more support than promised, a gold pound would require the depressive effect of a high bond rate, unemployment was bad enough as it was...[74] He got reassuring responses from the experts and his last two predecessors.[75] With a wary respect for Keynes, however, Churchill took seriously his fluent strictures against the "sharp hustle back to gold" in *The Nation* of 21 February.[76] Churchill directed them back to Otto Niemeyer, the Treasury's director of finance and a member of the Bradbury Committee, asserting, "The Treasury have never...faced the profound significance of what Mr. Keynes calls 'the paradox of unemployment amidst dearth.'"[77] Niemeyer returned confident reassurances.[78] On 17 March Churchill gave a dinner party and set the two sides debating, with his decision as prize. Present were P. J. Grigg, his principal private secretary and a neutral witness, and Niemeyer and Norman versus Keynes and McKenna. They went over the too familiar arguments, Keynes insisting that the true gap was really 10 percent and not the misleading 2.5 percent; the result would be more unemployment, strikes, and "permanent contraction." In the end Churchill turned to McKenna and mentioned McKenna's experience in politics, particularly as chancellor. Grigg recalled his words: "'Given the situation as it is, what decision would you take?'" McKenna had to admit, "'There is no escape; you have got to go back; but it will be hell.'" Grigg did not report Keynes as saying anything to this. Here, as at the Paris Peace Conference, was an example of the primacy of politics over economics, and Keynes had probably faltered, suffered a rare moment of weakness (and silence!) and refused to waste his spirit by failing once again. Grigg, as observer, concluded, "I thought at the time the ayes had it."[79] Three days later, Prime Minister Stanley Baldwin concurring, the government's decision to return to gold was made. Churchill would announce it on the convenient occasion of the budget speech on 28 April.[80]

Approaching the certain decision, Keynes nevertheless returned conscientiously to the hopeless struggle in a two-part article, "Is Sterling Overvalued?" in *The Nation* of 4 April and 18 April. Again he insisted upon the 10-percent gap.[81] His first public reaction to Churchill's announcement, however, was crippled by an odd mistake. He had assumed that the government had established a maximum but not a minimum price in gold for the pound, but this would not have meant a true return to the gold standard since the pound could have continued to float below parity.[82] In *The Nation,* upon correcting his mistake, he had to give up "most of the reasons for consolation which I found last week."[83] He soon found a better expression.

Viewing the decision in all of its awfulness as a fait accompli, Keynes slipped fluently into absolute condemnation in the form of three articles for the *Times*. Its editor, however, balked at their sense and amplitude, and Keynes placed them in Lord Beaverbrook's somewhat less distinguished but better paying *Evening Standard*. After appearing there on 22–24 July, they were expanded into a pamphlet and published less than a week later by the Hogarth Press as *The Economic Consequences of Mr. Churchill*.[84] The title, added in the pamphlet, was a mild ad hominem, simply too perfect not to be used after it had presented itself. Keynes was making a point analogous to that of the first *Economic Consequences*.

Keynes had begun unkindly by asking, "Why did he do such a silly thing?" Misleadingly, using an unkinder collective ad hominem, Keynes wrote that Churchill had been "gravely misled by the experts." With the pound made 10 percent dearer, he argued more relevantly, the export industries would have to cut wages in order to remain competitive: "Those who are attacked first are faced with a depression in their standard of life.... [I]t must be war until those who are economically weakest are beaten to the ground." For the pamphlet he added two new chapters to the three original article chapters, and one of them specified the chief victims: "Why should the coal miners suffer a lower standard of life than the other classes of labor?... *They* (and others to follow) are the 'moderate sacrifice' still necessary to ensure the stability of the gold standard."[85] In May 1926, after several months of makeshifts and unsatisfactory concessions, the miners acted out Keynes's argument.

Superbly intransigent, on 3 May the miners led workers in other key industries into the general strike of 1926, a shambling, nine-day affair that disheartened all Britain.[86] Keynes supported Lloyd George's effort to find a middle ground and expressed his own ambiguities in an article meant to elucidate the situation for American readers: "The strikers are not red revolutionaries.... The strike is a protest, a demonstration.... My feelings, as distinct from my judgment, are with the workers."[87] The government, using middle-class volunteer strikebreakers, called it an attack on the constitution and broke the general strike by 12 May. The miners themselves stayed out for seven months before drifting back on the employers' terms.

There were no victors. The gold-standard advocates had wanted a general reduction of wages *and* prices, leaving the workers' living standards intact, but it was impossible, as Keynes knew. The fact of the general strike, despite its collapse, prevented employers from attempting that general reduction. Combined with the overvalued pound, Britain's comparatively high wages meant no real improvement in the export trades. In the period of the greatest world prosperity it continued to experience unemployment above 10 percent. Keynes found his direst prophecies on the return to the gold standard cruelly confirmed.

Meanwhile, Keynes was trying to find a way out of the policy impasse by way of economic theory. As early as October 1923, writing in *The Nation* about unemployment, he had warned, "The most alarming aspect...is the possibility that existing conditions may not wholly explain it.... The doubt is a dreadful one."[88] Since mid-1924, while supporting ad hoc policy correctives, he had been laboring on the *Treatise on Money*, which might provide that explanation.

Notes

1. Keynes's figures, *CW*, 2: 100–101, 126; discussion, chap. 5, "Reparation," ibid., 71–142.
2. For the short- and long-run proportions of the problem, see David Felix, *Walther Rathenau and the Weimar Republic: The Politics of Reparations* (Baltimore, 1971), 67–79.
3. *CW*, 2: 170–79.
4. Ibid., 169–70.
5. Ibid., 160–89.
6. Harrod, *The Life*, 283.
7. Many of these details, ibid., 286–87; Moggridge, *MK*, 352–54.
8. Quoted, introduction (Polly Hill), John Maynard Keynes and Lydia Lopokova, *The Letters of John Maynard Keynes and Lydia Lopokova*, ed. Polly Hill and Richard Keynes (New York, 1990), 27.
9. Ibid., 28.
10. Frances Spalding, *Vanessa Bell* (New Haven and New York, 1983), 196.
11. See Milo Keynes, ed., *Lydia Lopokova* (London, 1983).
12. Letter to Jacques Raverat, 8 June 1924, in Virginia Woolf, *The Letters of Virginia Woolf*, vol. 3, edited by Nigel Nicolson (London, 1977), 115.
13. Letter, 24 October 1924, Keynes and Lopokova, *Lydia and Maynard*, 240.
14. As reflected in their letters, ibid., passim.
15. Moggridge, *MK*, 194, 348–52; *CW*, 12: 4. Harrod has Keynes *beginning* his speculating in 1919; see *The Life*, 288. Harrod later explicitly denied the wartime speculation in the press; see Skidelsky, *JMK* 1: 286–88.
16. Letter, Keynes to John Neville Keynes, 28 August 1914, quoted, Skidelsky, *JMK*, 1: 293.
17. Letter, Keynes to his associate, O. T. Falk, 18 September 1931, and editorial note, *CW*, 20: 611–12.
18. This account draws upon studies of Keynes's financial operations in chaps. 1–3 of vol. 12 of the *CW*, edited by Moggridge, and his *MK*, 348–52, 407–11, 585–86.

19. Moggridge, *MK*, 408.
20. Table, *CW*, 12:11.
21. Ibid.
22. "Keynes and King's," ibid., 88–92; table, p. 91.
23. Excerpt, letter, Keynes to O. T. Falk, 11 October 1938, ibid., 47.
24. Letter, Keynes to Kahn, 5 May 1938, ibid., 100–1.
25. Letters to F. C. Scott, 15 August 1934; 10 April 1940; 6 February 1942. Ibid., 55–57, 77–78, 81–83.
26. Under the general title, "Europe's Economic Outlook," ibid., 17: 242–78, including related correspondence and notes.
27. "New Reparations Settlement: Effect on World Trade," 28 August 1921, ibid., 249–56.
28. "New Reparations Settlement: Can Germany Pay?" ibid., 242–49; quotation, p. 248.
29. "Settlement of War Debts," 18 September 1921, ibid., 272–78.
30. Reprinted as *CW*, vol. 3; quotation, p. 5.
31. Keynes's articles, letters, etc., on Genoa, ibid, 17: 354–425. Keynes also got honoraria from £25 to £350 from other newspapers. On the conference see Carole Fink, *The Genoa Conference: European Diplomacy 1921–1922* (Chapel Hill, NC, 1984); Felix, *Walther Rathenau*, 127–46.
32. Keynes to E. T. Scott, his *Guardian* contact, 19 April 1922, *CW*, 17: 390.
33. Editorial note, ibid., 390.
34. Editorial notes, ibid., 400, 446–48; Harrod, *The Life*, 312–15.
35. Moggridge, *MK*, 376.
36. Published 4 January 1923, *CW*, 17: 448–54; quotations, pp. 452, 451, 450, 448.
37. "A Moratorium on War Debts," 4 August 1922, ibid., 18: 12–17.
38. "Hamburg Address," 26 August 1922, ibid., 18–26.
39. Editorial note, ibid., 62–63; Felix, *Walther Rathenau*, 179.
40. Keynes's plan, 23 December 1922, *CW*, 18: 97–99.
41. Letter, Keynes to Baldwin, 16 December 1922, ibid., 99–100; editorial note, 103.
42. Editorial note, ibid., 104.
43. Grasmere, the Summer Schools, and *The Nation*, ibid., 127; Harrod, *The Life*, 331–38; Moggridge, *MK*, 390–93.
44. Editorial Foreword, *CW*, 18: 123–26; quotations, pp. 125, 126.
45. *The Nation*, 8 and 15 August 1925, ibid., 9: 295–306; quotations, pp. 295, 296, 297, 298, 306.
46. "Liberalism and Labour," *The Nation*, 20 February 1926, from a talk at the Manchester Reform Club, 6 February, ibid., 307–11; quotations, pp. 309, 311.
47. Letter, 28 September 1913, quoted, editorial note, ibid., 13: 1.
48. "How Far are Bankers Responsible for Alternations of Crises and Depression?" Paper presented to the (London) Political Economy Club, London, 3 December 1913, ibid., 2–14; quotation, p. 6.
49. *CW*, 2: 1, 11–13.
50. Ibid., 149.
51. Chamberlain's notes, ibid., 17: 180–81.
52. "Memorandum on the Bank Rate," 5 February 1920, ibid., 181–84; quotation, pp. 183–84.
53. B. R. Mitchell, *European Historical Statistics 1750–1970* (New York, 1978: abridged edition), tables, pp. 66, 69.

54. .According to Chamberlain's notes, above, *CW,* 17: 180.
55. Reprinted as vol. 4 of the *CW.*
56. Ibid., 9: 272-94.
57. Discussion, ibid., 4: 154-59.
58. Ibid., 65.
59. Ibid., 19, part 1: 206-14; quotation, p. 208.
60. The fourth and last in a series of lectures, 5 December 1922, ibid., 60-76; quotation, p. 66.
61. Ibid., 4: 36.
62. Preface, ibid., xiv.
63. As expressed in the pamphlet *The End of Laissez-Faire, CW,* 9: 272-94; quotation, p. 272.
64. Ibid., 227, 287-88.
65. "Does Unemployment Need a Drastic Remedy?" *The Nation,* 24 May 1924, ibid., 19, part 1: 219-23; quotations, p. 222. Ibid., 347-49; quotation, p. 348.
66. Ibid., 9: 289, 285, 290, 292-93.
67. Quoted and discussed, R. M. O'Donnell, "The Unwritten Books and Papers of J. M. Keynes," 807-10.
68. Harrod, *The Life,* 357.
69. Detailed history of the return, D. E. Moggridge, *British Monetary Policy 1924-1931: The Norman Conquest of $4.86* (Cambridge, 1972), with later precisions in chap. 17, "The Return to Gold," of his *MK,* 414-45.
70. Keynes's testimony, *CW,* 19, part 1: 239-61; quotation, p. 242. The committee's official name was purposely noncommittal: Committee on the Currency and the Bank of England Note Issues.
71. Moggridge, *British Monetary Policy,* 49-50.
72. Quoted, ibid., 56.
73. Ibid., 61.
74. Quoted in full, ibid., Appendix 5, 260-62.
75. Ibid., 70-74.
76. "The Return Towards Gold," *CW,* 9: 192-200; quotation, p. 193.
77. Letter, 22 February 1925, quoted, Moggridge, *British Monetary Policy,* 76.
78. Undated letter, quoted, ibid., 76-77.
79. Account of the dinner, P. J. Grigg, *Prejudice and Judgment* (London, 1948), 182-95; quotations, pp. 183, 182.
80. Editorial note, *CW,* 19, part 1: 337.
81. Ibid., 349-54.
82. "The Gold Standard," *The Nation,* 2 May 1925, ibid., 357-61.
83. "The Gold Standard—A Correction," *The Nation,* 9 May 1925, ibid., 362-65; quotation, p. 362.
84. Editorial notes, ibid., 416, 417; "The Economic Consequences" (condensed by Keynes for republication), ibid., 9; 207-30.
85. *CW,* 9: 212, 211, 223.
86. See, for example, W. N. Medlicott, *Contemporary England 1914-1964* (London, 1976; 1st ed.: 1967), 223-30.
87. "Reflections on the Strike," (for *The New Republic,* but unpublished) *CW,* 19, part 2: 531-34; quotation, pp. 531-32.
88. "Population and Unemployment," *The Nation,* 6 October 1923, ibid., part 1: 120-24; quotation, p. 121.

4

Theorizing of the Middle Period:
A Treatise on Money

In Keynes's lifetime of inexorable success, his *Treatise on Money*, his only work to go beyond one volume, was the grand exception. In it all of his strengths and weaknesses were given space in which to play themselves out to the greatest extent: his gift for exquisitely refined syllogizing and fluent management of contradictions, practical intimacy with business and finance, mathematical and verbal artistry, a generalist's taste for history and other disciplines, skill in shaping of the material to fit the theory, and his faith in his intuition. A genius had released his creativity too freely. Yet the failure left behind a wealth of materials that would be reworked into *The General Theory*, his greatest achievement, with scintillating fragments left over for his distinguished service to nation and community of nations.

Keynes was building upon the work of Knut Wicksell, the great Swedish economist and contemporary of Marshall. Seeing stable prices as basic to economic stability, Wicksell concentrated on the investment-saving relation, subject of his brief book, *Interest and Prices* (German edition: 1898).[1] This relation was affected for good and ill by another relation, that between the two Wicksellian interest rates. One, which Wicksell called "the natural rate of interest on capital," was actually the rate of the return on capital, or profits in brief, the other being "the rate of the interest on loans" or the "market rate." If the natural rate (profits) was higher than the market rate (the cost of funds), entrepreneurs would be encouraged to borrow more to expand production, resulting in price increases and boom conditions. If, on the other hand, the market rate was greater than the natural rate, Wicksell concluded ominously, entrepreneurs would reduce investment and "prices will fall continuously and without limit."[2] Hence, price and general economic stability, the great objective of Keynes's *Tract on Monetary Reform,* was best achieved when the market rate was most nearly equal to (but still lower than) the natural rate. Wicksell's doubled relation, investment-saving/natural interest rate-market interest rate was the armature around which the theorist Keynes wound the elaborations of his *Treatise on Money.* Keynes the policymaker, meanwhile, was placing more and more emphasis on low interest rates to encourage business investment and so increase production and employment.

Encouraged by Keynes's ambiguities on the Wicksell-Keynes relation, Harrod and Moggridge have loyally attributed independent creation to him.[3] Thus, while Wicksell flourished a long generation before him, the *Treatise* discussed the great Swede as if he and Keynes were contemporaries, with Wicksell perhaps a half-step behind. It began with a suggestion of equality of effort and effect: "In substance and intention Wicksell's theory is closely akin...to the theory of this treatise..." But then Keynes continued the sentence with a comment that would reduce the value of Wicksell's contribution and so put his own above it: "...although he was not successful...in linking up his theory of the bank rate to the quantity equation." At another point Keynes wrote, "I feel that what I am trying to say is the same at root as what Wicksell is trying to say."[4] Here the late Professor Wicksell (1851–1926) seems to be still trying to keep up with Keynes. Inspection shows the absolute dependence of Keynes's *Treatise on Money* on Wicksell's *Interest and Prices.*[5]

It was actually in pursuit of Dennis Robertson's thinking, a fact that he more easily admitted, that Keynes conceived of his treatise. Robertson was evidently better acquainted than Keynes with the Continental economists, Wicksell notably. As we have seen from Robertson's prewar dissertation, he had pursued the quite Wicksellian concern with industrial fluctuations. Returned from the war, he had first written the graceful and illuminating *Money* (1922), which became a leading textbook on the subject, for Keynes (general editor of the Cambridge Economic Handbooks in one of his proliferating capacities). Returned to his older preoccupation, Robertson then undertook his 103-page, richly suggestive *Banking Policy and the Price Level: An Essay in the Theory of the Trade Cycle,* which would be published in January 1926, a profoundly Wicksellian—and somewhat Keynesian—exercise. Indeed its title more accurately describes Keynes's book than the one Keynes eventually chose. Keynes, meanwhile, was thinking out his basic idea and in July 1924, in a pattern he would repeat in the case of *The General Theory,* wrote the first of a series of tables of contents that served as outlines of the work-in-progress. He achieved a second table of contents on 9 October; on 30 November, he completed the third one, *and,* as he informed Lydia, "I have begun the new book!—today, and have written one page."[6] A few weeks earlier, on 12 October, he had written her, "I met Dennis and took him back to my room. I told him the contents of my egg and he told me the contents of his."[7]

Maynard and Dennis collaborated on both books, although the collaboration of Dennis most affected the origins and foundations of Maynard's book, while Maynard most affected the two major, penultimate chapters of Dennis's book, which comprised nearly half of the latter and much of its sense. In his introduction Dennis wrote that chapters 5 and 6 had been "rewritten...so drastically at [Keynes's] suggestion that I think neither of us now knows how much of the ideas therein contained is his and how much is mine."[8] In 1928, approaching completion of the *Treatise,* Maynard wrote Lydia, "Dennis came in last night and we had a long talk about the new theory. I think it will do...but it owes a great deal to him."[9] And to Wicksell, one might add.

Personally tender, professionally demanding, and profoundly different, Maynard and Dennis inflicted deep and complex agony upon each other. Maynard, objecting confidently to a thesis of Dennis, wrote Lydia, "I'm *sure* it's wrong; so afterwards I went round to bully him again and almost to say he ought to tear it up and withdraw it from publication."[10] This led to the collaborative chapters. For his part, Dennis, who had been moderately severe about Maynard's work, sent him a revised draft of his book, signaling, "I am so unconfident that I should always like to put at the top of everything I write, 'Nobody must believe a word of what follows.'"[11] These contrasting personal characteristics would lead to equally different theoretical and policy conclusions.

Richard Kahn, who would succeed Robertson as Keynes's junior collaborator-in-chief, commented dryly, "It is difficult...to pretend that Robertson's tortured writing and Keynes's tortured collaboration...were conducive to clarity of thought."[12] But the process *was* conducive to a creativity of thought, however obscure, out of which came brilliant work, however contradictory, by both collaborators. Robertson, realistically self-abnegating about his own professional specialty, took the position on page 1 that "far more weight must be attached than is now fashionable...to certain *real,* as opposed to monetary and psychological causes of fluctuation." On policy he argued that fluctuations could be "relatively desirable" and that the "*immediate* interest of the manual worker" could not be used as a standard against which to judge economic policy: "[I]t may well be that the ultimate interest even of the wage-earning class...is best served by a measure of industrial instability."[13] In pure theory Keynes might agree, but, as Robertson well knew, Keynes the policymaker balanced off Keynes the theorist. For the moment Keynes's policy toward his protégé's book was to ignore the conclusions already expressed or reserved for the final chapter and concentrate on the joint analysis of the classically Wicksellian investment-saving relation in chapters 5 and 6, which led well beyond Wicksell. In this way Keynes helped shape the analysis in a form that could lead, if he knew where he meant eventually to arrive, to *his* conclusions.

In those two chapters Robertson plunged into a new vocabulary articulating new conceptions, or, at least, variations of older ideas so original that they suggested new ways of thinking. Quirky, insecure emotionally beneath the intellectual insecurity, he was demanding too much of himself by his own standards and trying to achieve exquisite precision beyond the capacity of the economist's professional language. For saving he employed the word "lacking" to express its essential character as liquid wealth reserved for business investment. Among other examples "dislacking" meant consuming more than earned; "abortive lacking," hoarding; "automatic splashing," consuming more than intended; and "imaginary capital," national security or prestige as "immaterial wealth."[14] In attributing reality to what was lacking and its variants Robertson was according just importance to the *non*existence of various economic components. He was also noting the importance of intentions as well as faits accomplis. All this profoundly affected the contemporaneous construction of Keynes's *Treatise on Money* and, perhaps with a stronger effect in the long run, the foundations of *The General Theory,* loosening the cause-and-effect relationships of neoclassical economics for the first and helping effectively to deny them for the second. But then, as Robertson made clear, Keynes was an important originating force in the thinking behind the two chapters.

In the second of the jointly created chapters, however, Keynes permitted Robertson sufficient independence to move toward non-Keynesian conclusions. Robertson had already mentioned the positive values of fluctuations and instability. At a certain point in the trade cycle characterized by excessive prices, he went on in his expressive language, a responsible banking system had to restrain the boom "by churlishness" in meeting increased demand for circulating capital. (Keynes's prewar paper had advocated a similar caution.) But "a secondary fall" occurs, which further lowers prices and "begets a further 'unjustifiable' decline on the side of industrial output." Now, having changed his thinking, Keynes would demand easier rather than restrictive credit even before he had conceived of a complete theoretical rationale, and the discouragement of Robertson's last chapter further widened the difference between the two. Robertson emphasized the dangers of hampering recovery and doubted the value of "heroic capital development" and "the once heretical, but now perhaps over-respectable policy of 'public works.'"[15] If Keynes accepted most of the analysis, he rejected the hopelessness of his friend's policy advice. In the *Treatise on Money* and in his actions to influence policy he moved on toward *his* conclusions.[16]

Keynes began writing the treatise with a bold statement of the conception he intended to develop, entitling it "A Summary of the Author's Theory." This appeared in a draft of the proposed first chapter, written, as noted above, in November 1924. He explained that for numerous reasons the amount of money available for production was imperfectly coordinated with the need for it. One result was the credit cycle (also called, as Robertson preferred, the *trade* cycle),[17] with the "supposed remedies…capable…of aggravating the disease [while the] credit cycle itself, by causing…further fluctuations…tended to bring about its own repetition." Confidently, he continued, "If this analysis of the credit cycle is correct, it makes the nature of the cure fairly obvious." He had to grant, "Before, however, we can reach this goal, we must concentrate on a somewhat troublesome analysis."[18] Hence, he intended to comprehend the essential nature of the credit cycle and show how to correct its destructive fluctuations. In the end, if the cure was obvious, the way to achieve it, beginning with the analysis, was indeed troublesome. The process took six years and incorporated itself in at least seventeen successive draft tables of contents projecting Keynes's theorizing forward,[19] and an ultimate physical expression in 2 volumes, 7 "books," 38 chapters, and 689 pages.

At one point Keynes specified, "Booms and slumps are simply the expression of the results of an oscillation of the terms of credit about their equilibrium position." But at another he mentioned Ralph G. Hawtrey, director of financial enquiries at the Treasury and a prolific writer on monetary economics, as having "gone a good deal further than I...in arguing that the credit cycle is a 'purely monetary phenomenon.'"[20] In fact, scattering shreds of the problem throughout the treatise, Keynes argued alternately as if his credit cycle was a purely monetary phenomenon and as if every conceivable real factor, economic or otherwise, affected it.

To penetrate to the essence of his credit cycle Keynes felt obliged to develop a new instrument. Before the replacement is studied one should examine what it is that he proposed to replace. The accepted explanation for beginning to understand money and its function in the economy was the quantity theory and its mathematical instrument, the quantity equation. The equation can demonstrate many important aspects of the behavior of money by setting up an equality, hence its character as *equation,* between two pairs of variables. (The nonmathematical reader should be reassured that this explanation will not enter into mathematics any deeper than to mention the formula to be translated into plain English.) One such quantity equation is $MV=pY$, where M is the quantity of money in a given economy; V, the velocity of turnover of money in the purchase of newly produced goods (or services); p, the price index; and Y, the level of real income. Thus, at any moment, the amount of money multiplied by its turnover rate must equal the price expressed as an index times the amount of real income. This can be made more meaningful if we put it to work in situations known to the reader. What would happen if the amount of money doubled in a short time, as occurred in Germany or Russia in the early 1920s or, to pick a period nearer to us, the Russia of the early 1990s? If the V for velocity and the Y for real income did not change, a doubling of M, the money quantity, would require a doubling of p to maintain the equality. Thus, the price index or price paid for the average good or service would double. With this one has an elementary sense of inflation, an important phenomenon in the life of money.

One more step will add useful meaning. Suppose that M-money was doubled but the statisticians reported that prices had tripled. The equation would continue to be an equation and produce equality if V for velocity, for example, were increased as M increased. That makes sense. If a swift inflation is in progress, people would tend to turn their income into purchases faster because they realize that it was losing value as long as it was expressed in money. The German hyperinflation of 1923 was the classic example of accelerating money-quantity *and* money-velocity increases, with workers paid daily or more often so that they could hurry to make their purchases before prices increased again. Thus the quantity equation inexorably at work.

Wicksell had been unhappy with the quantity theory and devoted a chapter of *Interest and Prices* to attacking it as a "mere truism." But he pulled himself up short: "It is far easier to criticize the quantity theory than to repeal it by a better or more correct one." He devoted the rest of the chapter to showing the failures of the theory's opponents and concluded: "So it is no good; the quantity theory cannot be thrown overboard.... The quantity theory is the most competent of all the methods of interpretation that have so far been advanced of the oscillations of the general price level.... It must be put up with."[21] To Keynes, Wicksell was another of his teachers he was obliged to correct.

Keynes did so by saying: "The fundamental problem of monetary theory is not merely to establish identities or statical equations relating (e.g.) the turnover of monetary instruments to the turnover of things traded for money." Remaining in its character as a truism, as Wicksell himself had conceded, the quantity theory had failed to go beyond postulating identities. Hence, it had failed to "analyz[e] the different elements involved in such a manner as to exhibit the causal process by which the price level is determined." The old theory had also failed to develop a dynamic character and so pursue monetary phenomena in their movement through the economy. It will be simpler to begin with the first objection and leave the problem of dynamics for later.

In order "to exhibit the causal process" Keynes broke down the components of the economy into many more elements than the quantity theory felt competent to manage. Thus, his more complex analysis distinguished between "windfall profits" and those defined as the "normal remuneration of entrepreneurs," the earned equivalent of workers' wages as opposed to unearned good fortune. While Keynes explained the principle behind the distinction, he did not show how the earned and unearned parts of income could be identified in the real economy. Thus, as he remarked, "the income of holders of ordinary shares will usually include elements of each of these items."[22] One asks how the tax authorities could implement a law that set different tax rates on the shareholders' part of a given firm's earned and unearned income. The distinction, causing more problems wherever it appeared, ran all through the economy. Yet it was only one of the many that Keynes saw in money itself.

Money was subject to a continuing process of division. Initially Keynes categorized it into income and business and savings deposits. In another movement, however, he divided savings deposits into demand and time deposits.[23] Returning to them a dozen chapters later, he found that he had to "cut...across our division of the total quantity of money...into *industrial*...and *financial circulation*," the first comprehending all income deposits and part of business deposits, and the second taking the rest of the business deposits plus all of the savings deposits.[24] He did not explain how one could calculate with these multiple, shifting categories.

Under the rubric of money, inflation itself became a cluster of four categories. There were income inflation (wages, salaries, and normal profits), profit inflation ("windfall" profits), and commodity and capital inflation. Keynes was characterizing these inflations by their origins, the given variant of inflation expressing itself in disproportionate increases in given economic sectors, thus in earnings or windfall profits, or the prices of consumer or capital goods.[25] The logic of the *Treatise* could do nothing with such categories since, as Keynes had to concede, one form of inflation often led to others: "The occurrence of either a commodity inflation or of a capital inflation will tend to cause a profit inflation; and a profit inflation will bring about an income inflation."[26] One generally supportive interpreter wrote that Keynes had simply confused production increases with price increases.[27] Moreover, while Keynes had verbally and mathematically defined his four inflations, he refused to define the fundamental term "inflation" itself, as he had withheld the definition of "probability," crucial aspects of the *Treatise*'s money vanishing into the indefinable. With money lost in these confusions, Keynes was unable to develop his promised method of price-level determination. He was no more successful when he used his own apparatus to provide a dynamic theory.

In the *Tract on Monetary Reform*, one may recall, Keynes had satirized comparative statics, the method employed by the quantity theory, which permitted believing economists "only [to] tell us that when the storm is long past the ocean is flat again." The best the theorists of the old theory could do was to describe economic phenomena at given stages, without filling in the interstices between the stages. But neither he nor any other economist to date has produced a genuinely dynamic economics. One reason, among many, is the intrusion of noneconomic factors into the "tempestuous seasons" he wanted to study, for example, the political factors he noted in his two books on "economic consequences." Another reason is "chaotic behavior," which resists analysis. "[O]ff-equilibrium behavior remains to this day a rather fuzzy area of economic investigation," one dictionary of economics put it.[28]

The dynamics of the *Treatise* is barely more than promise. Keynes touched directly upon the transition process in four passages totaling a half-dozen pages in the whole book.[29] Only in the last is a suggestion of movement to be found. There Keynes conceived of a notation for monetary velocity that signified greater than normal or "unity" velocity when investment was "in excess," unity when investment and savings were equal, and less than unity when investment was deficient. This is possibly a pregnant conception, but it led to no actual examination of patterns of monetary fluctuations. Book 4, another heuristic effort, is promisingly entitled "The Dynamics of the Price Level" and seems to aim at its essence in the section, "The Problems of the Transition."[30] But Keynes fell upon an "essential awkwardness" due to the fact that a change in the "quantity of bank money is algebraically consistent for a time with more than one set of consequences."[31] Hurled back by too many such ambiguities, he was reduced to an essentially anecdotal narrative of insecurely specified causes and effects in various sectors of the financial economy. At one point in the final chapter, on international disequilibrium, Keynes dispensed with his dynamics to scramble to the security of "the new position of equilibrium as compared with the old," thus the theoretically spurned comparative statics.[32] (Remaining with this latter method, he made no effort to apply dynamics in *The General Theory*.) So much for the dynamics of the *Treatise*.

Keynes's replacement for the quantity equation, asserting their superiority in their name, was, collectively, his ten fundamental equations. They appeared, assigned to chapter 4 of Book 1, in the fifth known table of contents, dated 6 April 1925, some nine months after the first one.[33] From that point to the last draft table of contents the fundamental equations grew in importance from one chapter to eight chapters, making up all of Book 3. They increased beyond that. Keynes had then decided on a two-volume work, the first volume dealing with the pure theory of money, and the second, the applied theory. He shifted five of the eight fundamental-equation chapters from the first volume to the second volume as the ensemble of Book 5, and wrote three new chapters around the equations to replace them in volume 1. In sum the completed *Treatise* devoted 11 chapters and 181 pages to the fundamental equations. They were its engine and drive train as well.

What do the fundamental equations tell us? The final equation, when translated into words, arrives at this ultimate statement: "Price level of output as a whole equals production cost plus (unearned profit divided by total output)," or price equals cost plus profit.[34] Accusing the quantity equation of too simple a formulation, Keynes had produced an even simpler one, useless in theoretical exposition and empty of meaning. In its denial of supply-demand price determination, resting on the classical labor theory of value, it is also reactionary. The distinguished American-Israeli monetary economist Don Patinkin, the supportive interpreter mentioned above, concluded, "[H]e all too frequently shifted unawares across the slippery line that lies between tracing 'cause and effect' (as Keynes put it) and simply repeating tautologies inherent in those equations."[35] With its failed fundamental equations the *Treatise on Money* remains immobile at its starting point.

If the fundamental equations must be left behind, as economic science has confirmed, Keynes himself had reactionary second thoughts about the inadequacy of the quantity equation. At least twice he restored it in the *Treatise* to accomplish what his own equations failed to do for him. In volume 1 he tried to explain "The Relation of the Price Level to the Quantity of Money," as the section title put it, and had to call in the enemy for help. Introducing a new equation, he admitted that it "bears a family relationship to Professor Irving Fisher's familiar equation," which was a variant of the quantity equation.[36] Once again, at the beginning of volume 2, Keynes remarked disarmingly, "I may appear to the reader to be reverting to the old-fashioned 'quantity of money' approach." On the next page he granted it baldly, "Let us write our quantity equation as follows."[37]

Keynes the historian tried to strengthen his pure theory with the fifty-four-page chapter 30, "Historical Illustrations," which found inflation more beneficial then deflation in line with his recent thoughts on policy. In the case of Spain, France, and England he could see "an extraordinary correspondence between periods of profit inflation and of profit deflation, respectively, with that of national rise and decline." But then he had to grant that "the decline and fall of Rome was contemporaneous with the most prolonged and drastic inflation yet reported."[38] Other historical illustrations cooperated no better with the *Treatise*'s theory.

Like Keynes's equally unsuccessful theory of speculative "credit-cycling," the *Treatise* was a vain effort to anticipate the movement of the credit cycle. In his theorizing, the monetary authority operating through a central bank, unlike the private speculator, could go beyond anticipation and control or, at least, powerfully influence that movement in terms of its responsibility for the general welfare. This was the central message of the *Treatise on Money*—to grant extraordinary power and responsibility to the managers of money. Following Wicksell, Keynes saw the credit cycle being generated by price changes as related to costs, thus creating either profits or losses and leading to increases or decreases, respectively, in production and employment. The proper monetary leadership would try to reduce the oscillation with the help of stable prices and so maintain the economy in a continuing state of profitability by way of the appropriate levels of production and employment. It was for this reason that Keynes campaigned incessantly, after the postwar boom had broken, for lower interest rates, thus lower investment costs. Easy credit, however, remained a simplistic solution to a perverse problem. Indeed the prewar Keynes, one may recall, specifically counseled against it as productive of a boom surely enough, but a boom inevitably pursued by crisis and slump. The *Treatise* of the postwar Keynes only obscured the problem under a heap of irrelevant theoretical refinements.

Having failed to achieve an effective theory for a national economy like Great Britain's, Keynes shifted onto international terrain, where a sensible order of things might assist domestic reform. A powerful "supernational bank" would manage the value of gold according to a commodity index; it would also set the international bank rate and engage in open-market operations.[39] Looking back to Keynes's conception of a central bank for India, it looked forward to the International Monetary Fund and the World Bank, which Keynes would help conceive and bring into existence. But such a bank was much more powerful than the latter two *plus* the Federal Reserve Board, the Bank of England, and the Banque de France. While it was visionary to constructive effect, the idea that nations would give up command of their own economies to such a bank was, to use a favorite adjective of Keynes's, crazy.

When the *Treatise* was published, the contemporary reality joined perversely with a paralyzing theoretical error to make the book's acceptance even more difficult. Its model of the economy assumed constant output based on full employment, Keynes having innocently accepted that neoclassical assumption while attacking its theory. Great Britain's 10-percent unemployment for the period 1922–30 made the assumption look odd, and it appeared odder when the figure rose to almost 15 percent in 1930 itself before increasing to 22.5 percent in 1932. The *Treatise* did allow for unemployment, but it was usually placed just over the horizon, following a fall in prices, and not seen as a central concern. With the fundamental equations expressing the full-employment conception rigidly, Keynes was led to provide a reductio ad absurdum of his own logic. This became known as the "widow's cruse fallacy" from his reference to the Bible story about the miraculously refilled oil cruse of the widow who helped the prophet Elijah (1 Kings 17:9-16). Thus, he concluded that profits spent by entrepreneurs on "riotous living" had no other place to go except back to the entrepreneurial pockets as still more profits accrued, the pattern repeating itself indefinitely. On the other hand, if they had losses, saving to pay the losses generated an equal amount of additional losses, again in a repetitive series, this time ending in bankruptcy.[40] This is one of a number of examples, others to follow, in which Keynes became his own severest critic.

Keynes dealt with the apparent contradiction between book and reality in two ways, both constituting exceptions. In the year of the *Treatise*'s publication he inserted a ten-page section in volume 2 on "The Slump of 1930," in which he speculated on the possibility of a continuing decline, with increasing unemployment and a "far-reaching socialism" replacing "capitalist individualism."[41] If this matched up with what was threatening to happen in the real economy it denied the book's neoclassical theory. The other exception was his parable of a community producing and consuming one product, bananas. A thrift campaign then plunged it into a deep depression that might end with a production halt, total unemployment, and starvation for all. Once again, if this had its realistic suggestiveness, it was achieved by ignoring the *Treatise*'s theory.

The banana parable is worth pursuing for another reason, its seductive absurdity. One can speculate that its relation to the real circumstances justified its use precisely because it did not obey the *Treatise*'s economic laws. Indeed, the parable has received perhaps more attention than the rest of the book. But it is a false analogy, failing to relate to economic science as well as to the economics of the book. A one-product community cannot represent an economy. In that society there is nothing for which the one product can be exchanged, hence no exchange, no buyers and sellers acting independently—none of the economy's essential characteristics. The banana community is a production unit or aggregation of such units functioning under administrative and not economic laws. Yet the parable, seized upon out of desperation, has been taken seriously as an instructive analogy.

In another effort to break out past the theoretical limits of the *Treatise,* also veering into the pragmatic dimension, Keynes speculated on enlisting the monetary cranks as auxiliaries. At the very least they could serve to balance off those nay-sayers to reform, the bankers. The *Tract on Monetary Reform*'s doubts about the virtue of gold had called up a grateful correspondence from the heretics, who sensed in Keynes a fellow believer. Their 200 years of flourishing existence, he agreed, argued powerfully "that the orthodox arguments cannot be entirely satisfactory."[42] While questioning the cranks' lack of a theory of money and interest,[43] he was now more tolerant of their errors than he had formerly been in the case of John Hobson. Keynes agreed with them that the bankers were not trying to maintain the optimum level of employment.[44] His reasoning, advancing beyond the *Treatise,* was already en route to *The General Theory,* where his objections to the heretics' approach would be forgotten.

Keynes ended the book with an abrupt, three-page "Conclusion" attached to the final chapter. He had to grant that the book had not achieved what he had set out to do: "Is monetary theory more ready to take the critical leap forward which will bring it into contact with the real world?" His answer was a promise: "I believe that the atmosphere...is favorable to such a result." He was admitting that the result was still in the future. Referring to his ambition to create a dynamic theory, he similarly claimed for his treatise no greater role than that of "a contribution to this new phase of economic science."[45] And so he made his escape from the book—from the theory he could not think out.

Keynes should not have been so surprised and hurt by the negative comments among the many favorable and even awed reviews. He had been his own first critic, beginning to separate himself from the *Treatise* in the preface itself: "The ideas with which I have finished are widely different from those with which I began. . . . There are many skins which I have sloughed still littering these pages."[46] It was an extraordinary service that he demanded of his readers: identify those discarded parts and move sympathetically with the theorist to the indistinctly identified newer ideas. Whatever admissions he had made in the book, he still had faith in its fundamental statement, however ineffable, and defended it dexterously against reviews lacking sufficient sympathy to grasp it. But even the best reviews presented difficulties. The friendly fellow economist (and railway chairman) Josiah Stamp saluted it as "the most penetrating and epoch-making since Ricardo," but had to admit he did not understand all of it.[47] Similarly, the Harvard economist John H. Williams mentioned its "rare combination of penetration in theoretical analysis, grasp of mathematical statistical method, and felicity of expression." But he found important parts confusing and complained of a "sense of my shortcomings" in understanding the whole.[48] Two reviews were particularly painful.

In a long review article Dennis Robertson crystallized out his resistance to Keynes's newer ideas. In a covering note he had to write Maynard that he could not "subscribe to the fundamental analysis of your *Treatise*."[49] His comments, noting Keynes's prefatory doubts, agreed with him that the book failed to achieve the "harmonious synthesis" that his ideas needed, thus the contradictory introduction of the fundamental equations as both truisms and operative causes in the economy.[50] If Dennis was a friend, Friedrich von Hayek, the young but already formidable Austrian, then at the London School of Economics, was a friendly acquaintance. His two-part review began by agreeing with Robertson's that the *Treatise* was "the expression of a transitory phase in a process of rapid intellectual development." Protesting the "almost unbelievable" and "inconsistent use" of terms in such distinctions as the division of profits into earned and unearned, Hayek found the book's essential argument lacking a clear conception of capital and saving. More specifically, he found its author ignorant of the Austrian theory of capital, the source of the Wicksellian ideas upon which Keynes himself had built.[51] Keynes reacted personally as well as professionally to both reviews.

Keynes's basic public position was that neither critic had understood the book. "Mr. Robertson's difficulties" were due "to our minds not having met on certain large issues."[52] Privately he had written comments on the galley proofs and passed them on to Richard Kahn, whom he was finding useful as a personal editor and similarly collaborative replacement for Dennis. Kahn bravely defended Robertson on one point. At another criticism Keynes burst out, "Mr. Robertson's last paragraph... yes!—a mere relic of Sadistic—well, not so much barbarism as puritanism. But at this point psycho-analysis must take charge." Kahn advised, "I hope that you will decide to *omit*."[53] Keynes omitted. In the case of Hayek, Keynes began by finding his thought so rooted in a different theory that he could not comprehend new ideas. But then Keynes began "drifting into a review," in his words, of Hayek's *Prices and Production*, which he found "one of the most frightful muddles I have ever read." Hayek was a misdirected "remorseless logician...end[ing] up in Bedlam."[54] (In his response Hayek suggested that Keynes might be "trying to distract the attention of the reader...by abusing his opponent."[55] This writer easily agrees with the justice of either's critique of the other's work.)[56] Keynes's copy of the Hayek review had thirty-four penciled marks or comments, one of them regressing to adolescence: "He evidently has a passion which leads him to pick on me."[57] If Keynes's more professional expressions defended the book with his usual skill, he himself was not convinced.

On 5 January 1931, two months after the *Treatise* was published, Keynes wrote to an economist-correspondent, "My own feeling is that now at last I have things clearer in my own head, and I am itching to do it all over again."[58] From that January until May, Richard Kahn, Joan and E. A. G. (Austin) Robinson, and others among Keynes's younger professional associates gathered together in the "Circus," as it became known, "to digest it, to understand its implicit assumptions, and, inevitably, to criticize it."[59] With their help Keynes's thoughts on the *Treatise* were moving insensibly into the thoughts constructing *The General Theory*.

Notes

1. Knut Wicksell, *Interest and Prices* (*Geldzins und Güterpreise*), trans. R. F. Kahn (London, 1936). Keynes arranged the assignment for his protégé Kahn.
2. Ibid., 102, 120.
3. Harrod, *The Life*, 409; Moggridge, *MK*, 79.
4. *CW*, 5: 167, n. 177.
5. Keynes recommended publication of the English translation of *Interest and Prices* and a condensed English edition of Wicksell's lectures (this latter project not being carried out) in a letter and report to his old Eton friend Daniel Macmillan, 3 October 1932, ibid., 12: 862–65.
6. Keynes and Lopokova, *Lydia and Maynard*, 265. The sentence (rewritten) survives along with the page and more; see *CW*, 14: 19–22.

7. Keynes and Lopokova, *Lydia and Maynard*, 234.
8. Dennis H. Robertson, *Banking Policy and the Price Level* (London, 1926), 5.
9. Letter, 20 January 1928, quoted, editorial note, *CW*, 29: 2.
10. Letter, 22 May 1925, Keynes and Lopokova, *Lydia and Maynard*, 327.
11. Letter and memorandum, *CW*, 13: 29-33; quotation, p. 33.
12. Richard F. Kahn, *The Making of Keynes' General Theory* (Cambridge, 1984), 62.
13. Robertson, *Banking Policy*, 1, 22.
14. Ibid., 41, 45, 48, 45.
15. Ibid., 79, 81, 94, 96.
16. See J. R. Presley, *Robertsonian Economics* (London, 1978). Influenced by Keynesian thought, Presley found no more positive qualities in it than the modest creator claimed.
17. This is not to suggest that credit cycle and trade cycle are necessarily synonymous. *Credit* cycle implies that the cycle is essentially a money and credit phenomenon; *trade* cycle could suggest that nonmonetary factors are significant.
18. Draft chap., *CW*, 13: 19-22; quotations, p. 21.
19. Reprinted, ibid., 15-18, 27-29, 41-50, 78-82, 113-17.
20. Ibid., 5: 165; 6: 117.
21. Knut Wicksell, "The Quantity Theory and Its Opponents," *Interest and Prices*, 38-50; quotations, pp. 41, 43, 50.
22. *CW*, 5: 111-12.
23. Ibid., chap. 3, "The Analysis of Bank Money," pp. 30-43.
24. Ibid., 217-18.
25. Ibid., 140.
26. Ibid., 253.
27. Don Patinkin, *Keynes' Monetary Thought: A Study of Its Development* (Durham, NC, 1976), 36-37.
28. Entry, "Trade Cycle," *The New Palgrave*.
29. *CW*, 5: 120, 131-33, 137-38; ibid., 6: 4-5.
30. Book 4, ibid., 5: 217-326; "The Problems of Transition," ibid., 241-47.
31. Ibid., 243.
32. Ibid., 300.
33. Ibid., 13: 28.
34. In Keynes's notation, "$\pi = W_1 + Q/O$," ibid., 5: 124. Patinkin arrived at the same "translation," *Anticipations of the General Theory?* (Chicago, 1982), 7.
35. Patinkin, *Keynes' Monetary Thought*, 51.
36. *CW*, 5: 131-5; quotation, p. 135.
37. Ibid., 6: 4, 5.
38. Ibid., 132-86; quotations, pp. 143, 134.
39. Ibid., 356-64.
40. Ibid., 5: 125.
41. Ibid., 6: 338-47; quotations, p. 346.
42. Ibid., 193.
43. Ibid., 5: 160-61.
44. Ibid., 6: 198-99.
45. Ibid., 364-67; quotations, p. 365.
46. Ibid., 5: xvii.
47. Stamp, review, *Economic Journal* 41 (June 1931): 241-49; quotation, p. 242.
48. J. H. Williams, "The Monetary Doctrines of J. M. Keynes," *Quarterly Journal of Economics* 45 (August 1931): 547-87; quotations, pp. 547, 587

49. 2 May 1941, *CW,* 13: 201–12; quotation, p. 211.
50. Dennis H. Robertson, "Mr. Keynes's Theory of Money," *Economic Journal* 41 (September 1931): 395–411; quotation, p. 395.
51. Friedrich A. Hayek, "Reflections on the Pure Theory of Money of Mr. J. M. Keynes," *Economica* 11 (August 1931): 270–95; quotations, pp. 270, 271.
52. Keynes, "A Rejoinder," *Economic Journal* (September 1931), *CW,* 13: 219–36; quotation, p. 236.
53. "Addendum II: R. F. Kahn's Comments," ibid., 237–38.
54. Keynes, "The Pure Theory of Money: A Reply to Dr. Hayek," *Economica* (November 1931), ibid., 243–56; quotations, p. 252.
55. Friedrich A. Hayek, "A Rejoinder to Mr. Keynes," *Economica* 11 (November 1931): 398–403; quotation, p. 398.
56. See also Friedrich A. Hayek, *Prices and Production,* 2nd ed. (London, 1935). This edition was substantially altered as the result of many criticisms besides Keynes's.
57. Editorial note including quotation, *CW,* 13: 243.
58. Letter to Bertil Ohlin, ibid., 29: 8.
59. Moggridge, editorial note, ibid., 13: 338.

5

Policy-Making

Keynes's writing of the *Treatise on Money* was interwoven with his untiring efforts to make policy, the treatise itself to serve as its theoretical rationale. As early as 1923, as we have seen, Keynes had been emphasizing the dreary importance of unemployment and the need to do something about it. In 1924 he joined Lloyd George, both easily forgetting old differences, in the latter's proposal of public works as a solution. In *The Nation* of 24 May an article of Keynes's responded to one of Lloyd George's published there previously: "We have stuck in a rut. We need a new impulse, a jolt, an acceleration."[1] The nature of the cure, however, indicated that Keynes could not provide the economic theory to justify it. He could only suggest that the situation was so bad that one must not wait for the requisite long thoughts to come. He was also urging measures, already suggested in the *Tract on Monetary Reform* and elsewhere, that would therapeutically reverse the current deflation into a measure of inflation. He called one such measure a "great experiment," another confession of poverty in theory.[2] But the established doctrine dominated, as the return to gold in 1925 proved. Thus, while trying to erect his countervailing conception, Keynes continued his pragmatic wagers on policies that might conceivably work.

Not afraid to act the consummate busybody and perhaps falsely imagining that he was not doing enough, Keynes went off as a free-lance reformer on a merely regional level. In *The Nation* of 13 November 1926, he directed his critical attention upon "the apparently suicidal behavior of the leaders of Lancashire." They had failed to act decisively against the reduction in demand for cotton goods. He carried his solution personally to Manchester and hurled it at large audiences at three successive meetings. It was a cartel that would improve the efficiency of the better firms and kill off the weaker ones. The marginal firms,

85

however, refused to commit suicide on Dr. Keynes's prescription, and the action broke down by 1927.[3]

Earlier in 1926 Keynes engaged himself in a more appropriate action, a major effort by the Liberals to work both their own and the British economy's revival. After more than a year of wide and possibly deep study, the Liberal Industrial Inquiry, which included many members of the Grasmere group, produced the thick book, *Britain's Industrial Future*, in January 1928. In February, Maynard reported to Lydia that the book deservedly "has had a bad press." It was twice as long as necessary: "Any reader must be discouraged."[4] He had, however, slipped into it the advocacy of substantial publicly controlled capital expenditure, but was frustrated in an effort to make the program more exciting—and controversial. He had also proposed a somewhat socialistic reorganization of industry, the banker Robert H. Brand successfully objecting that such a measure would blunt vital profit-seeking initiatives in the economy and keeping the idea out of the published work.[5] All this had been in addition to Keynes's formal responsibility for two of the programs's five "books," unexciting treatises on business organization and finance. More to the point, another "book," perhaps under his influence, vaguely suggested the possibility of countercyclical public works. Whatever deficiencies in their program, the Liberals entered the election of May 1929 more richly outfitted with ideas than the two other parties.

The Liberal campaign, Keynes participating variously, was as lively as their program was earnest. On 1 March Lloyd George, at a meeting of Liberal Members of Parliament and candidates, pledged that the public-works projects he had in mind would reduce the number of unemployed by as much as 586,000 in a year. Keynes supported that claim in two polemical articles in Lord Beaverbrook's *Evening Standard*—on 19 March and 14 April—and, collaborating with Hubert Henderson, in the pamphlet *Can Lloyd George Do It?*, this last published on 10 May, twenty days before the election.[6] Keynes was using a primitive form of his (and Richard Kahn's) famous multiplier. According to this, the increased employment and hence spending generated by the public works would bring about a much greater indirect increase in employment to satisfy the new demand—thus the multiplier multiplying the effects of a given sum of productive investment.[7] Here Keynes the theorist and Keynes the politician and policymaker were fused.

The Conservative government, meanwhile, was composing a policy statement with two main arguments that were variable depending on the memorandum being used by the given spokesman. The ultimate document was the White Paper compounded of a Treasury memorandum plus four ministerial memoranda issued on 19 May.[8] One argument, the "Treasury view" proper, based itself on pure theory to the effect that the demand for loans financing public projects would compete with the demand of private entrepreneurs for loans, increasing interest rates and thus "crowding out" the weaker borrowers. Thus, public employment would tend to reduce private employment *pari passu*. The other argument, responding to the immediacy of the election campaign, said more modestly that Lloyd George's scheme would run into great practical difficulties because of its size. The term "Treasury view" was, however, usually taken to mean the first argument, and Chancellor of the Exchequer Winston Churchill had used it explicitly in his budget speech of 16 April: "It is the orthodox Treasury dogma, steadfastly held, that whatever might be the political or social advantages, very little additional employment and no permanent additional employment, can, in fact, and as a general rule, be created by State borrowing and State expenditure."[9] Once again Keynes was dealing with the economic consequences of Mr. Churchill.

Keynes and Henderson tried to counter Churchill's exposition of the Treasury view with an ad hoc rebuttal. They contended that the government could draw upon three new resources: the funds used to pay the unemployed who had since become employed as a result of public spending, the "rescue" of savings otherwise being lost through inadequate credit, and funds released by a possible reduction in foreign lending.[10] But the authors tacitly admitted the highly speculative nature of their argument by making no effort to quantify the results they claimed to expect. Moreover, the Treasury people could easily rebut the multiplier argument by pointing out that in pure theory the higher cost of funds would cancel out such positive effects. Against this, the *Treatise on Money* providing no direct help, Keynes could produce neither a specific logical defense nor a counter-theory in which the Treasury view would be seen as irrelevant. In any case, the Liberals could not convince enough of the electorate that they possessed a solution to stagnation and unemployment.

In the politics of 1929 the enterprise of the Liberals and Keynes failed. "The bold plans...which were to be so largely incorporated into British policy during the next twenty years, were either derided as unworkable by the Tories or calmly annexed by the Labour Party."[11] In the election the Liberals, with 5,308,510 votes, got 2 million more than in 1924, but the Conservatives had 8,656,473 votes, an increase of two-thirds of a million, while 8,389,512 votes went to Labour. Votes were not accurately translatable into Parliamentary seats; Labour, with fewer votes, won more than the Conservatives, 288 to 260, while the substantial Liberal figure produced only 59 seats, just 19 more than in 1924. Labour took office again, while the Liberal party was confirmed in its state of near-extinction. "This really marked the end of Keynes's active public life as a party politician," Harrod wrote.[12] Inapt as a party man, Keynes could respond more than willingly when the Labour government sought his services as policymaker in a double capacity.

Keynes's function as chairman of the Liberal *Nation* hardly conflicted with his new role or roles, while any suggestion of ambiguity soon vanished. Given the state of the party, its journal of opinion was beginning to founder and lose more money in the process. Keynes's solution was to unite it, beginning with the issue of 18 February 1931, with the further left *New Statesman* as the *Athenaeum* had been united with *it*, the party of the second part fading away. Keynes would become chairman of the new enterprise and install Kingsley Martin, a bright young man on whom he had had his eye since 1923, as editor. In the new circumstances Keynes would find himself in the character of a constitutional monarch, more ruled than ruling, and Martin, engaging bright Marxists as subeditors, would lean toward Labour and more left than that as well.[13]

On 5 November 1929, just a few days after the Wall Street crash and the beginning of the Great Depression, Philip Snowden, again chancellor of the exchequer, appointed Keynes and fourteen other experts to the Committee on Finance and Industry. On 25 November, Ramsay MacDonald, again prime minister, invited Keynes and seven other experts to a luncheon at 10 Downing Street on 2 December, the purpose of which was to advise him to do what he wanted to do, improve the economic advice his office was receiving. This meant another appointment for Keynes. The man and the circumstances were extraordinarily well met. Keynes had been preparing precisely for such opportunities, the first calling upon his longer thoughts and the second challenging him to deal with the swiftly developing economic crisis.

Whatever its theoretical limitations, the *Treatise on Money* concentrated Keynes's mind usefully upon the investment-saving relation and its application to Britain's problems. That relation emphasized the terrific need, as the Depression gathered force, of reducing interest rates as much as possible to restore the abysmally discouraged business investment. Another way to achieve this end was the policy of protection in case the cost of investment funds could not be sufficiently lowered; the neoclassical free trader Keynes was willing to accept these implications as well. If the theory he employed was too narrow, the richly experienced pragmatist Keynes could envision the best policy solutions and trust he would duly expand it to support them upon a base of professional right reason. Moreover, his theorizing, as we have seen, had got beyond the *Treatise* before he had sent the final proofs to press and, with the help of the Circus, was continuing to move swiftly forward.

The Committee on Finance and Industry, to be known eponymously after its chairman, a Scottish barrister and future jurist unrelated to the publishing family, had been conceived before the crash as a response to Britain's unique, long-enduring depression. While it also perforce sought a solution for the crisis that befell it, the Macmillan Committee's mission dictated justice to all serious viewpoints, an inclusiveness that would delay recommendations until too much damage was done. Keynes's other opportunity, however, placed a greater premium on speed. With his precise sensitivity to the economic and political implications, Keynes responded swiftly to MacDonald's vague demand for better economic advice. If he was always eager to give it, Keynes now saw the chance to impress his prescriptions upon a huge and shapeless emergency pathetically in need of an economist's unique abilities and experience. He produced two memoranda laying down a policy for MacDonald and sketching the agency to implement it. While dealing with two distinct areas of operation, both demanded utopian extremes of good economic behavior. The emergency might provide an opportunity for doing Mooreian good.

Keynes's first memorandum, written soon after the 2 December luncheon, launched itself into full speed with its first sentence: "The Prime Minister to [call for] a drastic reorganization and reequipment of the industry of the country on a considered plan...and for a determined onslaught by all sections of the community on the problem of unemployment." To this Keynes wanted "subjoined a number of statements as follows from various authorities": the Bank of England and the chairmen of the five major joint stock banks would promise ample credit, while the leading trade unions and employers' associations, observing a truce, would agree to the status quo in wages during 1930, and other organizations would cooperate in the same sense.[14]

The second memorandum, following a second luncheon on 9 December, proposed an "Economic General Staff" headed by a "considerable officer of the state." It would "engage in continuous study of current problems affecting national economic policy." The idea, including the name, had been published a half-dozen years earlier by William H. Beveridge, future creator of the Beveridge Plan, in Keynes's *Nation.*[15] To this Keynes had added the possibility of improving "the distribution of wealth" and the explicit objective of achieving "the deliberate and purposive guidance of the evolution of our economic life," thus a conscious movement toward the democratic socialism he had been advocating since the mid-1920s.[16]

Both proposals vanished like dreams on a gray winter morning. The socialist prime minister knew utopianism too well to take it seriously as policy. In any case the powerful interest groups were giving sufficient evidence that they would not make the risky sacrifices Keynes had so effortlessly imagined for them. The economic general staff would take form as the Economic Advisory Council; composed of worthy experts like Keynes and a senior economist assisted by a small staff, it would meet monthly with a distracted prime minister. The EAC would serve perhaps even more usefully, given the political context, as a defense of the prime minister against charges of economic illiteracy and nonfeasance. Of course, on second thought, Keynes knew better than to expect grand administrative and economic solutions. He could equably attend the two subsequent December meetings in which his—and others'—ambitious ideas were ground down to harmlessness, MacDonald commenting on the cabinet secretary's "most useful criticism" at one point.[17] By the time the newly constituted EAC held its first formal meeting, on 17 February 1930, Keynes had undertaken practical measures to make the most of what he had to accept as a modest agency of economic advice. At least the object of that advice was the head of government and personally hospitable to Keynes's ideas.

One other Englishman of consequence had agreed with Keynes on the urgent need for large-scale action and, like him, made proposals to that end. He was the acutely ambitious Oswald Mosley, who had, in fact, anticipated Keynes and the Wall Street crash. On 11 September 1929, as chancellor of the Duchy of Lancaster, a noncabinet post, Mosley suggested a great road-building program and the creation of a body much like the EAC. He followed that plan with a second, grander one on 16 January 1930, which demanded extensive governmental reorganization and specified a £200-million government loan for general public works as well as road construction. Concerned about disturbing the financial markets, he sent a copy of his conception to Keynes.[18] Responding sympathetically and professionally, Keynes took account of the "crowding-out" argument of the Treasury view: "Any new investment and...any increase of employment...[tend] to raise the rate of interest." He aggressively refused to permit the argument to inhibit action: "To object to additional borrowing...on this ground is a most desperate fallacy."[19] Mosley's proposal went to the cabinet's Unemployment Policy Committee and, with the cabinet concurring on 8 May, the committee rejected it flatly: "[W]e must not be rushed into shoveling out public money."[20] Mosley resigned from the government on 20 May. In 1931 he left the Labour party to found his New party, and, by 1932, a British fascist movement. In 1933, when Keynes was advocating a policy of protection and national self-sufficiency, Mosley congratulated him on his "fascist economics." Keynes responded to the effect that his ideas were meant "not to embrace you but to save the country from you."[21]

Keynes and Mosley were struggling against the intensified perversity of the economic science of the time. Neoclassical economics knew no response to depression except to reduce expenditures and increase taxes. The rationale was that balanced budgets would eventually encourage business expansion, but meanwhile it meant bankruptcy, unemployment, and desperation. Many neoclassical economists, Dennis Robertson and Arthur Pigou among many others, did indeed support measures that would counter the terrific deflation, but they were crippled, as Keynes would point out, by their inability to justify those measures theoretically. Uninhibited in this manner, Keynes was moving to jettison the old theory and replace it with one that fit the problem. Meanwhile the dominant policy, enforced by bankers domestically and internationally, was obediently carried out by all governments until 1933, when Hitler and Roosevelt, however differently motivated, would undertake their expansive policies. Before then unemployment paralyzed the Weimar Republic as it continued to remit reparation installments and tried to find money to support the jobless. Events were ferociously validating the prophecies of *The Economic Consequences of the Peace*.

Unlike Mosley, Keynes remained to function within the constraints as given. Accommodating himself to the slow ruminations of the Macmillan Committee, which had begun meeting on 21 November 1929, he concentrated first on the EAC's potentials. He dropped his utopian ambitions and slipped easily back into his character as a tireless member of committees. It meant acceptance of lost time as the British economy bumped its way downward. Before the EAC's first meeting he had persuaded Hubert Henderson to leave the moribund *Nation,* reject another offer, and accept the post of its senior economist.[22] With his man in place, Keynes persuaded MacDonald at that first meeting to create a Committee of the Economic Outlook "to attempt a diagnosis" of the essential nature of the economic problem.[23] As committee chairman he tried to move its members to quick, appropriate recommendations—and failed. While the other economist on the committee, the Fabian G. D. H. Cole, supported his expansionist ideas, the two business members wanted wage reductions and other deflationary measures. The result was two diametrically opposed reports in May, with the union representative on the committee impartially signing neither.[24] At the EAC's last meeting before the summer, merely frustrated, Keynes resiliently suggested a new committee composed solely of economists. This was based on another utopian belief, albeit a lesser one, that sane economists, like dentists on teeth, could agree on a substantial number of scientific truths. Once again MacDonald gave Keynes what he wanted, creating the EAC's Committee of Economists, accepting four out of six of his nominations for its members, and making Richard Kahn one of the two joint secretaries. Keynes's nominees were Henderson, Pigou, Josiah Stamp, and Lionel Robbins, the last the youngest professor of economics in England and presumed respectful of Keynes's seniority and position. Keynes had to let the summer slip by in holidays, but MacDonald offered a measure of hope; he indicated that he wanted the committee's report in hand to meet the new session of Parliament on 28 October.[25]

Keynes directed a blizzard of two memoranda and four other papers at the committee members and commanded them to five long meetings in September and October. He had ruthlessly reduced his recommendations down to protection in first line (while retaining public works as supplementary) because an effective tariff system could be achieved by "a single act of legislation…not likely to be particularly unpopular."[26] But he had picked capable people with strong minds. It was actually

Robbins, once a guild socialist but now staunchly neoclassical, who offered the greatest resistance. Keynes fell into "fits of almost ungovernable anger" to bully him and created a law forbidding a minority-of-one report. Robbins said he would take his case to the cabinet. Remarking on his "emotional state," Keynes gave up. The younger man's dissent, entrenched in free-trade principle, insisted, "A tariff is an affirmation of separation, a refusal to cooperate, a declaration of rivalry." Against such national-suicidal sentiments in a period of ruthless economic nationalism, Keynes can be excused his moment of purposeful fury.[27]

Even if Keynes had been free to write the Committee of Economists' report himself, the result would have been no different. With most members supporting Philip Snowden on his free-trade principles, MacDonald was unable to command the cabinet on economic policy. The first and most telling response of the cabinet, which got the report on 24 October, was to delay discussing it until early December. The decision was an anticlimax. A cabinet committee dominated by Snowden found it a "disappointing document" lacking "practical propositions."[28] The Committee of Economists had taken over the initiative from the EAC itself, and the rejection of the report's recommendations only confirmed the council's ineffectiveness in the government's operations. By 1931 it had faded into insignificance. So ended Keynes's endeavors with this approximation of an economic general staff. Again refusing to give up, he could only redirect his energies elsewhere and submit to an even slower pace of dealing with economic disaster.

Keynes's long and frequently intense labors on the Macmillan Committee preceded, paralleled, and succeeded his efforts on the EAC. By the time it had submitted its report on 1 July 1931, the committee had held about a hundred meetings evenly divided between examining fifty-seven expert witnesses, as well as discussion and drafting sessions.[29] Taking the most initiatives of the fifteen members, he participated aggressively in all the major aspects of the committee's operations.

Keynes also served as a seminar leader on the application of his *Treatise on Money* to the economic situation. The point was to exploit the particular expertise of the members, and Keynes's theorizing merited five sessions from 20 February to 7 March 1930. On that first day, Hugh P. Macmillan, the chairman, spoke for most members in finding the *Treatise*'s investment-saving relation "extraordinarily useful" as illumination. On the second day, however, Keynes's parable of the bananas, lacking the force of a true analogy, met general bafflement and specific rejection by Professor T. E. Gregory of the London School of Economics, the only other economist on the committee. When Keynes rather loosely reported that the Cambridge economists were "now satisfied, I think, that [the *Treatise*] is accurate," Macmillan adjudicated, "I cannot believe that finality has been reached even in an exposition by you."[30]

Testing the *Treatise* in this way, Keynes was being driven to appreciate its practical limits. Thus, the investment-saving relation began promisingly in his sense by implying that a lowering of interest rates would encourage enterprise by reducing the cost of funds, a policy that he had long urged. As early as the second day of his exposition, however, he had to concede that the encouragement might not work in "a chronic state of underinvestment, bad profits, unemployment and so forth." In the final session he had to admit that it could be like pushing a worm forward by the tail: "[I]f there are no...borrowers ready to come forward...then it may very easily prove to be a bit of a fiasco."[31] His pure theory had nothing more to say.

While his theory had failed him, Keynes as applied economist effortlessly dazzled and solidly impressed his fellow committee members. Over the sessions of 28 February and 6–7 March he discussed at considerable length the possibilities of seven practical corrective actions.[32] Reviewing the option of leaving the gold standard, he coolly stipulated the political impossibility: "There is no likelihood of such a remedy being accepted in the present circumstances." Dismissing other action as ineffectual or unpolitic, he arrived at protection, consistent with his policy at the EAC. Yet he could not forbear dwelling also on "my own favorite remedy" of public works, in the long run "the one to which I attach much the greatest importance." He could conclude that either remedy would strengthen the other. Macmillan could confidently speak for all: "[W]e are greatly indebted to you for your exposition, not only of the orthodox view...but also the more startling views...with which you developed your argument."[33] Again this was not belief but respect qualified by skepticism.

In the sense of theory and the long run, projecting beyond the committee's mission to the ideas leading to *The General Theory*, Keynes's most important intervention was his encounter with a Treasury spokesman. At issue was the proposal for large-scale investment in public works, which the Treasury view had opposed essentially with its "crowding-out" thesis. Having lost the argument in the politics of the election of 1929, Keynes was all the more eager to win now. In two days of questioning and testimony, on 16 and 22 May 1930, he could put the opposing position to the test in the person of Sir Richard Hopkins, the Treasury's controller of finance and the dramatically perfect adversary. "Diminutive... with the general appearance... of an extremely intelligent monkey... on the subject of finance [Hopkins] was an intellectual match for anyone in his generation" in the competent opinion of Lionel Robbins.[34] Questioning other Treasury policies, Keynes sought to find weaknesses in general while approaching the Treasury view by indirection, but Hopkins remained imperturbable.[35] It was Macmillan, perhaps tiring of the preliminaries, who brought up the real issue. Moving easily with him, Hopkins remarked on the "exceedingly able and lively pamphlet in which Mr. Keynes rather severely, though not unkindly, beat the Treasury about the head." He defended the Treasury view with both arguments mentioned here, the first about the practical difficulties of undertaking any large public works. Only then did he arrive at the crowding-out thesis: "[I]t does make a hole in the capital... available." At this Keynes complained that Treasury policy "bends so much that I find difficulty getting hold of it?" Hopkins equably responded, "Yes, I do not think these views are capable of being put in the rigid form of a theoretical doctrine." Keynes gave up, "I find... that the Treasury view has been gravely misjudged?" Hopkins was gracious, "But I should be very sorry if Mr. Keynes thought all his strictures on the Treasury were quite unjustified. Many of them were very fairly earned!" Macmillan concluded, "I think we may characterize it as a drawn battle!"[36]

A draw meant that Keynes had lost. Confronted again with the crowding-out thesis, he had failed to win the fellow committee members. Yet a rebuttal was indeed possible and Sir Richard, discussing popular reactions to given schemes, had, in fact, suggested it: "[T]he atmosphere in which schemes may be undertaken will itself condition the immediate consequences which they produce."[37] Thus, popular psychology, expressing confidence, or lack of it, expectations, and intuitions generally, had its effect as well. It was friendly territory to Keynes, who could agree with Sir Richard that such factors made the difference between success and failure. Appropriately applied to any economic proposition, they could soften its angularities to the point where it would give way and permit practical actions passing the test of common sense. Another factor might outflank the problem. An inflationary situation might well enliven enterprise by encouraging purchases and reducing concern about the cost of funds. In the circumstances, however, Keynes could not blurt aloud so disreputable a solution despite his earlier public expressions in the *Tract on Monetary Reform* and the press. The point was to achieve an inflationary effect without uttering the word "inflation," but he lacked the right formula, which required a volatile mixture of economics and politics. In the present tense he had to concede defeat.

Keynes got no better results out of a succession of other expert witnesses. The practitioners among them—bankers, businessmen, and labor leaders—were barren of ideas except for those affecting the specific defense or amelioration of their situation. The banker-in-chief, Governor Montagu Norman of the Bank of England, limited himself to seeing "the salvation of industry...first of all...in rationalization." The other committee members had already agreed with Keynes on the limits to the effect of mere efficiency improvements and could go on to join him in incredulity when Norman, trying to avoid his responsibility for the depressive consequences of a high bank rate, denied that the rate affected business activity: "No, I do not think one necessarily governs the other."[38] Departing "thoroughly depressed," Norman modulated his statements in a later appearance before the committee without providing useful enlightenment.[39] The governor might betray the sterility of the policy he represented, but negating his negation hardly advanced Keynes's policy with the committee.

The economists were no more helpful than the practical men. Among them, Dennis Robertson and Arthur Pigou ran too true to form, Robertson in his pessimism and Pigou in his neoclassical remove from economic immediacy. Under Keynes's insistence Robertson granted that public works might have a positive effect, but would virtuously finance them through taxation, thus taking away with one hand most, at least, of what the other was giving to the economy.[40] Pigou began agreeably for Keynes: "The first point I want to stress is that the center of the whole thing is the volume of unemployment." But he then produced a statement of such even-handed ambiguity that it could paralyze all action: "[T]he cause of unemployment is either that the real rate of wages is all right, but there is not enough demand; or if one takes the demand as given, one can say that the rate of real wages is too high." About policies favored by Keynes, he applied a criticism that could be stored for use against *The General Theory*: "But all these devices such as devaluation and inflation...act only insofar as the workers are so to speak bamboozled."[41] Pigou knew too much for comfort, his own as well as the nation's.

Accepting the languors of the Macmillan Committee's mission, aware of the penalties for time lost, Keynes nevertheless fought indefatigably to make the most of its eventual report, however tardy it might be. After the testimony of the winter and spring of 1930, the committee, like the Economic Advisory Council, adjourned for the summer months. As recounted above, Keynes could distract himself with his hopes for the recommendations of the latter's Committee of Economists. In the fall, as the report containing those recommendations expired of neglect, he participated in a round dozen of Macmillan Committee sessions preparing its collective thinking for *its* report. From January to the end of May 1931, the period during which his Circus was reinterpreting the *Treatise of Money*, he engaged in thirty drafting sessions. A member of the drafting subcommittee, he quickly wrote out an outline, which the report followed approximately.[42] He had to struggle against the counter-effects of his dominating initiatives. Thus, Macmillan had cautioned during the fall discussions that the report's monetary part should be "express[ed] in different language [from the *Treatise*] as it might be said that the committee swallowed Mr. Keynes's arguments whole."[43] In the course of the drafting, undeterred, Keynes wrote a memorandum pressing for the "drastic reduction of the whole complex of market rates of interest," which was "analyzed...at considerable length in my book."[44] Professor Gregory, already practiced in resisting Keynes, protested in a counter-memorandum that the committee was "being presented with an ultimatum: 'If you do not accept the explanation of the trade cycle as set forth by me, the alternative is to say that there is no explanation...that, in fact, economic theory breaks down.'"[45] The result was a substantial setback to Keynes's ambitions for the committee's report: "[T]he chairman decided to draft a fairly flat concluding note for the body of the report and left [it to the] members...to make their own proposals in the form of addenda."[46] Like the EAC's Committee of Economists, the Macmillan Committee would produce a report vulnerable for its lack of consensus.

Keynes refused to give up. Trying to save something, he organized a party of six among the fifteen committee members who signed the twenty-page Addendum I articulating somewhat more affirmative ideas. Among his supporters were Reginald McKenna, his loyal companion of earlier policy struggles, the labor leader Ernest Bevin, and a leader of the cooperative movement. But Keynes had to soften his proposals for the sake of agreement and failed, in the end, to achieve it, Bevin and the cooperative representative appending a reservation to the addendum preferring devaluation (which Keynes himself preferred in general but not in the circumstances) over protection.[47] In sum Addendum I proposed protection and public works, but failed to specify the character of the latter. Thus, Keynes accepted the possibility of increased taxes, which he contended would cancel out too much of the expansive value of the expenditures. The report proper raised itself upon a lucid rendering of the problem, which owed much to his analysis, and collapsed into feeble hopes of international banking cooperation and a series of disagreements expressing themselves in four addenda, five "reservations," and a "memorandum of dissent," this last by the enduring John Bradbury, the former Treasury joint secretary, who opposed *all* economic intervention as delaying the natural neoclassical recovery. As in the case of the Committee of Economists' report, it made no difference.

The country's consensual thinking was such that on 11 February 1931, while the Macmillan people were drafting their report, all three political parties joined in creating a competitive committee embodying ideas essentially like Bradbury's. Each party had further supported the principle by delegating two of its members to the Committee on National Expenditure, as it was named, although twenty-one Labour backbenchers broke discipline and voted against the measure. The new committee owed its existence to an initiative of Keynes's Liberal party, which gave it the mission of "advis[ing] on reductions in the national expenditure," thus deflation piled on deflation as the only conceivable policy.[48] The neoclassical principle was enforced by the international banking community, which would provide Britain financial backing only if it demonstrated its probity by rigorous economies, and by the great financial crisis of 1931 making that backing acutely desirable. The crisis had begun in May with the failure of Austria's Creditanstalt and intensified with the collapse of a major German bank in July. Still in July it struck Britain and its overvalued pound. In the financial storm, the Macmillan report, delivered on 1 July, was cast aside as wrong and irrelevant.

And so, following the defeat of the Liberals and their expansive, somewhat Keynesian platform in May 1929, Keynes as policymaker, while contemporaneously accepting his failure as theorist in his *Treatise on Money*, had to endure the rejection of his proposals of descending ambition: the great cooperative "onslaught" on unemployment and the creation of a strong economic general staff during the actual process creating the ineffectual Economic Advisory Council in late 1929 into early 1930, the EAC's eventual report calling for protection but burdened with a dissenting opinion in the fall of 1930, and the Macmillan Committee's too long gestated "flat" report in July 1931 with his variously qualified minority addendum recommending protection and mysteriously financed public works. Keynes's use of the *New Statesman* at the time to argue protection publicly had not helped. When the Macmillan Committee thereupon vanished from the screen of history, he seemed to have achieved nothing for all of his great and varied efforts.

There followed a jumble of events emphasizing the relation between Keynes's correctness as economist-and-prophet and his inability to translate his policy advice into action. On 30 May, as the European financial crisis was beginning and just after completing his work on the Macmillan Committee report, he sailed for the United States, in the first of two important visits in the 1930s, to tell the Americans what to do about *their* depression. In Chicago, in late June and ending on 1 July, moving beyond the *Treatise on Money* toward suggestions of *The General Theory*, he gave three lectures and led a discussion on unemployment.[49] (The future practical economics of Franklin Delano Roosevelt and the New Deal would converge with his developing conceptions, an ideological alliance that would be affirmed in a meeting of Keynes with Roosevelt during his second visit to America in 1934.) Back in England later in July 1931, Keynes could only passively take account of the widely unmourned demise of the Macmillan Committee and its report.

In August, MacDonald, seeing no alternative, began following the economy advice of the Committee on National Expenditure, lost the support of most of his party, and, with Snowden remaining as chancellor, formed the National Government dominated by Conservatives. On 21 September, the persisting and intensifying weakness of the pound nevertheless forced Britain off the gold standard. Keynes, who had denounced the economy measures as "replete with folly and injustice,"[50] patriotically advised the government on the technicalities of exchange control in connection with the devaluation. (This was when he patriotically refused to permit his investment group to sell sterling and avoid a huge loss.) He was seeing too much of his advice vindicated.

If, approaching this moment, Keynes had preferred protection over devaluation, it had been a political and not an economic decision, and he was delighted at the outcome. For a talk in November his notes read, "The lucky way in which we got off gold."[51] The pound dropped below $4.00 and unemployment stabilized at just over 20 percent in 1933 and then fell consistently to reach 11.3 percent in 1937. As for protection, the National Government put through the Import Duties Act at Keynes's suggested figure of 10 percent in early February 1932. The country's situation was still difficult, and the threatening rise of Hitler in the years 1930 to 1933, creating dangers from another flank, meant an unbearable vindication. Accommodating himself to his modest role in a new governmental committee, Keynes was working away at *The General Theory*. If that theory did what he intended, it would be the appropriate vindication.

All Keynes's failures would prove to be marvelously constructive for Britain and himself. With his help the Economic Advisory Council and the Macmillan Committee, although shunted aside, established a precedent for the use of professional economists and their science at the center of government; in one form or another their operations would be taken up by other agencies. The Macmillan Committee would be followed by various ad hoc bodies. On 14 July 1931, during the crisis of that summer, MacDonald had called into life the Committee on Economic Information (CEI) as a part of the EAC, but actually to preserve its usable functions, thus to provide objective information instead of politically controversial advice, while letting the EAC itself disappear. Although Keynes had to see his friend Josiah Stamp become chairman, he cheerfully accepted membership in it and could continue, interpreting information into advice whenever he could, to influence the government from within as well as without. The EAC was officially dissolved in 1938, while the information committee became the nucleus of Britain's wartime economic staff, first as the Survey of War Plans under Josiah Stamp and presently, conceived more broadly, as the Economic Section of the Cabinet Office.[52] By that time, Keynes, too great a figure to be contained within any government office, was again influencing policy on the highest level.

The most important effects of the EAC and the Macmillan Committee were channeled through Keynes's mind. His intense policy-making of the period from late 1929 to mid-1931 and his own and the Circus's doubts about the *Treatise on Money* led him away from the *Treatise* and into the fashioning of *The General Theory*. His experiences of 1929–31 had further confirmed his earlier lessons that economic policy, however true the theory behind it, was helpless without political acceptance. While Keynes was a passionate theorist, he would not be content until he had transformed his theory into active policy. In the fall of 1931 he gathered up his most significant writings of the last dozen years for a volume he originally called "Essays in Prophecy," but, by publication date in November, had unerringly entitled *Essays in Persuasion*.[53] His whole working life was an essay *to persuade*. One reason why the *Treatise*, right or wrong as economic theory, had failed to persuade, he could see, was that its full-employment assumption did not address the Depression and its unemployment. His next book would not make that mistake. *The General Theory*, centered on economic distress, would be politically correct.

Notes

1. This was the article in which Keynes had speculated on the "true socialism of the future" (chap. 3 above): "Does Unemployment Need a Drastic Remedy?" *CW*, 19, part 1: 219-23; quotation, p. 220.
2. Talk at League of Nations Conference on Unemployment, 25-27 March 1924, ibid., 191.
3. Keynes, "The Position of the Lancashire Cotton Trade," ibid., part 2: 578-85; quotation, p. 578. See chap. 7, "Industrial Reorganization: Cotton," ibid., 578-637; Harrod, *The Life*, 379-86; Moggridge, *MK*, 449-52; and Skidelsky, *JMK*, 2: 261-63. In 1929 another, more limited attempt, backed by the Bank of England and blessed by Keynes, carried out some mergers improving the cotton industry's competitiveness without solving the basic problem.
4. Liberal Industrial Inquiry, *Britain's Industrial Future* (London, 1928); Maynard's letter to Lydia, 5 February 1928, *CW*, 19, part 2: 735.
5. Liberal Industrial Inquiry, *Britain's Industrial Future*, 110-15; Skidelsky, *JMK*, 2: 265-67.
6. Reprinted, *CW*, 9: 86-125.
7. Ibid., 102-10.
8. See Peter Clarke, *The Keynesian Revolution in the Making 1924-1936* (Oxford, 1988), 47-69, 91-97.
9. As quoted in *Can Lloyd George Do It?*, *CW*, 9: 115.
10. Ibid., 116.
11. Medlicott, *Contemporary England*, 240.
12. Harrod, *The Life*, 396.
13. See Keynes-Martin correspondence (which begins in 1923), *CW*, 28: 1-222.
14. "The Industrial Situation" (undated), ibid., 20: 18-22; quotations, pp. 18, 19.
15. William H. Beveridge, "An Economic General Staff," *The Nation*, 34 (29 December 1923): 485-86; and 34 (5 January 1924): 509-10.
16. "Economic General Staff," 10 December 1929, *CW*, 20: 22-27; quotations, pp. 25, 22, 27.

17. Susan Howson and Donald Winch, *The Economic Advisory Council 1930-1939: A Study of Economic Advice During Depression and Recovery* (Cambridge, 1977), 20-26; quotation, p. 21.
18. Editorial note, *CW,* 20: 312; letter to Keynes, 6 February 1930, ibid., 312-13. See Sir Oswald Mosley, *My Life* (London, 1968), 178-83; Robert Skidelsky, *Oswald Mosley* (London, 1975), 171.
19. Letter to Mosley, 8 February 1930, *CW,* 20: 313-15; quotation, pp. 314-15.
20. Cabinet: Conclusions of the Meetings of the Cabinet, Public Record Office, London (hereafter PRO), CAB 23/64.
21. Quoted, Skidelsky, *Oswald Mosley,* n. 305-6.
22. Editorial note, *CW,* 20: 28.
23. Meeting, 17 February 1930, Minutes, Cabinet Papers 58: Economic Advisory Council, PRO, CAB 58/2.
24. Editorial note, *CW,* 20: 326-27; the Keynes-Cole report, Howson and Winch, *The Economic Advisory Council,* 165-80.
25. Howson and Winch, *The Economic Advisory Council,* 41-42.
26. "Memorandum by Mr. J. M. Keynes to the Committee of Economists," *CW,* 13: 178-200. "A Proposal for Tariffs Plus Bounties," ibid., 20: 416-19; quotation, p. 417. Document selection, but not the final report, chap. 4, "The Committee of Economists," ibid., 402-66.
27. Lionel Robbins, *Autobiography of an Economist* (London, 1971), 150-53; quotations, pp. 151, 152. Cabinet Papers 58: Economic Advisory Council, Committee of Economists: Report, 24 October 1930, pp. 1-42, including "Report by Professor Robbins" (pp. 39-42; quotation, p. 41), PRO, EAC (H) 127.
28. Quoted, Howson and Winch, *The Economic Advisory Council,* 78; reception of report by EAC and cabinet, ibid., 73-81.
29. Committee on Finance and Industry, *Report,* Cmd. 3897 (London, 1931; reprint, 1969), 1, 187-88; editorial note, *CW,* 20: 38. See *CW,* chap. 2, "The Macmillan Committee," 38-311; Committee on Finance and Industry, *Minutes of Evidence Taken Before the Committee of Finance and Industry,* 2 vols. (London, 1931).
30. Minutes of discussions, 20 and 21 February 1930, *CW,* 20: 38-93; quotations, pp. 65, 86, 87.
31. Sessions, 21 February, 7 March 1930, ibid., 82, 149.
32. Minutes, ibid., 94-117, 119-48, 148-57.
33. Minutes, ibid., 100, 126, 156.
34. Robbins, *Autobiography,* 187.
35. Committee on Finance and Industry, *Minutes of Evidence Taken Before the Committee on Finance and Industry,* 2: 1-24. This part of the Keynes-Hopkins encounter was not reprinted in vol. 20 of the *CW.*
36. Hopkins testimony, comments by Keynes and Macmillan, *CW,* 20: 166-79; quotations, pp. 167, 171, 172, 179.
37. Ibid., 170.
38. Norman's testimony, 26 March 1930, Committee on Finance and Industry, *Minutes of Evidence Taken Before the Committee on Finance and Industry,* 1: 210-19; quotation, p. 215.
39. Sayers, *The Bank of England,* 1: 336.
40. It would not necessarily cancel all of the advantage because of taxpayers' reduced savings as well as reduced consumption.

41. Pigou's testimony, 28 and 29 May 1930, Committee on Finance and Industry, *Minutes of Evidence Taken Before the Committee of Finance and Industry,* 2: 46-58, 78-93; quotations, pp. 46, 47, 58.
42. Editorial notes, *CW,* 20: 270, 271; draft outline, ibid., 270-71.
43. Committee on Finance and Industry: Discussions, 24 October 1930, p. 26, PRO, T 200/5.
44. Memorandum, Committee on Finance and Industry, 7 April 1931, *CW,* 20: 272-74; quotation, p. 273.
45. "Comment on J. M. K.'s Comment," ibid., 274-76; quotation, p. 275.
46. Editorial note, ibid., 280.
47. Committee on Finance and Industry, *Report,* ibid., 190-209; reservation, pp. 209-10.
48. Quoted, Medlicott, *Contemporary England,* 253.
49. *CW,* 13: 343-67; ibid., 20: 529-44.
50. Keynes, "The Economy Bill," *New Statesman* (19 September 1931), *CW,* 9: 145-49; quotation, p. 145.
51. Ibid., 21: 12.
52. Howson and Winch, *The Advisory Council,* 106-8; history of the CEI, pp. 106-53.
53. Moggridge, *MK,* 529.

6

Theorizing: Toward the Final Statement

Keynes's theorizing from 1930 to 1936—from *Treatise on Money* to *General Theory*—begins with the precisely destructive criticism of the first, continues with the blindingly genial construction of the second, and secures its new conception with more criticism, now precisely constructive.

Giving the lead himself, Keynes was master, indeed lord in one collaborator's eyes, of the process of criticism throughout. As noted above in chapter 4, his preface to the *Treatise* gave the first signal in referring to the "sloughed…skins" left behind, followed by a more privately expressed indication of January 1931 on his "itch[ ] to do it all over again." The Circus, operating in the first half of 1931, was only obeying orders under Keynes's Law of Criticism. Three other critics of the theorizing—Ralph G. Hawtrey of the Treasury and the former protégés Dennis Robertson and Roy Harrod—would each develop sharply illustrative positions in relation to that law. As can be seen in the various interchanges between Keynes and his friendly critics, he commanded rigorous correction, which he frequently accepted in utter docility, but made an exception of his fundamental, intuitively conceived theses. His intuition remained the last instance.

The Circus quickly joined with Keynes in dismantling the *Treatise* while retaining the usable parts. Besides Richard Kahn and Joan and Austin Robinson, it consisted of Piero Sraffa, an Italian of subtle, scholarly intellect established at Cambridge as another Keynes protégé, and, from Oxford that year, James E. Meade, a future Nobel laureate for his work on international trade, plus a few intermittent participants among the research students or faculty acceptable to the entrance board of Kahn, Austin Robinson, and Sraffa. Dennis Robertson was "sarcastic about the Circus and came to only one meeting," according to Joan Robinson's memory.[1] Loyally, the Circus admitted that the other *Treatise* critics, Keynes in the lead, had good arguments.

"From the point of view of a humble mortal like myself, Keynes seemed to play the role of God in a morality play; he dominated the play but rarely appeared himself on the stage," Meade remembered. "Kahn was the Messenger Angel who brought messages and problems from Keynes to the Circus and who went back to Heaven with the result of our deliberations."[2] Exploiting Kahn's judgment, developed during the *Treatise* revisions, Keynes could hear a simple and ordered melody of meaning rather than the natural cacophony of undisciplined young voices. Harrod, entering the process after the Circus completed its collective work, noted Keynes's ability ruthlessly to concentrate on his objective and blind himself to irrelevant or conflicting views, even and perhaps most particularly, those that he had held himself: "Once more he went into a great tunnel, from which he was to emerge with *The General Theory.*"[3]

The book's basic conceptions, if not already created, quickly made their appearance: the investment-saving relation from the *Treatise,* the marginal efficiency of capital replacing its Wicksellian natural rate of interest and the MEC-interest rate relation replacing its natural interest rate-market interest rate relation; the multiplier; effective demand; involuntary unemployment; and liquidity preference, inter alia. Most of these are familiar or almost so, thus the multiplier already figuring in Keynes's pamphleteering of 1929; the MEC is *expected* profits, the "expected," however, adding a major change in theorizing, while liquidity preference is a preference for cash that tends to be excessive, this also representing a significant variation. Just what each means and their arrangement into a system-and-model remain to be elucidated in a close viewing of the completed *General Theory.*

What does Keynes say about his theorizing? In an important letter to Roy Harrod a half-year after the book appeared, he wrote promisingly, "I have been much preoccupied with the causation, so to speak, of my own progress of mind from the [neo]classical position to my present views." Intriguingly, he mentioned "moments of transition which were for me personally moments of illumination." He emphasized the conception of effective demand, his master conception: "To me the most extraordinary thing regarded historically... is the complete disappearance of the theory... *after* it had been for a quarter of a century the most discussed thing in economics." He specified, "One of the most important transitions for me, after my *Treatise on Money* had been published [31 October 1930], was suddenly realizing this." It was the second illumination: "It only came after I had enunciated to myself the psychological law that, when income increases, the gap between income and consumption will increase,—a conclusion of vast importance to my own thinking." This growing gap was the essence of his consumption theory; he did not, however, explain how it related to effective demand and *why* it was so important *and* "psychological." In any case chapter fragments he left behind and his account agree that he arrived at his consumption and effective demand, still in 1930 or, at the latest, 1931.

"Then, appreciably later, came the notion of interest being the measure of liquidity preference, which became quite clear in my mind the moment I thought of it." This was not much later, a matter of months and still in 1932, since his second draft table of contents of 1932 had changed the first one's "bearishness," a *Treatise* locution, to "liquidity preference." Keynes concluded, "And last of all, after an immense amount of muddling and many drafts, the proper definition of the marginal efficiency of capital linked up one thing with another."[4] The last table of contents of 1933 had listed the marginal efficiency of capital,[5] which "linked up" with the interest rate (thus necessarily with liquidity preference) because entrepreneurs would not reasonably proceed with their enterprises unless the MEC's promised profits were greater than the cost of funds, in other words, the interest rate. If Keynes's letter establishes the dating of the essential parts of *The General Theory*, it is, however, disappointingly but unsurprisingly incommunicative about his deeper vision of the basic ideas that composed it and how he made his inspired connections among them. His intuition asserting its claim here, they remain illuminations, a series of epiphanies vouchsafed only to the seer.

The Circus had vigorously assisted this process of breaking out past the *Treatise*. While accepting the Keynesian-Wicksellian investment-saving relation as central, its members questioned Keynes's assumption of constant output. Their discussion of his "widow's cruse fallacy" pointed to his error: the constant (maximum) output had led to his magical conclusion that entrepreneurial spending "devoted to riotous living" never depleted entrepreneurial coffers.[6] The multiplier could then play its crucial part in the work of destruction-construction. Its function simply refused to fit into the *Treatise* model of the economy, since the model's constant-output character restricted the multiplier effect to increasing prices. Although also seeming to promise magical results, the multiplier was founded on much more realistic assumptions, thus the subnormal output and employment of the Depression they were then living through. Hence, it needed another model in which to do its work of increasing output (*and* employment). And so Kahn and the others easily joined Keynes in the inexorable impulsion toward a new theory.

The refinement of the multiplier formed its own chapter in the theory's creation. A year earlier, while serving with Keynes's Committee of Economists of the Economic Advisory Council, Kahn had tried to develop it further from the version in the Keynes-Henderson pamphlet. Arthur Pigou and Henderson, however, the latter beginning to resist Keynes's threatening attitude toward neoclassical assumptions, successfully objected to using it as part of the argument in the committee's report.[7] Kahn persisted and revised his original draft into his famous multiplier article, published in the *Economic Journal* of June 1931. Supporting his thesis with a deft mathematical demonstration, he posited that "at times of intense depression when nearly all industries have at their disposal a large surplus of unused plants and labor," the multiplier effect would be great: "The amount of secondary employment is then large and the rise in prices is small."[8] With this, eliding Kahn's "small" price increase, Keynes could simply reverse the *Treatise*'s constant output and changing prices into *The General Theory*'s falling output (and employment) and prices assumed to be constant.

Before it could be fitted into the new theory, however, the multiplier required further refinement. In strict mathematics, as originally conceived by Keynes, it was too good. One additional farthing, inexorably counted, spun around the economy to produce full employment, but, as inexorably, continued on inconveniently toward infinity. Kahn tamed the multiplier (which he called a "ratio") by imagining leakages of the new income into increased imports and income payments to former dole recipients. This provided for the eventual extinction of the extra investment funds after a greater or lesser number of swings around the economy from investment to income and saving, the last transforming itself into newer (and less) investment, newer (and less) income, and so on. In the Circus discussions James Meade had already pointed out that all the leakages eventually summed up exactly to the total of the initial investment and

Kahn had adopted the idea (known as "Mr. Meade's relation") in his article.[9] And so Keynes's young associates returned his multiplier to him exquisitely calibrated.

Before he absorbed the new multiplier into *The General Theory,* naming it for the first time, Keynes made use of it in a series of four articles in the London *Times* of 13–16 March 1933. In the series, entitled "The Means to Prosperity," he advocated a public-works program whose promise was amplified by the improved multiplier. He followed that with the article "The Multiplier" in the *New Statesman* of 1 April.[10] Standing alone, however, the new instrument was intriguing but not convincing. It would do its work appropriately as an essential component of the mechanism Keynes was building around it. With it, meanwhile, he was well launched on the whole endeavor.

Keynes's great organizing conception, seized upon as early as 1930 or 1931, was effective demand. He was attacking Say's Law, which held that supply necessarily created an equal demand in the global sense, because it generated precisely the income level that could consume everything produced. The professionally respectable Thomas Malthus, the first professor of political economy in England, countered Say with the theory of "gluts," which denied his abstract thesis. (If Keynes executed a major reversal of thought from *Treatise* to *General Theory,* Malthus had been even more absolute in moving from his great *Essay on the Principle of Population* [1798], which conceived of an ever-expanding population with an insatiable demand, to his *Principles of Political Economy* [1820], with its problem of unconsumed production.) Keynes went back to Malthus, but brought in another conception, involuntary unemployment, as an integral element in his new theory. His effective demand would require no more than thirty pages of hard, abstract reasoning to take its place as the introductory general statement of *The General Theory.*

Keynes would then break down the global economy into its major areas of consumption and investment. About the first, he would propose that the maldistribution of income in an advanced economy would prevent the total *consumption* of its rising production levels, that the poorer classes lacked the buying power to buy and consume all the products they had labored to produce. While consumption was surely as important as investment, it represented a simpler problem and would require less argumentation.

Investment called up the complexities and mysteries of money and interest, and here the monetary economist Keynes could expand much more on the foundation of his long experience and thought. Beyond that his genius showed itself in bringing consumption and investment together to construct the grand but simple model of his economy. If its less prosperous inhabitants consumed too little, the well-to-do with money to spare, impelled by their *liquidity preference,* tended to spare too little for business investment and demand too high a price—the interest rate— for what they did spare. Thus, investment, like consumption, *consumed* too little of the goods and services needed in its economic sector, the production process. Another significant connection between consumption and investment was incorporated in the multiplier, which, as noted here already, translated income resulting from business investment—the work force's income particularly—into multiple rounds of consumption.

One can pursue the development of *The General Theory,* much like that of the *Treatise on Money,* by following its trail of draft tables of contents, chapter drafts or fragments of chapters, and correspondence. To this, student notes add a few more oddments of evidence. Keynes's set of eight lectures had been entitled "The Pure Theory of Money" through the fall of 1929, when he interrupted the series during his period of intense involvement with policy-making in 1929–31. Resuming the lectures on 10 October 1932, he called attention to their new title, "The Monetary Theory of Production": "Gentlemen, the change...is significant."[11] *The General Theory* began life with the new lecture title as its working title heading the first two, going back to 1932, of six known draft tables of contents.[12] Keynes used the same title for a *Festschrift* article, dating from late 1932, explaining in it that "the main reason why the problem of crises is unsolved...is to be found in the lack of what might be termed a *monetary theory of production.*" The conventional theory posited a *"real-exchange economy"* in which money was assumed to be neutral: "The theory which I desiderate would deal...with an economy in which money plays a part of its own and affects motives and decisions and is, in short, one of the operative factors in the situation."[13] In 1933, signaling Keynes's emphasis on the problem, the manuscript working title became "The Monetary Theory of Employment." But the second and third tables of contents of that year, in line with Keynes's greater claims for his theory, were now headed by "The General Theory of Employment."[14] He would return to this last title for a major article in 1937, his ultimate defense of the published work. In mid-1934, preceding the first version in galley proofs dated 11 October, the last draft table of contents bore the complete title "The General Theory of Employment, Interest and Money."[15]

The end product would comprise six "books" and twenty-four chapters. The first table of contents—in 1932—had been a fragment ending with only the title of Book 4; it had eleven chapters, whose titles were closer in sense to the *Treatise* than to *The General Theory*. As noted above, the second one, also of 1932, dropped "bearishness," the *Treatise*'s approximation, for "liquidity preference" among its chapter headings. Of the three tables of contents of 1933 the first had expanded to seventeen chapters and suggested more emphasis on employment in a chapter heading as well as in its own title. The last of 1933, dated December, listed five "books" in twenty-one chapters and mentioned most of the published work's themes in its chapter titles, including the opening attack on Say's Law, liquidity preference explicitly seen "as determining the rate of interest," the multiplier, the marginal efficiency of capital, and the problematic of real as opposed to money wages. Its Book 4 was entitled "The Theory of Prices," but the next table of contents, from about mid-1934, definitively demoted prices to an inessential chapter, another indication of the movement away from *Treatise* to *General Theory*. The table of contents of mid-1934 launched effective demand against Say's Law precisely as would the published *General Theory*, with the same titles for Book 1 and its three chapters, and promised virtually all of the work's other conceptions. The table of contents dated June 1935 and printed on galley proofs went to six books and twenty-eight chapters; very nearly everything was in place.[16] Five chapters would be dropped or consolidated into others. More important, two crucial chapters would be added to consolidate the argument in two movements, chapter 18, "The General Theory of Employment Re-Stated" for the pure economic theory, and the more inclusive, final chapter 24, "Concluding Notes on the Social Philosophy Towards Which *The General Theory* Might Lead." These last touches were supremely, genially right. With these chapters' precision and expansiveness, respectively, Keynes had completed structuring the book and its argument in a form making the most of what he had to say.

The chapter fragments dated vaguely "during 1931–32" show major ideas racing pell-mell one after another. One early fragment entitled

"The Monetary Theory of Production" specified its concentration on "increases and decreases in the volume of output and employment" as characteristic of an economy using money, thus a close approach to Keynes's formal statement of effective demand. Related to this, the next fragment, "The Instability of a Profit-Seeking Organization of Production," specified, "[T]here is no presumption whatever that the equilibrium output will be anywhere near the optimum output." Addressing the investment side of the economy, it also expressed the thesis, remarkable at first sight, that "it might be truer to say that the amount of saving...depends on the amount of investment, than the other way round." One might note the close connection between theory and policy here, always the case with Keynes, if not always so acutely articulated. The message was: take care of investment and saving could take care of itself and finance future investment. In a situation tending toward suboptimum output and employment, Keynes continued, a policy of taxation and spending favoring the "relatively poor" over the "richer classes...is likely to increase the spending of the former more than it decreases the spending of the latter," hence the theoretical grounding of corrective action with populist appeal. Now, having just dealt with the investment side he began to develop the part played by consumption, the other major component of the economy.[17] With this he had the basic structure sketched out. He had begun with the abstract general statement of effective demand, that not all demand was "effective," that the difference between effective demand and total demand comprised the unused labor, hence the unemployment, which Keynes defined significantly as "involuntary," and unused resources. He had yet to provide the proof of his general argument in general terms, but he was already dividing the global economy into the substantial specifics of insufficient investment and consumption whose sense, at this point, was beginning to be easier to see and *feel*.

Keynes proceeded first with the larger details affecting investment. Two other chapter fragments attributed to 1932 and both entitled "The Parameters of a Monetary Economy" conceived of the as yet unnamed marginal efficiency of capital, laid down the essence of what Keynes would call "The General Theory of the Rate of Interest," thus "the market rate of interest is a thing of itself, dependent on liquidity preference and the quantity of money," and fitted them into a dynamic relationship driving the book's economy: "The market rate of interest and the anticipated productivity of capital...having conjoined...we can deduce the volume of capital development."[18] He was still giving more attention to investment (and the economy as a whole) than consumption, but had only to maintain this momentum of creative thinking to arrive expeditiously at his goal of a balanced theory integrating investment and consumption in a global model—and justifying grand policy.

The student notes of the lectures, which were an immediate expression of Keynes's theorizing, tell their part of the story through 1935. According to Professor Thomas Rymes, who edited and summarized the notes, from a total of nine students, the most thorough and complete were by the Canadians Lorie Tarshis, who would himself become a proper Keynesian professor of economics, and Robert B. Bryce, an early implementer of Keynesian theory in a governmental career capped by the position of Canada's deputy minister of finance. Rymes found that both Tarshis and Bryce "were so disenchanted after their first year... of economics at Cambridge that they wished to discontinue such studies."[19] Their second thoughts are another proof of Keynes's powers of persuasion.

Keynes got to the thesis of *The General Theory*'s Book 1 on effective demand and output as a whole in his lectures of the fall of 1933. He was urging the existence of involuntary unemployment, as he defined it, to prove the existence of an effective demand smaller than the total demand necessary to consume the economy's production total. Tarshis noted how he interpreted the distinction between real and money wages: "In Keynes's theory, real wages do not depend on money wages but on other forces.... If the reduction of the real value of the existing wage [through increased prices] would not lead to a withdrawal [from the labor force], then it means unemployment is presumably involuntary." Detached, Bryce permitted Keynes to announce the denouement: "Mockingly, Keynes suggests that there may be no escape for labor from high wages in a slump"—thus from unemployment. If *The General Theory* would not express it quite that way, it was perhaps an even more accurate rendition of the perversity, as Keynes had come to see it, of the uninhibited free-enterprise economy. Furthermore, to state the problem approximately in such terms was to move toward solving it. There could be a practical resolution if one managed investment and consumption in the light of his *expectations,* a psychological factor to which he would attribute great importance. If employment had fallen, Tarshis wrote, then "either con-

sumption or investment or both must be increased by changing expectations, the propensity to spend, or investment.... We could, except in
unusual circumstances, make employment a maximum."[20] During the
Great Depression such a possibility was immensely cheering.

Using the figure of Alfred Marshall negatively as exemplar of neoclassical economics, Keynes developed his interest theory as related to
liquidity preference and insufficient investment. In 1933 he accused his
former master of circular reasoning and the ability to escape its consequences sneakily: "[T]he argument vanishes into smoke.... You cannot find much truth in him, and yet you cannot convict him of error."
Keynes rejected "the ordinary theory of interest...which I was brought
up on, and I think I taught it once...but it doesn't hold one drop of
water." The notes fail to record his argument beyond that assertion. When
he announced in the last lecture of 1934, "The rate of interest has nothing to do with the propensity to save, but only with liquidity preference," Bryce's notes read: "But oh this is too damn much!"[21] But Bryce,
like Tarshis, successfully reduced his resistances and confusions, and
joined him in seeing, as Keynes himself would put it, with Keynes's
spectacles.

How much originality can be claimed for Keynes? Most of the individual conceptions of *The General Theory* were familiar before he seized
upon them. Liquidity preference as name and phenomenon, clearly exhibiting his personal stamp, is more purely Keynesian than the others.
Despite its earlier history, Donald Moggridge would claim effective demand for him as well by a deft reversal of apparent cause and effect:
"Another indication of Keynes's growing confidence in his new ideas
was that he began to find predecessors for them."[22] Moggridge's argument was that Keynes, revising his essay on Malthus of 1922, had attributed his ideas to Malthus in a new passage written around the
beginning of 1933.[23] But this collides with the fact that, as quoted above
from Keynes's letter to Harrod in 1936, Keynes himself had referred to
Malthus and his contemporaries as making effective demand "the most
discussed thing in economics." It is too easy to find other references to
effective demand among the underconsumptionist thinkers. The dispute
is wasted effort.

Most of the specific *General Theory* concepts were commonplace in
the history of economic thought. Indeed all great ideas are compounded
of many known components, thus the Copernican system and Newton's

vaster conception, and the relaying of economic thought successively by the Physiocrats, Adam Smith, Ricardo, Marx, the marginalists, Walras, and Marshall. In every case the *whole* was original. Similarly, Keynes's *General Theory* as completely fitted together and set to work was radically different from all other economic conceptions. As part of this general scheme, Keynes had used the multiplier, common property of so many theorists,[24] in an original way to relate consumption to investment and so integrate the two parts of his economy, the "real" and the monetary. Still another dimension of Keynes's genius, although barely articulated in *The General Theory*, was to conjoin economy with politics and policy-making in another even grander scheme, as I shall argue. Again one must grant that the sum—a historical force like Marx's *Capital*—belongs to Keynes alone.

With the work of the Circus done, Richard Kahn and Joan Robinson continued, now as individuals, to function actively as critics of the work-in-progress. Kahn remained the chief critic and she might well have felt diminished in the circumstances, Keynes writing her on one occasion, in March 1934, "I am going through a stiff week's supervision from R. F. K. on my M. S. [*sic*]. He is a marvelous critic and suggester and improver—there never was anyone in the history of the world to whom it was so helpful to submit one's stuff."[25] Or perhaps not, since, as Keynes knew, she and Kahn were lovers. Regarding himself as lord of the university domain, Maynard twice, according to his conscientious reports to Lydia in early 1932 and late 1933, strode—evidently without knocking—into Kahn's quarters to find him making love to Joan Robinson on the floor. Easily applying his logician's skills, Maynard explained the first instance as a "conversation...on The Pure Theory of Monopoly" and the second, "the only convenient way of examining mathematical diagrams."[26] More seriously, one can feel a pang of sympathy for young Kahn, caught between the emotional and intellectual seductions of such powerful figures and never able to win his personal or professional independence. He became an increasingly reclusive bachelor, and his book on Keynes and *The General Theory* cited here, which was published less than a decade before his death, shows his lifelong captivity to Keynes's thought.

The masterful Keynes was eager for Kahn's approval up to a point. On 15 January 1935 he writes Kahn confidingly, "I have done two more chapters for you, if you have time to look at them.... I rather want to

know what you think of my latest concerning the fundamental characteristics of interest which...is, I think, rather beautiful, if it is correct."[27] Keynes was firm when, however, he thought Kahn's mind had
failed to meet his. On "user cost," a nonessential factor to which he
devoted too much thought (and a seldom-read appendix to chapter 6 of
the book), he said he was rewriting a passage they had discussed, but
was not accepting Kahn's advice on one point: "It still does not appeal
to my intuition."[28]

Kahn knew better than to challenge Keynes's Law of Criticism, but
he came close to it at one point. In a note he found that "this all reads
most beautifully." But, in a long string of comments on the galley proof
that it accompanied, he addressed the troublesome definitions of saving
and investment, firmly denied that these were, as Keynes would have
them in one passage, "'different names for the same thing,'" and called
them *different* things (that is the whole point)."[29] In the event, Keynes
accepted the reassurance while rejecting the correction. In *The General
Theory* saving and investment began as "merely different aspects of the
same thing," leaving behind a contradiction that Kahn had not been able
to smooth away. On that galley, however, Kahn had also offered a three-
line set of verbal equations, beginning, "income = value of output =
consumption + investment." For *The General Theory,* Keynes rearranged
the second line, while retaining its sense, and adopted the whole set.[30]

Joan Robinson, although Keynes too clearly favored Kahn, was more
inclined to license him to do what he wanted to do. In May 1932, reacting to his formulations, she began cautiously, "Austin and Kahn and I
were rather worried by some points in your last lecture.... Please for-
give the somewhat dogmatic air with which we write.... P. S. Please
why are you allowed to talk about prime cost but we are not allowed to
talk about short-period supply price?"[31] After more correspondence,
Keynes announced himself "open to conviction," but held his ground: "I
lack at present sufficient evidence to the contrary to induce me to scrap
all my present half-forged weapons;—though that is no reason why you
should not go on constructing your own."[32] After still more interchanges
she retreated "I feel very much ashamed of giving you trouble by not
saying where our method dovetails into yours.... With apologies." Writing on the next day, Keynes firmly doubted the dovetailing.[33] The pattern was repeated in 1935 upon the dispatch of the *General Theory* proofs,
Mrs. Robinson beginning, "I hope it is not an impertinence...to say

that I am very much delighted with your book"—and adding a long list of suggestions.[34]

If that was not enough, Keynes successively bundled up prepublication and postpublication letters from the consistently resistant Ralph Hawtrey for Joan Robinson's comment and support. To the first packet she returned, "I certainly don't think an archangel could have taken more trouble to be fair and to be clear. I darkly suspect that Hawtrey hasn't really taken in the theory of the rate of interest."[35] To the second she offered, "I read these letters with great tho' painful interest.... It is no good talking to him until he has taken in the multiplier."[36]

One might ask why Keynes had bothered with Hawtrey, who, in long, carefully reasoned disquisitions, had shown himself to be essentially negative toward the *Treatise on Money*.[37] But, in his solid separateness and total good will—he was also an Apostle—the slightly senior Hawtrey represented a challenge which Keynes simply could not resist. Also, Hawtrey could usefully correct errors missed by Keynes's young followers. His general emphasis on the operative importance of money brought him close to much of Keynes's thinking, but he remained firmly neoclassical in fundamental theory, which he was articulating in more than twenty books between 1913 and 1967. His biographer agrees that he was justly ranked in the "second tier among the economists of his period."[38] Despite his usefulness, his vigorous logic frequently left Keynes, as he thought, too narrow a channel freely to express his views. Thus, on the precise character of investment, Hawtrey argued, somewhat as had Richard Kahn, "You do not adhere to your own definition"; he then detailed a way of maintaining consistency and concluded, "I feel sure that this procedure will be much closer to the ideas you are setting out to expound."[39] Keynes often refused to permit Hawtrey to help him in this manner.[40] He had already indicated that his greater argument might be thereby jeopardized "*I*...fear I cannot materially change..."; he went on: "...though here your comments...have been very helpful, and I will do my best to deal with them." His best took the form of explaining the inconsistency without changing it.[41] After that he usually averted his attention when Hawtrey returned to the charge. Hawtrey, along with others, did succeed in getting Keynes to give up the conception of quasi-rent, which Keynes had adopted from Marshall to mean a particular kind of profit. After an initial defense, Keynes saw that his "use of the term was possibly confusing and certainly unnecessary."[42] He settled on extending his marginal efficiency of capital to cover the instances where quasi-rent had been employed. Hawtrey's punishingly long letters, with their masses of detail, served Keynes's purposes while frustrating his will to persuade.

Neither interlocutor could quite let go. On 7 November 1935, Hawtrey began another letter with an apology: "I hope you will have patience with me if I pursue some of my criticisms further."[43] Keynes returned, "If this correspondence does not fatigue you, there is nothing I like better."[44] In his last word before publication he could not forbear responding *seriatim* and at length to Hawtrey's arguments in a later letter, ending, "So many points are still seen through your spectacles and not through mine!"[45]

Then there was Dennis Robertson. Despite their reciprocal unhappiness about the *Treatise,* Maynard and Dennis could not keep themselves from risking a disturbing disagreement again. Their correspondence on the new book began in January 1935 with an intricate entanglement on its special definitions, out of which Maynard could profitably conclude that he should, at least, "rewrite the passages in question."[46] Dennis then settled down to a long, detailed critique in two letters a week apart. "Some points," he did his best to begin with a positive reaction, "are obviously superb, in your old philosopho-economic manner," but he had to concede that "you won't want it to be judged by them." He found the treatment of effective demand confusing and went on to disagree about the behavior of labor, an important argument supporting the logic of Keynes's effective demand. "I don't think I'm unsympathetic to what I feel to be the newest and practically the most important thing which you are saying," he insisted.

A superb professional, Robertson went on to show his unerring sensitivity to the great issues of economic science and to Keynes's genius in that regard, namely, to recognize "that in the postwar world there have been certain long-term depressive influences at work," which Dennis found of a kind unique to the twentieth century. If Maynard was proved correct, which was not at all unlikely, Dennis could cheerily volunteer, shifting the rationale, as Maynard did so fluently, from theory to policy, "I may often be found agreeing with you in practice on the need for Govt work programmes,—even for Gesellian [i.e., inflationary] taxing schemes and what not." He had not been able, however, to avoid responding negatively, justified frequently by simple incomprehension, to a long series of the book's theses: "[A] large part of your theoretical structure is still to me almost complete mumbo-jumbo!"—hastening to add feelingly and contritely, "Yours ever—in spite of these bites at the hand that fed me."[47]

Maynard punished Dennis with a curt, three-sentence note, to which he appended a considerable rebuttal formally entitled, "COMMENTS ON D. H. R.'S CRITICISMS." Accepting a few technical corrections, he quarreled with the main points. Dennis had found his conception of "own-rates of interest" incomprehensible, and he granted, "I admit the obscurity of this chapter." He continued superbly, "A time may come when I am, so to speak, sufficiently familiar with my own ideas to make it easier." He went on to give Dennis more precise commands on the type of criticism he should provide: "[Y]ou must...either differ from me much more or much less. You make no frontal attack on any of my main points." Maynard would have been happier if Dennis had indeed broken Keynes's Law of Criticism. He complained, "Yet there is not really a single point of importance where I succeeded in making you change your mind." Dennis had said as much. Maynard could only match this ultimate denial with an ultimate, warmly angry dismissal: "[T]his book is a purely theoretical work, not a collection of wisecracks. *Everything* turns on the mumbo-jumbo and so long as that is still obscure to you our minds have not really met."[48] After another exchange they agreed to suspend discussion.[49]

On 10 October, more than a half-year later and four months before publication of *The General Theory,* Maynard wrote, "My Dear Dennis, How are you and what have you been doing in the vacation?" The rest of his letter discussed the corrections he was making; he proposed to send "page proofs as they come along." He had modified a number of passages that Dennis had criticized but doubted that Dennis would be satisfied.[50] Dennis responded somewhat more warmly but preferred to wait until he was dispensed of university chores in December and could have the book as published in his hand.[51] And so he relieved himself of any responsibility for more changes. Their letters would resume with unabated intensity.

The two senior, independent-minded economists Hawtrey and Robertson, like the dependent juniors of the Circus, had, whatever they may have thought, tried to avoid criticizing Keynes's major theses while guiding him in best expressing them. One person, the junior, the loyal

Roy Harrod, actually disobeyed Keynes's Law and confronted a central thesis with a straightforward, reasoned rebuttal. The exception proved the rule precisely.

Teaching at Oxford, Harrod had not been able to join the Circus although he would doubtless have qualified as a competent member. (In 1922, as a promising Oxford classics, philosophy, and history student, he had been selected to teach economics; he elected to spend a sabbatical year learning it in Cambridge; Keynes took him up.)[52] Keynes brought him in as critic with the dispatch of galley proofs in mid-1935: "I am extremely anxious to know how it strikes you."[53] With enormous conscientiousness Harrod studied the proofs for three weeks, sending off five detailed critiques over a week's period.[54] Of course he contributed useful technical corrections and improvements. Like Robertson, finding no less than a "howling paradox," he raised questions about Keynes's view of labor behavior as relating to involuntary unemployment and effective demand. Incidentally, pointing up Keynes's remarkable nonrecognition of the considerable achievement, Harrod took issue with one footnote "because it neglects the analysis of imperfect competition...achieved by...your Joan Robinson!"[55] These were only irritants.

Harrod's major point, to which he devoted two long letters on 1 August followed by four others that month, was on Keynes's treatment of the central issue of interest theory.[56] Keynes argued that the investment-saving equality, which he assumed (although not consistently), vitiated the use by neoclassical interest theory of supply-and-demand reasoning to determine the interest rate. To this Harrod countered that, for example, the number of German lessons given was always equal to the number taken, yet "there is...no reason to doubt that the price of a German lesson is determined by the supply and demand functions in the ordinary way." He concluded strongly that Keynes's argument was "specious and indeed invalid." Keynes had spoken at Oxford the previous February; Harrod now reported on the reception of his interest theory: "[T]his was the most criticized part of your address.... Frankly it convinced no one." He argued that it was another Keynesian thesis that defeated neoclassical interest theory, namely, "that there are changes in other things which are so relevant and of such overpowering importance that the old s[upply]-and-d[emand] analysis had better be put away." Thus, Harrod, now slipping back under the sway of Keynes's Law, could conclude his sense of Keynes's logic: "[T]he level of income and the rate of interest are indeterminate unless you bring in another equation, which you do in fact, viz., the liquidity preference schedule."[57] QED, but not, Harrod correctly feared, satisfactory to Keynes.

Before Keynes responded Harrod hastened to strengthen his arguments. In his second letter of 1 August he began, "I am thinking of the effectiveness of your work," which would be "diminished if you try to eradicate very deep-rooted habits of thought *unnecessarily.* One of these is the supply-and-demand analysis."[58]

There followed, besides other letters, a triple exchange on interest theory: the premonitory calm, accompanied by flurries, before the storm.[59] Harrod went on, before it broke, to confess to a greater and more damaging disagreement. On 21 August, he admitted, "Having reread ch. 15 [the future chapter 14, "The Classical Theory of the Rate of Interest"], I am now more depressed about it than I was before, when in the first flush of enthusiasm I was ready to swallow anything."[60] He was right to have been troubled.

"There was a dreadful moment when he wrote to say he suspected I had not understood," Harrod wrote in the biography,[61] thus Keynes's powerful letter of 27 August: "It is, I am sure, a big question of substance.... And I think that your acceptance of my constructive parts can only be partial if you do not accept my critical sections." Repeatedly responding to Harrod personally in this manner, Keynes reminded him of his *personal* responsibility for his criticism: "I am frightfully afraid of the tendency, of which I see some signs in you, to appear to accept my constructive part and to find some accommodation between this and deeply cherished views which would in fact only be possible if my constructive part had been partially misunderstood." To Keynes it would mean that his basic theses would be "water off a duck's back...unless I am sufficiently strong in my criticism to force the [neo]classicals to make rejoinders. I *want,* so to speak, to raise a dust; because it is only out of the controversy that will arise that what I am saying will get understood." He specified that Harrod was limiting the neoclassical error to its failure to account for the effect of income changes on the interest rate: "But the fact is that [it] is not my view...far from it." With this Keynes went on to compound his attack on neoclassical interest theory with some indications of his own replacement for it, the General Theory of the Rate of Interest: "My theory is that the rate of interest is the price which brings the demand for liquidity into equilibrium with the amount of liquidity available." And here we have supply (Keynes's "amount of liquidity available" or cash) and demand for it in the apparently familiar situation of equilibrium. At the mention of the term a reader trained in neoclassical economics would begin to feel he or she was beginning to understand what Keynes was saying.

Keynes, however, would not permit the retention of the comfortable old belief. He was in earnest and absolute. He proceeded to attack neoclassical theory using Harrod's example of the German lessons. "But suppose that whenever the price of a German lesson went down the demand schedule [i.e., curve (line) in a graphical illustration] also shifted its position,—the whole thing would have no meaning."[62] Keynes's point demands examination and understanding, impossible in a quick reading; we need a diagram. Harrod said that supply and demand determined price in the following manner:

Figure 6.1
The Pricing of German Lessons 1—
The Neoclassical Supply-and-Demand Price

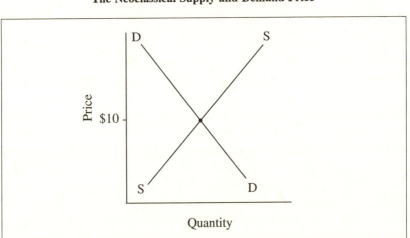

Price = $10 as determined by intersection of S–S supply and D–D demand curves.

For those who have not experienced it or who would like their memories refreshed, this is a good place to address the simple logic of supply and demand. Keynes's theorizing raises important questions about this logic. On the diagram the supply and demand curves (lines whether curved or straight) are abstractions expressing willingness to sell and buy. Behind the supply curve is a number of sellers who propose to sell given quantities at given prices, the quantities expressed horizontally, thus on the horizontal axis, and the prices vertically, on the vertical axis. The normal supply curve rises from southwest toward northeast, expressing the fact that the sellers (whose numbers might be increasing) would be willing to sell more as the price rises. The opposite is true of the demand curve, which falls from northwest toward southeast. This expresses the fact that buyers (perhaps more of them) will buy more as the price *decreases*. In the market, which the whole diagram illustrates, a process of bargaining takes place. The resolution is achieved at the intersection of the two curves. At that point the desires of sellers and buyers can be matched; in other words, equal quantities, as measured on the horizontal axis, are being offered and demanded at the price indicated on the vertical axis. If, for example, Keynes's lower price were arbitrarily introduced, then there would be less offered than bought; the buyers would be bargained up to the intersection, which indicates the point of equality. Similarly, at a price above the intersection there would be less demanded than offered; the sellers would be bargained down to the point of equality. This logic, according to neoclassical economics, is behind every sale-and-purchase on every free market.

The intersection of supply of German-language lessons by teachers and the demand for those lessons by learners, let us say, results in a price of $10 (per hour) in a given urban location in a given time span. Keynes now introduces a lower price, which, he says, leads to a shift in the demand schedule, expressed by a curve (line) on a graph. According to neoclassical theory, which Keynes has not yet overthrown, he has reversed cause and effect. Logically he had no right to introduce a price decline as an uncaused cause. Neoclassical theory reasons that a shift of one or both curves, expressing decreased demand or increased supply, must, as cause, take place *first,* the price then falling in the circumstances. Referring to the diagram, a neoclassical economist would say that Keynes had moved the intersection of supply and demand, which represents the price as determined in this manner, *before* supply or demand themselves had moved, an impossibility in geometry as in sense or economy, thus:

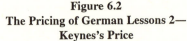

Figure 6.2
The Pricing of German Lessons 2—
Keynes's Price

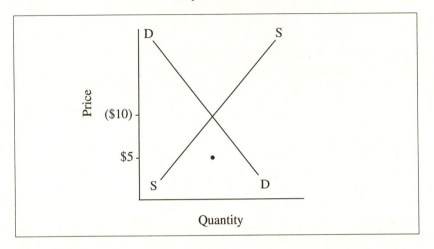

Price = Any arbitrary figure, e.g., $5, but it could be 0 or infinity, since it was determined without reference to S–S supply and D–D demand curves.

This is only a limited objection to a partial statement of Keynes's.

In his letter Keynes did indeed provide a theoretical justification for his attack on neoclassical supply-and-demand determination of the interest rate. This was his theory of liquidity preference. On the basis of liquidity preference, and speaking of supply-and-demand schedules for money, Keynes announced, "In truth there are no such things as these schedules. They are completely bogus." He was denying what he had taught, one might recall (chapter 2 above), as a prewar economics lecturer. He concluded devastatingly for neoclassical theory, if correct: "Without bringing in liquidity preference the position of equilibrium is entirely indeterminate, and any method, such as the [neo]classical one, which endeavors to arrive at the rate of interest without bringing in liquidity preference is bound to be circular in the worst possible sense of the word." While Harrod, with his copy of the *General Theory* proofs, might be expected to understand, the reader is not so equipped. Further explication is in the book and we must wait to see just how liquidity preference works in the economy before we can rationally agree or disagree. In his last word, implicitly thanking Harrod for acceptable corrections and lifting him up after condign punishment, Keynes wrote, "I have rewritten effective demand, income, and user cost radically."[63]

Keynes was absolutely correct in theory and policy. Keynesian and neoclassical interest theory could not coexist. The best that Harrod would grant him was that he had contributed a qualification of neoclassical theory. Besides being logically wrong, Harrod's advice was a formula for compromise and cowardice. Keynes proposed a revolution in economic theory and policy. A revolution meant annihilating neoclassical theory and erecting a new theory in its place.

Harrod doubtless understood the letter immediately. He knew that Keynes's good will toward him could be overwhelmed, as it had happened in the case of Dennis Robertson, if he persisted in half-defending the old theory. He yielded surely not to Keynes's logic, since that logic subsumed unproved theses, some of which he still questioned, but to Keynes's demonstration of force. In doing so he would go on to make an important contribution to the force of *The General Theory*. "No, no; you do me throughout great injustice," his long letter of 30 August began, "I have understood you much better than you think." Sacrificing his carefully posited example of the German lessons, Harrod quoted Keynes's arbitrary change in the price of lessons and the resultant annihilation of the neoclassical supply-and-demand pricing process: "I agree entirely." He quoted Keynes's statement, "'Any method...to arrive at the rate of interest without bringing in liquidity preference is bound to be circular.'" To this Harrod wrote, "Yes, if income is variable. No, if income is constant. But, you say, income *is* variable. Granted."

Going beyond surrender, Harrod then gave a detailed explication of Keynes's explication of neoclassical interest theory and added a complex diagram illustrating it.[64] In the biography Harrod said that the "diagram purport[ed] to reconcile the [neo]classical theory with his theory." It did nothing of the sort. Had it done so, Keynes would have rejected it out of hand. The diagram, expressing Keynes's hostile interpretation of neoclassical theory, permitted him to shatter it with one blow. Keynes immediately recognized its enormous value in achieving his ends, and used it in *The General Theory*, as Harrod happily noted, "the only diagram in it!"[65]

"I absolve you completely of misunderstanding my theory," Keynes began his reply. Harrod's dreadful moment had passed. "It could not be stated better." As for the diagram, it was "both correct and very useful as a help to exposition, and I shall like to appropriate it." He found one area where Harrod needed correction and supplied it firmly and mildly. Now he rewarded his young friend: "Will you come down for a night or two?" In a footnote to the letter he augmented the reward: "You will see that I have, in a sense, shifted my ground in the above. I have gained a great deal from your hard knocks, and would like some more."[66]

In his surrender letter Harrod had decorously arranged the tatters of his dignity. He resolutely insisted that Keynes was going too far in denying that the rate of interest had anything to do with saving. He objected to Keynes's defense of the mercantilist thinkers as "rationaliz[ing] isolated pieces of common sense too much," while that common sense was "embodied in a hopelessly confused notion of [the] economic system as a whole."[67] (With Joan Robinson's support Keynes retained his defense of the mercantilists.)[68] Harrod had first agreed on the necessity of the "radical reconstruction" of economic theory along the lines of his own diagrammatic scheme of major Keynesian theses. He now pronounced, in a final access of courage, "No further criticism of the [neo]classical system is required. All your subsequent criticism is fussy, irrelevant, dubious, hair-splitting and hair-raising."[69] Keynes could graciously concede to Harrod this last word.

Keynes had managed all the criticism to fit his purposes, the refinement of a new thought system intuitively established by 1933. Kahn and the other helpers had collaborated with him in organizing the elements of that system, but all of those elements were derived from Keynes's earlier thought as expressed in the *Treatise* and his other writings. Easily sloughing off given fundamental objections, Keynes could cheerfully accept assistance in the refinement process from selected aliens-in-theory as well as from friendly reasoners. By the beginning of 1935, as he dispatched the proofs, he was concentrating on the defense of his new theory against the shock reaction he anticipated, indeed as he was purposefully provoking, from the established economic theorists.

In the fall of 1934 Keynes had pleasurably participated in a debate in the public prints about Karl Marx and Soviet Russia as incorporation of Marx's ideas. This permitted him, assisted by his visits to Russia and emanations from Lydia's family, once again to paint contemporary Russia as monstrous and put his rival Marx in his place. On 1 January 1935, before he had begun to send the proofs to his helpful critics, Keynes wrote to George Bernard Shaw, who was touting Marxism-Leninism-

Stalinism: "There must be *something* in what you say, because there generally is." Keynes had read the Marx-Engels correspondence "without making much progress." (He did not mention *Capital*.) Perversely, "I prefer Engels of the two." Keynes thought "they invented a certain method of carrying on and a vile manner of writing, both of which their successors have maintained with fidelity." As for the claims that "they discovered a clue to the economic riddle...I can discover nothing but out-of-date controversializing."

Keynes changed the subject to himself. "To understand my state of mind, however, you have to know that I believe myself to be writing a book on economic theory which will largely revolutionize...the way the world thinks about economic problems." It remained for his theory to be "duly assimilated and mixed with politics and feelings and passions." He did not propose to "predict what the final upshot will be in its effect on action and affairs. But there will be a great change.... I can't expect you, or anyone else, to believe this at the present stage. But for myself I don't merely hope what I say,—in my own mind I'm quite sure."[70]

Keynes was saying what all the evidence shows to be true about his theorizing, that it was a passionately pragmatic exercise meant to be mixed with politics and feelings in order to achieve that great change in action and affairs. The thinking was secondary to the effect, or as Marx himself had put it: "The philosophers have only *interpreted* the world in various ways; the point is to *change* it."[71]

Notes

1. Joan Robinson, *Contributions to Modern Economics* (Oxford, 1978), xiv.
2. Quoted (p. 250), Paul Lambert, "The Evolution of Keynes's Thought from the *Treatise on Money* to *The General Theory*," *Annals of Public and Co-operative Economy* 40 (July–September 1969): 243–63. Lambert, editor of the *Annals*, said Meade spoke these words in conversation with him and two others.
3. Harrod, *The Life*, 437.
4. Letter, Keynes to Harrod, 30 August 1936, *CW*, 14: 84–86. The *CW* edition printed the letter with a few errors, which have been corrected in the parts quoted here.
5. Ibid., 13: 421.
6. Ibid., 5: 125.
7. Howson and Winch, *The Economic Advisory Council*, 49.
8. Richard F. Kahn, "The Relation of Home Investment to Unemployment," *Economic Journal* 41 (June 1931): 173–98; quotations, p. 182.
9. Kahn's account, Kahn, *The Making of Keynes' General Theory*, 98–100. A Danish economist added another leakage factor, savings of the newly employed: Jens

Warming, "International Difficulties Arising out of the Financing of Public Works During Depression," *Economic Journal* 42 (June 1932): 211–24.

10. See "The Means to Prosperity," *CW,* 9: 335–66. This is the version published in the United States, into which the multiplier article was inserted.

11. Lorie Tarshis, "The Keynesian Revolution: What It Meant in the 1930s," unpublished typescript, quoted, Skidelsky, *JMK,* 2: 460.

12. *CW,* 29: 49–50.

13. Keynes, "A Monetary Theory of Production," ibid., 13: 408–11; quotation (and editorial note re date), p. 408.

14. Ibid., 29: 62, 63; ibid., 13: 421. Interpreters of Keynes have disputed whether he arrived at the essence of *The General Theory* in 1932 or 1933, but the answer depends on whether one's requirements are general or specific. Clarke, *The Keynesian Revolution,* opts for 1932 (p. 267) as the moment Keynes seized upon effective demand as his organizing conception; see his discussion of differing opinions (pp. 256–82). Robert W. Dimand, *The Origins of the Keynesian Revolution,* (Stanford, CA, 1988), picks 1933 because Keynes lacked labor-market and supply-function theories until then (p. 155).

15. Editorial note and table of contents, *CW,* 13: 423.

16. Ibid., 421–22, 424, 525–26.

17. Editorial note dating the fragments, ibid., 380; the fragments, ibid., 381–96; quotations, pp. 381, 387, 388, 393.

18. The fragments, ibid., 390–405; quotations, p. 399.

19. Thomas K. Rymes, *Keynes's Lectures: Notes of a Representative Student* (London, 1989), 8. See introduction, pp. 3–26.

20. Ibid., first and sixth lectures, 16 October, 20 November 1933, pp. 85–90, 111–17; quotations, pp. 88, 113–14.

21. Ibid., seventh lecture, 27 November 1933, pp. 117–22; quotation, p. 121 (another student, M. Fallgatter). Seventh lecture, 3 December 1934, pp. 154–58; quotation, n. 158.

22. Moggridge, *Keynes,* 1980 edition, 109.

23. Editorial note, *CW,* 10: n. 71.

24. Discussion of multiplier in, for example, Kahn, *The Making of Keynes'* General Theory, 91–104; Clarke, *The Keynesian Revolution,* 246–55, including an appendix on its mathematics, pp. 254–55; Dimand, *The Origins of the Keynesian Revolution,* 111–17; Paul Lambert, "The Evolution of Keynes's Thought," 243–63, especially pp. 245–51; Neville Cain, "Cambridge and Its Revolution: A Perspective on the Multiplier and Effective Demand," *Economic Record* 55 (June 1979): 108–17.

25. Letter, 29 March 1934, quoted, editorial note, *CW,* 13: 422.

26. Letters to Lydia, 1 February 1932, 13 October 1933, quoted, Skidelsky, *JMK,* 2: 449, 495.

27. Quoted, editorial note, *CW,* 13: 525.

28. Letter, 4 September 1935, ibid., 634–35; quotation, p. 634.

29. Undated comments, but clearly from 1935, ibid., 637.

30. Ibid., 7: 74, 63.

31. Ibid., 13: 376.

32. Ibid., 376–77; Keynes's letter, 9 May 1932, pp. 377–78.

33. Letters, 11 and 12 May 1932, ibid., 379–80.

34. Letter and notes, 16 June 1935, ibid., 638–45; quotation, p. 638; other letters, pp. 645–52.

35. Letter, 2 December 1935, ibid., 612–13.
36. Letter, 29 May 1936, ibid., 14: 34.
37. The Keynes-Hawtrey interchanges on the *Treatise* began when the Macmillan Committee asked Hawtrey's opinion of it; see editorial note, ibid., 13: 126. The correspondence, ibid., 130–73; ibid., 29: 10–11.
38. Patrick Deutscher, *R. G. Hawtrey and the Development of Economics* (London, 1990), 1. See especially introduction, pp. 1–7.
39. Letter, 1 October 1935, *CW,* 13: 583–85; quotations, pp. 583, 585.
40. For example, in letters from Hawtrey, 7 and 20 November 1935, ibid., 599, 611–12.
41. Letter, 24 September 1935, ibid., 580–82; quotation, p. 580.
42. Letters, 4 and 24 September (cited above), 1935, ibid., 576–77, 580–82; quotation, p. 580.
43. Ibid., 595.
44. Ibid., 600.
45. Letter, 6 January 1936, ibid., 626–33; quotation, p. 627.
46. Letter, 29 January 1935, ibid., 494–96; quotation, p. 496.
47. 3 and 10 February 1935, ibid., 496–506, 506–11; quotations, pp. 497, 506, 507.
48. Letter, 20 February 1935, ibid., 511–20; quotations, pp. 519, 520.
49. Letters, 11 and 14 March 1935, ibid., 520–23.
50. Ibid., 523–24; quotations, p. 523.
51. 11 October 1935, ibid., 524.
52. Harrod, *The Life,* 313–30.
53. Letter, 5 June 1935, *CW,* 13: 526–27.
54. Letters, 31 July, 1 (two), 3, and 6 August 1935, ibid., 527–37.
55. Letter (cited above), 31 July 1935, ibid., 527–30; quotations, pp. 528, 529.
56. Letters (the first four cited above) of 1 (both), 3, and 6 August, and also 12 and 21 August 1935, ibid., 530–33, 533–34, 534, 535–37, 539–40, 544–546.
57. Ibid., 530–33; quotations, pp. 531, 532.
58. Ibid., 533–34, quotation, p. 533.
59. Ibid., 537–47.
60. Ibid., 544–46; quotation, p. 544.
61. Harrod, *The Life,* 453.
62. *CW,* 13: 547–53; quotations, pp. 547–48, 548, 549, 550.
63. Resuming Keynes's letter of 27 August 1935, ibid., 551, 553.
64. Letter, 30 August 1935, ibid., 553–57; quotations, pp. 553, 554.
65. Harrod, *The Life,* 453.
66. Letter, 10 September 1935, *CW,* 13: 557–59; quotations, pp. 557, 559. The letter contained a copy of Harrod's diagram, p. 557.
67. Ibid., 555.
68. Letters, 3 and 7 September 1935, ibid., 650–51.
69. Ibid., 556.
70. Ibid., 24: 42; the last two paragraphs were excerpted in ibid., 13: 492–93.
71. Thesis XI of his *Theses on Feuerbach,* in, for example, Marx and Engels, *The Marx-Engels Reader,* 2d ed., ed. Robert C. Tucker (New York, 1978), 145.

7

The General Theory as Abstraction

While *The General Theory* is one of the greatest puzzles in the history of ideas, its basic statement is simple enough. It contended that the modern economy slipped into stagnation and unemployment because of defects in both its real and its monetary sectors. In the real sector consumption failed to keep up with rising production; in the monetary sector the price of funds—the interest rate for short—was too high and discouraged business investment. Thus, laggard consumption and investment joined in generating stagnation and unemployment. Book 3 addressed consumption; Book 4, the interest rate as it affected investment. Book 1, introducing the argument in its thirty pages, viewed the economy in an all-encompassing manner. It dealt necessarily with consumption and investment by way of pure abstractions, which expressed the existence of a global economic leakage.

Book 1 exemplified the abstract character of the whole work. Although Keynes drew upon his rich experience for examples, *The General Theory* rested heavily upon abstractions, much more so than did the *Treatise on Money*. Requiring great alertness from the reader, the later work constantly shuttles between selected realities and grand abstractions. Keynes was frank about claiming to comprehend the vastness and complexity of the modern economy in 389 pages.

Superb in his ambition, Keynes made his first statement in the title: "I have called this book *The General Theory of Employment, Interest and Money,*" he began chapter 1. He would argue that both classical and neoclassical theory were "applicable to a special case only and not to the *general* case." The traditional theory, his *Treatise on Money* fatally sharing in the defect, was true only in the ideal situation of the full-employment economy; his general theory would address the general case.

"Moreover," Keynes emphasized the practicality and pressing timeliness of his enterprise in the Depression year 1936, "the characteristics of the special case...happen not to be those of the economic society in which we actually live, with the result that its teaching is misleading and disastrous if we attempt to apply it to the facts of experience."[1]

Keynes's attack on the enemy theory went so far as to rob it of its name, as was shown already in his correspondence with the Circus members and other supportive critics. In a footnote he explained that he was lumping such economists as Marshall and Pigou, universally termed neoclassical, with their classical predecessors, thus Adam Smith and David Ricardo, inter alia, and calling all of them "classical."[2] Yet the essence of his attack was directed against the neoclassicals as contemporaneously dominant.

In the preface, dated 13 December 1935, Keynes confidingly invited his readers to join him in a struggle for liberation: "The composition of this book has been...a long struggle of escape, and so must the reading of it be for most readers if the author's assault upon them is to be successful—a struggle of escape from habitual modes of thought and expression." Disarmingly, he confessed, "It is astonishing what foolish things one can temporarily believe if one thinks too long alone."[3]

Keynes's title is not particularly accurate. He had, as the previous chapter noted, appended "Interest and Money" to his earlier working title. Yet employment would not be the subject of any of the "books" or even chapters; reversed into unemployment, it was the great product of the model Keynes constructed. He was really presenting a general theory of *output* and employment as effects, the insufficiency of the one associated with the insufficiency of the other. Instead, his title offered a mixed bag of one effect, employment, and two causes, one of the latter, moreover, being redundant: either "money" or "interest" could be dropped, since the one implied the other. The imbalance was emphasized by the failure to mention consumption. It would have been more accurate to call it the general *monetary* theory of either output and employment or consumption and (rather than interest or money) investment, the "monetary," as suggested by Keynes's lecture title of "The Monetary Theory of Production," retaining his emphasis on money as related to production or output. Yet these alternatives are not as intriguing as the words Keynes chose. The author has the right to select a suggestive and impressionistic title that might be a bit askew, but was not quite misleading.

Book 1, the most general of *The General Theory*'s six books, led to a confrontation of the two global abstractions, Say's Law and Keynes's Law of Effective Demand. It did so over a tortuous route dealing with employment, or rather unemployment, and the behavior of contemporary British labor. It had begun by attacking another pure, if more limited, abstraction—neoclassical employment theory. It would contend with one great classical and one related, significant neoclassical abstraction. In both cases it would use the same conjoint examples of economic reality—unemployment and British labor behavior—as the test to find both wanting.

Keynes challenged neoclassical employment theory on the question of voluntary or involuntary employment. The neoclassicals argued rigorously that except for various anomalies and short-term situations, there was no such thing as involuntary unemployment. It was difficult to put such a thesis to the man in the street during the 1930s, when unemployment was so ferociously rampant, but the neoclassical Keynes could grant that most, if not all of it, could still be defined as *voluntary* unemployment. This was the case if it were "due to the refusal or inability of a unit of labor, as a result of legislation or social practices or of combination for collective bargaining or of slow response to change or of mere human obstinacy, to accept a reward corresponding to the value of the product attributable to its marginal productivity,"[4] that is, its value to the employer. The policymaker and Liberal publicist Keynes had experienced the refusal of labor, as acted out in the General Strike of 1926, to be satisfied with a wage that employers believed was equal to its marginal productivity. The same factor, as the Keynes of the Economic Advisory Council and the Macmillan Committee dealt with it, was at work after the worldwide Depression struck. In both cases the pragmatic Keynes, accepting British labor's obstinacy as given, preferred to work around it by the inflationary effect achieved through devaluation or tariffs. In *The General Theory,* however, the theorist Keynes had another solution: neoclassical theory was wrong and he would replace it with a correct theory.

In essence, Keynes, now putting his neoclassical training behind him, argued that an important part of what neoclassical economics called voluntary employment was actually involuntary. According to "traditional theory," as he put it, "the existing level of real wages accurately measures the marginal disutility of labor." The "marginal *dis*utility" was the complex of negative aspects of working that the real wages had to counterbalance before the worker accepted employment. To Keynes this was false, although he did not question neoclassical theory's related postulate that employers could receive in return the value of the marginal productivity, in other words, the marginal *utility*, from hiring a given volume of labor. But, from the point of view of the workers, the situation was not symmetrical: "Does it follow...that the existing level of real wages accurately measures the marginal disutility of labor?" Neoclassical theory, supporting its affirmative answer, said that if workers offered their services up to the point where the negative aspects of working balanced off the positive, there could be no (involuntary) unemployment. It was here that Keynes objected: "Not necessarily. For, although a reduction in the existing money-wage would lead to a withdrawal of labor, it does not follow that a fall in the value of the existing money-wage...would do so, if it were due to a rise in...price[s]...." Thus, "it may be the case that within a certain range the demand of labor is for a minimum money-wage and not for a minimum real wage."5 While limited by various qualifications, Keynes's thesis nevertheless became absolute. He argued that the result was substantial unemployment that was *involuntary*—a statement with which the millions of Depression unemployed would poignantly agree—and hence, neoclassical employment theory was *generally* invalid.

Keynes was developing and putting to work his famous conception of the "money illusion," which, he was aware, seemed to show the action of the workers as irrational. Why should a nominal figure overweigh the material value of commodities bought with it? Scintillating with confidence and rhetorical skills, the adept logician of the treatises on probability and money set out to turn its meaning inside out and prove that the money illusion was more realistic than the concern for real wages: "Thus it is fortunate that the workers...are instinctively more reasonable economists than the classical school." He argued that organized labor groups fought to protect their *relative* real wage as compared with the real wage of other groups. This effort revolved, he insisted, around money wages, not real wages, since prices were beyond trade-union control. "Every trade union will put up some resistance to a cut in money wages, however small," he concluded. "But...no trade union would dream of striking on every occasion of a rise in the cost of living." Keynes's whole argument depended on this distinction, as enforced by trade-union leadership, between real and money-wages. On this basis he denied the argument of the neoclassicals that the workers' conduct was an "obstacle to any increase in aggregate employment."[6] Consequently, unemployment was due to a failure of the laissez-faire system: and once again he could argue that neoclassical theory was in error.

At this point one should examine what Keynes had achieved with his reasoning. He was beginning to clear the position for *his* employment theory by showing, as he thought, the failure of the traditional theory. Beginning with a small part of reality, he was arriving at very large, very abstract statements. One should note that Keynes forgot his important and plural qualifications—"it may be" and "within a certain range"— and ended with his unqualified grand conclusion. In that regard, about the money illusion generally, one is impelled to bring in other parts of reality.

The historian Keynes had studied inflation through the centuries. During the German hyperinflation, which he knew very well and which he had anticipated in his unsuccessful speculations, the workers brushed past concerns of relative wages to ask what their absolute wages would buy on a given day. In the last twenty days of the inflationary period, from 1 November to 20 November 1923, for example, the German mark lost about 97 percent of its value. At the end the employers kept up with these changes by increasing wages daily or more often in order to retain those workers. Two or three years earlier, during War Communism (1918–21), most of the Russian workers deserted the factories to disappear into the countryside, the paper money of the desperate Soviet economy having failed to buy such necessities as food. After World War II, given the inflationary bias (encouraged by Keynesianism), unions hired economists to calculate cost-of-living increases to be inserted in wage contracts, thus specifying a close approximation of the real wage over time. Keynes's strained logic cannot hold up against such realities and many other objections that are only too easy to articulate.

It proved impossible for Keynes himself consistently to apply his money-illusion logic. When he moved on to consumption in Book 3, he saw his representative economic men differently. From that perspective, examining "the principal objective factors which influence the propensity to consume," he began, "Consumption is obviously much more a function of (in some sense) *real* income than of money-income."[7] Workers have always shown that they know to relate their money income to their always real consumption, indeed much more confidently than a Keynes pausing to insert the parenthetical and mysterious "(in some sense)" into his relation.

In Bertrand Russell's review of the *Treatise on Probability* he noted how Keynes used minor irregularities to call into question the laws of probability. Keynes's attack on the neoclassical theory of employment used the same method. The fact is that odd circumstances and labor conduct could well produce a situation of unemployment that was voluntary *in general* despite the many cases where it was individually *involuntary*. Thus, Britain's 10-percent unemployment of the 1920s was due, as we have seen, to a combination of the overvalued pound and the resistance of Britain's powerful unions to wage reductions. The unions were maintaining an established pattern. "In the nineteenth century, when organized workers faced a falling demand for their labor during depressions, they usually preferred to see some of their number discharged rather than to share the loss by having all work for lower wages," John A. Garraty wrote in his magisterial *Unemployment in History*. In the Great Depression of the 1930s it was no different, with union leaders rejecting responsibility for the unemployed, who tended to drop out of their organizations.[8] This tangle of economic and social perversity, which few attempted to think through, greatly strengthened the persuasive character of Keynes's argument.

Claiming success in this first assault against neoclassical economics, thus against its theory of employment, Keynes then proceeded against Say's Law, the ultimate abstraction representing the total economy. In his *Traité d'économie politique* (1803), Jean-Baptiste Say so expressed his Law of Markets: "A man who applies his labor to the investing of objects with value by the creation of utility of some sort, cannot expect such a value to be appreciated and paid for, unless other men have the means of purchasing it. Now, of what do these means consist? Of other values of other products, likewise the fruits of industry, capital and land."[9] Keynes actually quoted John Stuart Mill's version from his *Principles of Political Economy* (1848): "'What constitutes the means of payment for commodities is simply commodities. Each person's means of paying for the productions of other people consist of those which he himself possesses.'" Every commodity (or service), when created, simultaneously took on the double character of a value and the capacity to purchase a comparable value. Keynes summarized, "From the time of Say and

Ricardo the classical economists have taught that supply creates its own demand."[10] Keynes was attempting to pry open and break the simple global identity that Say's Law expressed, to the effect that supply and demand are two aspects of the same global wealth and had to be equal. One might more easily argue that the sense of the identity was too large to be fitted to a given sector of reality, that it was effectively, if not theoretically, irrelevant. But Keynes, as he had made clear to Roy Harrod, would not settle for half measures. He would argue that supply did *not* equal demand because of the workings of *effective* demand, that Say's Law was not a true law.

Keynes was drawing upon the historical support of Thomas Malthus. As recounted in the previous chapter, Keynes revised his original essay on Malthus to emphasize the importance of effective demand in his predecessor's thought. This emphasis tended, moreover, to lead away from the population theory, which Keynes did not mention and which is identified with the name of Malthus today. Malthus, Keynes had to concede, had succumbed to David Ricardo in their debate and failed to provide his effective demand with persuasive logical support: "[T]he almost total obliteration of Malthus' line of approach has been a disaster to the progress of economics," Keynes commented in his essay.[11] "Ricardo conquered England as completely as the Holy Inquisition conquered Spain," he resumed in *The General Theory*. "The great puzzle of Effective Demand with which Malthus had wrestled vanished from economic literature."[12] Keynes proposed to restore it.

Reviving effective demand and confronting Say's Law, Keynes now undertook his demonstration of the global imbalance of supply and demand.[13] Rather than reasoning directly with them, however, he set up an equivalence between supply and production costs, and between demand and expected proceeds. He did this by way of a mathematical demonstration using functions, thus "aggregate supply function" and "aggregate demand function." At this point a critical or naive reading should ask why Keynes did not deal directly with supply and demand. It would make for a simpler, clearer demonstration. A suspicious reading might interpret that Keynes did not because he could not, that the paralogician of the two *Treatises* needed confusion rather than clarity to gain his ends. But we should let him continue.

With the functions, Keynes set up the two triple linkages: (1) supply-aggregate supply function-production costs and (2) demand-aggregate demand function-expected proceeds, thereupon to proceed with their respective final units. We can, at least, leapfrog the *functions* and the mathematical sophistication they require of us. Representing an unhelpful complication, they are not necessary for the sense of the operation.[14] Keynes justified these equivalences by assuming correctly that entrepreneurs would increase supply until *production costs* began to threaten to become greater than *expected proceeds*. At that point the economy would be at equilibrium. There would be no inherent tendency to increase or decrease production, thus supply, and purchases providing the expected proceeds, thus demand. Yet Keynes argued that a situation of greater or lesser unemployment might occur. He was denying the neoclassical claim that the labor market should also be in equilibrium as part of a general equilibrium condition comprehending full employment. Once again, although it subsumed within itself the equilibrium between production costs and expected proceeds, Keynes arrived at his situation of global *dis*equilibrium characterized by unemployment.

With entrepreneurs limiting production to maximum proceeds as determined by equilibrium, why should only labor be in disequilibrium? Keynes's reason continued to rest upon his money illusion, which he argued was more realistic than a concern for real wages. But, as we have seen, the money illusion is really an illusion, implying perverse, self-defeating action by labor. If the workers reasoned like the entrepreneurs they would prefer somewhat less to no pay at all. In the economy he was conceiving, Keynes refused to let them think on this level of reality.

In regard to Keynes's posited global disequilibrium accompanied by unemployment, let us reexamine the propositions that make supply equal to production costs, and demand equal to expected proceeds, which have been stipulated to let him develop his argument. Global supply and demand are huge abstractions, which Keynes tried to manage by analogy. He reasoned, credibly in one sense, that production costs and expected proceeds could substitute for the larger terms because, as noted above, the equilibrium point of production costs and expected proceeds set the limits for global supply and global demand, respectively. This was because of the expected losses beyond that point. One must, however, be aware that Keynes is himself, like the neoclassicals he condemned for it, taking an ideal situation for a real one. In the real world production costs do not of themselves determine prices, are not necessarily covered by sales proceeds, and, in sum, are not always interchangeable with global supply. As for *expected* proceeds, these are psychological, not economic, realities; not measurable by economic gauges. Hence, an eventual inequality of production costs and expected proceeds, which can always occur if the expected proceeds fail to be *realized*, proves nothing about unqualified supply and demand. In any case, to return from larger or smaller abstractions to the real situation of labor, belief in a global disequilibrium depends on assuming that workers willingly remain in a state of disequilibrium, meaning unemployment for many and fear of it for the others.

At least three exegetes have used essentially the same diagram, apparently thrice invented or reinvented, to express the sense of Keynes's view of the relation of labor to the aggregate supply and demand functions. The similarity is doubtless due to the fact that his conception is clear enough in what it claims, although the indefatigable Don Patinkin, in presenting *his* diagram, remarked, "How many painful struggles to understand this chapter [chapter 3, on effective demand] could thereby have been avoided."[15] It is more likely that the difficulty lies not in *understanding* Keynes, but in believing he said what he said. On the theory, therefore, that the diagram itself is not needed for comprehension, this writer will spare his readers the sight of it. In all three cases the interpreters illustrated the contradictory economic situation, as expressed above in words, in which the whole economy was in equilibrium with the exception of the labor market, where many workers remained fixed in the unemployed state. If the workers, however, were free to move, the curve that illustrates *all* the supply factors including labor supply would itself move to the point of equilibrium *without* exception. In that case total demand would equal effective demand, returning us to unqualified demand, this equaling unqualified supply. We arrive back under the sway of Say's Law. Given Keynes's genius for the contradictory, we should not be surprised to find him joining us there.

Besides its use of equivalences for supply and demand, Keynes's attack on Say's Law reaches backward and forward for its arguments. Part of his reasoning depended on that used against voluntary unemployment, namely, the money illusion. Having already discussed the subject in chapter 2, "The Postulates of Classical Economics," he returned to it in the distant chapter 19, "Changes in Money-Wages," where he extended it around the figure of Arthur Pigou as exemplar of neoclassical economics. His argument depended on Pigou's alleged failure to allow, as he had, for money-wages as against real wages and admit the importance of involuntary unemployment. With this Keynes had circled back to the beginning of his unproven contentions in chapter 2. If this was a loop of logic moving in both directions, another argument pointed exclusively forward. Thus, drawing upon his future logic of Books 3 and 4, Keynes now mentioned the deficiencies to be revealed in the propensity to consume and the inducement to invest, with the resultant "paradox of poverty in the midst of plenty" and "obvious and outrageous...defects of the economic system."[16] These were promises waiting to be substantiated. We experience another rhetorical maneuver, the use of past and future arguments to strengthen the inadequate logic of present proof.

The back-and-forth shuttle is a significant part of *The General Theory*'s structure (as I suggested above in the previous chapter on Keynes's theorizing). It was noted that chapter 18, "The General Theory of Employment Re-Stated," completed the discussion of pure theory, with six chapters remaining. Leaving the three chapters of the final Book 6 to speculations on various matters, including Keynes's social philosophy, Book 5's three chapters are reprises on the theory of Book 1. This was indicated above by the reference to chapter 19's resumption of the treatment of money-wages. Similarly, in chapter 20, "The Employment Function," Keynes continues the analysis of effective demand he first undertook in chapters 2 and 3. If, however, he was trying to improve the original argument, he frustrated his purpose, because we find him contradicting it!

Keynes began by seeing deficient effective demand as characterizing the modern economy and producing "under-employment of labor in the sense that there are men unemployed who would be willing to work at less than the existing real wage." In his next sentence he imagines, "Consequently, as effective demand increases, employment increases, though at a real wage equal to or less than the existing one, until a point comes at which there is no surplus of labor available at the then existing real wage." Making no effort to bring in the "money illusion," he saw the workers at one point unwilling to work "unless money-wages rise... *faster* than prices," thus demanding real-wage increases. In this way the system can move toward the ultimate equilibrium, arriving there, according to Keynes himself, on the next page: "[F]ull employment will be reached."[17] The denouement is an isolated moment, an inconspicuous and overlooked contradiction in a logic repetitively arriving at the opposite conclusion. Even without such apparent slips Keynes cannot make his Law of Effective Demand prevail over Say's Law. He has failed with the greater abstraction as he failed with the neoclassical theory of employment.

Keynes's whole effort in Book 1 had to fail because it was an attack on a true identity. To give him every opportunity he has been allowed to make his case here, but a more rigorous logic would have stopped him. The fact that supply *is* demand in a global sense is self-evident. Indeed Keynes had felt obliged to admit it before attacking the proposition. Thus, he granted as "indubitable" the fact that "the income derived in the aggregate by all the elements in the community concerned in a productive activity necessarily has a value exactly equal to the *value* of the output."[18] If the income has the same value as the output, then the demand generated by that income equals the supply represented by that output: Keynes had restated Say's Law. Having conceded the truth of the law, he then tried to withdraw the admission by setting up the double equivalence chains of supply-aggregate supply function-production costs and demand-aggregate demand function-expected proceeds. He found the exceptions upon which he built his denial in the linguistic or conceptual flaws or ambiguities of either linkage. It was too easy to show that his demonstration failed on its own terms, that Keynes could not produce true involuntary unemployment; but one should return to the Say's Law identity as if one had never left. Keynes's indubitable greatness was not exceptionally licensed to change the laws of right reason.

Yet according to reason's dictates, strictly speaking, Keynes had lost nothing. Furthermore, he went on to gain a great deal from the confusions he wrought. The logic of *The General Theory* does not need the argument of Book 1. As noted earlier Keynes had divided the economy between consumption and investment, assigning Book 3 to the one and Book 4 to the other. If one or, better, both of them could prove the endemic failure of their sectors to use up supply in the form of consumption and investment values, respectively, he could prove the existence of fatal or debilitating flaws in the laissez-faire economy. Whatever Book 1 could prove would be redundant.

Book 1 did anticipate the function of Book 4 in that employment and labor behavior affect business investment and output. Keynes, however, was simply trying to prove the existence of disequilibrium as a theoretical possibility and took the unexamined unemployment essentially as evidence of it. He did not, as he would in Books 3 and 4, try to show how the economy actually caused the unemployment along with stagnation. Rather, restricting his argument purely to the defensive, he tried to absolve labor behavior of being, in his phase, "an obstacle to any increase in aggregate employment." This led to his thesis of labor's rational behavior and the realistic money illusion. Consequently, the best that Book 1 could do for his argument was to suggest that a breakdown had to occur *somewhere* in the economy. The unemployment of Book 1 was an abstract correlative, but a failed one, of the real problem or problems Keynes would examine later.

Book 1's argument came very close to perpetuating perfect circularity. Keynes had begun with unemployment and went on to argue that the system naturally led to stagnation, the most human and perhaps most important aspect of which was—unemployment. It can be absolved only if its labor behavior is limited in its effects to providing a theoretical suggestion of a situation of *general* disequilibrium.

Unemployment poses another puzzle: Why, in view of the central importance Keynes attributed to it, did he not examine it directly? Although appropriate to Book 4, he dropped it as an object of study and concentrated on money and interest. Unemployment was shunted to the end, or beyond it, of *The General Theory*—as one great result of the general failure.

What do Keynes's friendly interpreters make of his Law of Effective Demand and Say's Law? Many prefer to avoid the subject; the few direct studies show embarrassment. After calling effective demand one of Keynes's "major 'breakthroughs,'" Don Patinkin, upon closer examination in a later passage of his *Keynes' Monetary Theory,* said Keynes's discussion of it was "one of the most problematic" in *The General Theory.* Keynes had failed, Patinkin wrote, to develop a theory of demand for labor consistent with the assumption of unemployment-and-disequilibrium on which the book was based.[19] In his exemplary Keynesian textbook, *Economics,* Paul A. Samuelson buried Say's Law variously. In the most recent edition he wrote suggestively that *The General Theory* "mortally wounded the belief in Say's Law." He did not say that the new theory had wounded the law itself. In an earlier edition he had written, "The simple-minded belief in Say's Law was banished,"[20] as if a simple-minded belief were a dangerous person exiled to Siberia—while a sophisticated belief would apparently escape banishment. Neither Patinkin nor Samuelson could bring himself to say that Keynes had *refuted* Say's Law, but then Keynes never quite said it himself.

Book 1 was much more than an exercise in pure logic and economics. It was an overture sounding themes, some of them noneconomic, which will be developed in the rest of *The General Theory*. It encourages the reader to think and especially, to *feel* with the writer, while blinding him with its convoluted confusions. It provided generations of students with pathetic verities for belief through empathy. One could debate endlessly about the realism of the money illusion, the voluntarism in involuntary employment, and the defects in demand or effective demand. The Keynesian conceptions were so manifestly counter-rational that critics wondered uneasily if Keynes had not come into possession of new truths. And indeed he had. Book 1, however overstrained its logic, communicates with its exercises around and about unemployment a sense of the whole tragedy, of the pity of it all—an abstraction with enough body to be warm-blooded.

Notes

1. *CW,* 7 (*The General Theory of Employment, Interest and Money*): 3.
2. Ibid., n. 3.
3. Ibid., viii, vii.
4. Ibid., 6.
5. Ibid., 8.
6. Discussion, ibid., 13–15; quotations, pp. 14, 15. Keynes went on to argue that there was a "more fundamental objection" to neoclassical theory (ibid., 10), but it was a restatement of his original argument.
7. Ibid., 91.
8. John A. Garraty, *Unemployment in History* (New York, 1978), 190–93; quotation, p. 190.
9. Excerpt from an 1832 translation of the *Traité,* Henry Hazlitt, ed., *The Critics of Keynesian Economics* (New Rochelle, NY, 1977; 1st ed.: 1960), 12–13.
10. Quotation from J. S. Mill and Keynes's comment, *CW,* 7: 18.
11. "Thomas Robert Malthus," ibid., 10 (*Essays in Biography*): 71–108; quotation, p. 98.
12. Ibid., 7: 32.
13. Ibid., chap. 3, "The Principle of Effective Demand," pp. 23–34.
14. See ibid., 25–30. Keynes's aggregate supply function is written $Z = \phi(N)$; the aggregate demand function, $D = f(N)$, where N = employment of N men.
15. Patinkin, *Keynes' Monetary Thought,* 87; the diagram, p. 88. He was apparently unaware that essentially the same diagram was created earlier: Dudley Dillard, *The Economics of J. M. Keynes* (New York, 1948), 30. Another apparently origi-

nal invention was Victoria Chick, *Macroeconomics After Keynes: A Reconsideration of the* General Theory (Cambridge, MA, 1983), 63.
16. *CW,* 7: 30–32; quotations, pp. 30, 31.
17. Ibid., 289, 290.
18. Ibid., 20.
19. Patinkin, *Keynes' Monetary Thought,* chap. 9, "The Theory of Effective Demand in the *General Theory,*" pp. 83–94; quotations, pp. 23 (chap. 2), 84. He found more flaws in his later article, "A Critique of Keynes's Theory of Effective Demand," in *Anticipations of the* General Theory? (Chicago, 1982), 123–58.
20. Paul A. Samuelson and William D. Nordhaus, *Economics,* 14th ed. (New York, 1992), 379; Samuelson, *Economics,* 10th ed. (New York, 1976), 845.

8

Consumption and the Propensity to It

"Consumption—to repeat the obvious—is the sole end and object of all economic activity," Keynes wrote toward the end of his first chapter on the subject.[1] The logic incorporated in the structure of the General Theory as model gave consumption equal importance with investment as affected by liquidity preference and the interest rate, but that sense was not at all obvious to the reader. Actually Keynes apportioned a modest amount of attention to consumption in *The General Theory*. Book 3, devoted to that subject, consists of three chapters (one of them not essentially on consumption)—no more than forty-two pages and barely a third of the length of Book 4, which examines investment and related factors. And if Keynes had interrupted his argument to give consumption its due, he had begun that first chapter on it: "The ultimate object of our analysis is to discover what determines the volume of employment."[2]

Keynes did not, in fact, address consumption directly, nor had he promised to do so. He was being precise when he entitled Book 3 "The Propensity to Consume." Keynes was not discussing consumption but a *potentiality* leading toward it, and the discussion consistently treats it as part of a relation achieving, or failing to achieve, full employment. The major concern is not to consume but to consume enough to exhaust the total goods and services produced and so maintain a healthy economy. Keynes does not take advantage of the opportunity to deal with such real stuff as the materials maintaining life. He does not study people consuming food, alcohol, houses, paintings, first editions, newspapers, vacations, plus fours, and haircuts. Consistent with this, anticipating Book 4 on "The Inducement to Invest," we shall see that Keynes will similarly reject the opportunity to address reality in the form of the *production* of the goods (and services) for consumption. Using the word "invest"

145

in the sense of an entrepreneur putting money into capital outlays, Keynes will study the impulsion to produce those goods. Again he will be examining a potentiality and a relation, although at greater length than in the case of consumption. The monetary economist Keynes, while giving himself the task of dealing with the whole economy, is nevertheless remaining at a remove from it by using money and finance as mediators. As the title of his first draft chapter indicated, he was indeed writing a general *monetary* theory of the whole economy from consumption back to production.

Keynes had already signaled the great problem of the consumption and investment relation in Book 1, when he discussed effective demand: "The propensity to consume and the rate of new investment determine between them the volume of employment." The result was only too likely to be "deficient effective demand" and unemployment. This was when he introduced the "paradox of poverty in the midst of plenty." He sketched the outlines of the problem: "Moreover the richer the community, the wider will tend to be the gap between its actual and its potential production." While a poor community consumed the "greater part of its output...the wealthy community will have to discover much ampler opportunities for investment if the saving propensities of its wealthier members are to be compatible with the employment of its poorer members." Worse than that, the opportunities for further investment were "less attractive" for a wealthy community because of its already substantial accumulation of capital; Keynes pointed beyond Book 3's consumption to Book 4's investment: "unless the rate of interest falls at a sufficiently rapid rate."[3] Compounded in the argument was the powerful implication that equalizing or redistributing incomes would improve the general economic well-being. The problem of consumption was logically, pathetically, and threateningly defined as inherent in the system before Keynes would go on to explain what caused it and precisely how it manifested itself.

Yet Keynes never made his case against consumption, although Book 1 had promised it eloquently and, following his direct discussion in Book 3, he would reason in later passages of *The General Theory* and other writings as if he had, in fact, done so. It was another example of shuttling among past, present, and future to strengthen the argument.

The direct discussion of the presumed consumption gap took less than three pages,[4] the rest of Book 3 contributing nothing essential to its logic.

Except for those few pages the first two chapters dealt discursively and not very illuminatingly with various aspects of the propensity to consume interesting to Keynes. The third and longest chapter addressed the multiplier and consumption, again a mathematical relation, and will be more usefully examined when we see how Keynes fitted together the components of his General Theory. We double back to the confrontation with consumption.

"A higher absolute level of income will tend, as a rule, to widen the gap between income and consumption," Keynes began his argument. "For the satisfaction of the immediate primary needs of a man and his family is usually a stronger motive than the motives towards accumulation, which only acquire effective sway when a margin of comfort has been attained." That was the whole argument, but Keynes's thesis leapt to its conclusion in the next sentence. "These reasons will lead, as a rule, to a greater *proportion* of income being saved as real income increases. But whether or not a greater proportion is saved..."[5] One must interrupt Keynes here to puzzle out this ambiguous statement. Two expert readers drew diametrically opposed senses from it. In his review of *The General Theory,* Frank Knight complained of the ambiguity but concluded that Keynes was positing only an *absolute* increase and not necessarily a *proportionately* greater amount saved.[6] Another economist assumed the contrary in the *Quarterly Journal of Economics* of November 1938. Asked for clarification by Arthur Pigou, who saw the latter review, Keynes, besides assuring him that sense, published a long letter specifying an *absolute* increase in the amount saved in the journal's issue of August 1939.[7] With this statement defining the limits of his claim, Keynes had permitted his fundamental argument on consumption to abort itself.

For if merely a greater absolute amount of income were saved, the consequence would not be a consumption gap at all. This was why Knight had "puzzled some time over the question as to just why the author so emphasized the increase of saving with increased income, making the natural assumption that an increase meant an increased proportion."[8] If a given economy had achieved full employment at, say, a proportion of 90 percent consumption and 10 percent saving, and if income increased, a greater *absolute* amount of saving would have to take place simply to maintain the 9–1 consumption-saving ratio. The danger of deficient consumption would arise only if a greater *proportional* amount were saved (and, correspondingly, a lesser *proportional* amount were consumed). If income were doubled, say, from $100 billion to $200 billion, the 9–1 ratio would not change if saving also doubled, going from $10 billion to $20 billion, an absolute but not a proportional increase. If, however, saving had increased only to, say, $15 billion, then there would have been an absolute increase but a proportional *decrease,* saving falling from 10 percent to 7.5 percent of income (and a proportional *increase* of consumption from 90 percent to 92.5 percent of income). If saving had instead gone to $40 billion and 20 percent of income, this would indeed have been a proportional increase. The consumption-saving ratio would have fallen from 9–1 to 4–1, with a consumption gap resulting in a failure to consume everything produced and a condition of disequilibrium, deflation, and depression. This would provide a strong argument for income redistribution.

But if, as Keynes had written initially, the proportional saving increase was only *likely* but not *certain,* then his logic cannot proceed as if the alternative possibility were nonexistent—surely not after he had himself proposed it: "whether or not a greater proportion is saved..." In any case, while later positing only an absolute increase, he had adduced no facts and only exiguous argument in *The General Theory* to suggest the *likelihood* he claimed to perceive. In his precision in the *Quarterly Journal of Economics,* he put it: "I give reasons for expecting that, *as a rule,* a greater *proportion* of income will be saved, as real income increases." He had, in fact, not given plural reasons but the singular speculation on the consumption motives of "a man and his family." Keynes went on to grant, "This is a mere statement of opinion, which requires more statistical examination than I have given it."[9]

The example of the family man, moreover, raised other questions. In the same paragraph Keynes had gone from the savings pattern of "a man" to that of "any modern community," as if there were no difference between them. Is he taking the "man" or the "man and his family" as a model of the community or is he anthropomorphizing the community? In logic Keynes has no right to transfer such patterns between the two as if there were no significant difference between them. Indeed, eleven pages later, he remarked on "the large amount of income, varying perhaps from one-third to two-thirds of the total accumulation in a modern industrial community... which is withheld by Central and Local Government, by Institutions and by Business Corporations..."; he had to distinguish these savers from individuals or individual households, and he continued: "...for motives analogous to, but not identical with, those actuating individuals." With this admission Keynes granted that his argument risked being a non sequitur to the extent of the magnitude of institutional saving. However "analogous" the motives of such institutional savers might be, their saving rationale and pattern were so different from individual actions that they required separate studies, something *The General Theory* did not attempt beyond conceding certain differences.[10] Yet Keynes's argument proceeded as if the essential characteristics of saving flowed from his family man.

Keynes had already developed another dubious argument in the space provided by his consumption gap. Thus, *The General Theory* had the gap threatening to reduce the need for production, and hence for employment. In a "digression," as he called it, on capital expansion in Britain and the United States, he asserted forebodingly that the more capital created in the past, the less would be needed in the present and future. Keynes concluded, "The greater, moreover, the consumption for which we have provided in advance, the more difficult it is to find something further to provide for in advance, and the greater our dependence on present consumption as a source of demand."[11] The whole argument had proceeded with specific reference to the Depression, as if the consumption gap, with all its ambiguity, had to have concomitantly *depressive* effects.[12] But the force of the argument is based on the assumption of *disproportionate* increases in saving; merely absolute ones would leave consumption with its healthy hunger for more that has kept capitalistic economies expanding to this moment.

Later, after having emerged from the book, Keynes seems to have completed the process of believing what he set out to prove: the fact of a greater *proportional* amount saved. This is the sense of it as expressed in his letter to Roy Harrod (cited above in chapter 6) on the flash of intuition that was the theoretical breakthrough to *The General Theory*, namely, the "psychological law" of the consumption gap.[13] A few months after this letter, defending the book against four economist-critics, Keynes repeated the same thought on the consumption gap with almost the same words in his important article, "The General Theory of Employment": "This psychological law was of the utmost importance in the development of my own thought."[14] In neither instance did Keynes specify that the gap would be proportionately greater, but the conception would not have had the significance he attributed to it if it had merely meant an absolute increase.

The Keynesian conception of the income-consumption/saving relation breaks down. Keynes never made the effort to prove the proportionality of the consumption gap that his conclusions required. Nevertheless, he proceeded as if his model had worked perfectly. Loyal readers followed. Vast research activities, particularly in the empiricist United States, endeavored to undergird his argument with established or newly assembled facts describing a modern economy.

In *The General Theory* itself Keynes could test his ideas against earlier research by the pioneering economic statisticians Colin Clark and Simon Kuznets. Keynes had to content himself with a cautious reading. He found the Kuznets figures "very precarious." Moreover, "if single years are taken in isolation, the results look rather wild." Undeterred, he found more acceptable figures if the years were (arbitrarily) taken in pairs, namely, "a marginal propensity to consume not exceeding 60-70%."[15] ("Marginal propensity to consume" refers to the last unit of income—the one on the "margin"—which the consumer receives, and proposes to spend, in this instance at Keynes's estimated 60-70 percent rate.) In this way his extrapolations argued for a weakness in consumption but were too obviously biased to merit the uncritical acceptance they met.

Influenced by Keynes and the Depression, economists worried extravagantly and uselessly during World War II about the consumption collapse to be expected with the end of war-generated demand. Later, in 1948, the Harvard economist John H. Williams noted in "An Appraisal of Keynesian Economics": "Thus far, the forecasts have been almost uniformly bad." Instead of a collapse or even decline, economists had to explain the appearance of a "secular upward drift" in the consumption function. Later work of Kuznets, reported in his paper, "Capital Formation, 1879-1938," saw consumption as a constant fraction of income, but with a moderate tendency in the 1920s for the consumption proportion to *increase*. Similarly, Colin Clark found that savings had been a diminishing fraction of the growing national income in England for at least a generation. Williams concluded, "We have nothing left of this basic concept of the Keynesian theory other than that consumption is an important component of income and deserves all the study we can give it."[16]

Meanwhile, successively newer generations of researchers, careless in their reading of *The General Theory* but true to Keynes's spirit, understood his claim to mean a proportional increase in the propensity to save (or proportional decline in the propensity to consume) as aggravated by income inequality. Two early studies, however, tended to deny both the existence of a consumption lag *and* the negative effects of inequality.

The first study promptly led the hopeful research into a dead end. In 1947, Harold Lubell, a Harvard graduate student and former staff member of the Federal Reserve System, used governmental studies specifically to relate inequality to consumption expenditure in the article "Effects of Redistribution of Income on Consumers' Expenditures." He concluded that "if the present data are correct, too much emphasis should not be placed on income redistribution for the solution of the savings-investment problem." Lubell used data for 1941 that showed persons with annual incomes over $10,000 saving 29 percent of those incomes, while persons with incomes below $500 were dissaving $87, that is, spending their savings or borrowing to that extent to maintain a bearable living standard. Positing complete or partial movements to equality, namely, 100 percent, 50 percent, and 10 percent, he calculated that the resultant increases would mean 4.1 percent, 2.4 percent, or .5 percent increases, respectively, in all expenditures. Hence, "no redistribution of any feasible severity will bring about a large enough change in any expenditure to offer a major contribution to the problem of increasing the demand."[17] His figures inevitably reflected the mathematical commonplace that averaging the income of members of any known society would mean mediocre incomes for each member. Still, if the combination of these research results with an awareness of the statistical limitations deterred some researchers, others rose to the challenge of proving Keynes to have been right.

Keynes had assumed that income as received during a given period under examination was the only significant factor in determining consumption spending: the *absolute income hypothesis*. (This term has nothing to do with the distinction he had made between absolute and proportional increases/decreases in saving/consumption. The researchers assumed that *proportional* increases/decreases in saving/consumption—necessary to generate the consumption lag in Keynes's preferred theory—were *absolutely* determined by income.) Another study, arriving at the *relative-income* hypothesis, showed the relation of consumption to income to be much more complex and problematic than that. In his widely cited book *Income, Saving, and the Theory of Consumer Behavior* (1949), James S. Duesenberry, who was teaching at Harvard, actually saw a "Drive Toward Higher Consumption," as a subheading announced it, because of the "character of our culture," rising living standards, and "habit formation." He went on to see income inequality encouraging rather than reducing consumption because of the "emulation" factor, poorer persons spending more on the example of the wealthier. Duesenberry specifically challenged Keynes's absolute-income hypothesis and instead posited consumption and saving as dependent on a series of factors: interest rates, the relation between current and expected income, income- and age-distribution, and the rate of income growth. Additionally, he pointed out that according to one set of data, blacks saved three times as much as whites of the corresponding income levels. He reasoned that such blacks were in a higher relative position in their own community and felt wealthier than the absolute figures indicated, thus the relative-income hypothesis.[18] If Duesenberry was right in just one or two of these various senses, consumption according to Keynes could hardly serve the operational requirements of his *General Theory*—to produce the promised stagnation in production and employment.

A number of variants of the absolute- and-relative income hypotheses appeared, the most significant being the Tobin Modification of the relative-income conception, with wealth as well as income influencing consumption—to explain blacks' lower spending as due to less wealth. Other hypotheses included: the life-cycle hypothesis of households consuming a constant proportion of their expected lifetime income; Milton Friedman's similar permanent-income hypothesis, which placed more emphasis on wealth and shortened a household's planning horizon to three years; and the thesis of "real balance effects," which also emphasized wealth in the form of real net liquid assets encouraging consumption. The result of this theorizing and research was to distance economic thinking from the theory of Keynes that had inspired it. For while the new work produced useful insights about consumer behavior, it made no difference to the validity of Keynes's consumption theory whether Friedman's permanent-income hypothesis or the real-balance effects of Arthur Pigou and Don Patinkin were more nearly correct. If, as all their

studies showed, consumption was only partially and perhaps secondarily influenced by unqualified income as compared with other factors,
then Keynes's hypothesis was called into question as much by Keynesians
like James Tobin and Patinkin as by the non-Keynesians Pigou and
Friedman. The point is that the tremendous amount of work invested in
strengthening the consumption part of *The General Theory* succeeded
in gravely weakening it—or worse.

At various junctures from the 1950s, these and many other research
efforts have been reviewed by historically minded economic writers.
Some of the later writers themselves attempted to improve upon what
they saw as neglected opportunities or failures. In 1959 "The New Theories of the Consumption Function" noted the fundamental disagreement
among interpretations and found major problems in statistical completeness and credibility.[19] In 1962 "Research in Household Behavior" sur-
veyed the field since World War II, emphasized "the need for reconciling
the different theories of the consumption function," and concluded, "It
is amazing how little attention is being given to the improvement of data
collection techniques, and how much empirical analysis is focused on
attempting to explain what may be no more than errors of observation."[20]

Similarly, two surveys in the 1970s found inadequate research, more
disagreement among researchers, and, in any case, a failure to substan-
tiate Keynes's hypothesis. In 1975, Alan J. Blinder of Princeton, prolific
author of many theoretical writings and a well-regarded Keynesian textbook, declared himself "shocked" to discover that the consensus rejecting Keynes's hypothesis had never been "subjected to a direct empirical
test." He thereupon carried out such a test and ended by supporting that
rejection. Indeed, although a representative of mainstream Keynesianism,
Blinder had to grant that "equalizing the income distribution will either
have no bearing on or (slightly) reduce aggregate consumption."[21] In
1977, Ronald G. Bodkin, a member of the more radical post-Keynesian
school, reviewed all the researches noted here (except Blinder's) and
concluded that "the plethora of attempts at empirical verification" had
shown that Keynes's consumption function "apparently displayed no
such tendency" as attributed to it by Keynes.[22] The negative consensus
held.

In 1986 two economists in England noted that "over the past decade
the aggregate consumption function in the United Kingdom had been
the subject of intensive econometric scrutiny," but that most of that re-

search had assumed Keynes's absolute income hypothesis to be wrong. (Besides the British research, they had reviewed the work of the American Alan Blinder.) They proposed to rehabilitate Keynes's theory by another approach, radically different in one regard. They refused to limit themselves to past results and instead undertook to base their argument on a computer-constructed projection into the future. Using data on British family expenditures for the years 1963–82, they carried out "simulations experiments" for the period 1983–2000. They achieved the conclusion that by the end of the simulation period a social situation of "more inequality" saved five times as much as "less inequality"—the opposite of the results reported by Blinder, among many others. Thus, they could argue that "more equality" would reduce saving and increase consumer spending. But their "experiments" upon the future were protected from any testing against present reality, and, as noted above, were mounted upon the extremely vague classifications of "more inequality" and "less" of the same. Moreover, the priority they granted "social justice" and their stated ambition to create "an instrument of demand management policy"[23] are indications of a powerful left-wing bias that could easily produce the desired results from such a computer simulation.

If one takes a few steps backward to put everything into perspective, one can see a huge fact dominating the history of Keynesian theorizing about consumption and saving: it has remained in the dark tunnel of the psychology of the Great Depression, with its enfeebled consumption, that dominated the writing and conclusions of *The General Theory*. But Keynes himself had escaped from that tunnel by November 1939 when he wrote the newspaper series later published as *How to Pay for the War*; in it he advocated policies to deal with the inflationary effects of wartime prosperity and its *expanding* consumption. Indeed, the Keynes of 1939 had been anticipated by the Keynes of 1919, who wrote *The Economic Consequences of the Peace*. This comparably significant work had a view of consumption and saving totally opposed to that of *The General Theory*, and one that is more relevant to present problems. Keynes had eloquently written then, "If the rich had spent their wealth on their own enjoyment, the world would long ago have found such a regime intolerable." Without limiting such consumption, there could not have been such positive results as the stream of new products from the "immense accumulations of fixed capital." This capital was built up of the savings of the "capitalistic classes," who had been allowed to claim most of the benefits of capitalism "on the tacit underlying condition that they consumed very little of [those benefits] in practice."[24] If this represented polemical exaggeration, so did the consumption theory of *The General Theory* in the opposite sense. A balanced judgment, with Keynes's formal agreement, at least, sees consumption as the purpose of the economy and the appropriate savings level as a necessity in providing the materials of consumption.

The Keynesian consensus in economic theory did not pursue Keynes's post-*General Theory* view and, accepting what had become canonical, continued to emphasize the need to strengthen aggregate demand—even after it was long obvious that demand was healthy and growing. It took the inflation of the 1970s to call up "supply side" economics as a way to right the balance. This essentially pragmatic response has not, however, led to a general examination of the origins of the problem in *The General Theory*'s statement on consumption.

It is, after all, increases in saving that make one essential difference between an advanced economy and a less developed one. The New Stone Age, with its exquisitely chipped arrowheads and molded pots, saved more than the Old Stone Age—and much less than the Middle, Victorian, or Space ages. One should not fear a secular upward drift in saving, which is necessary in order to finance such improvements as arrowheads and computers. Most of the world is wretchedly poor and must save more to improve its condition.

Wants and needs are insatiable everywhere. The comparative statistics, ranging in recent years from a per-capita annual income of less than $100 in poorer Third World countries to about $25,000 for the more advanced economies, fairly shriek it out. Restricting himself to the West, the monetary economist Harry G. Johnson (1922–1977) proposed that Keynes's notion of satiated consumption and capital saturation was "clearly untenable except on the implicit assumption that the standard of life enjoyed by the masses…is already close to the maximum they deserve."[25] Ultimately, the argument must consider life itself. The figures for life expectancy accompanying the per-capita income figures accompany them upward. People in the more prosperous countries live twice as long as do those in the poorest parts of the world. We can continue to lengthen life for everyone as we expand and refine our capital equipment. We are living with the great Malthusian problem, the side of Malthus Keynes purposefully forgot. The world's capacity to maintain life is always limited; we can push back those limits, as we have done up to now, by continuing to improve the world's general productive capacity. As life and population increase, the limits become more threatening with the ecological strains and the growth of economic costs. With demographers predicting a doubling of the world population in a generation or so, the crueler Malthus makes us forget the Keynesian Malthus. There is no limit to consumption—to demand. The slackening in demand Keynes observed in the 1930s was a back eddy resulting from a minor external anomaly in a broad Amazonian flow forward. Even at its worst it took place at the same time when a large part of the world's population was slowly dying of malnutrition or somewhat more quickly of famine or curable disease. The victims could not translate their desire for life into the *demand* a neoclassical or Keynesian economist could recognize. Facing reality—enormity—Keynes's imagination failed him.

In place of a grander imagination, Keynes, concentrating on the specifics of the British situation, indulged in the pyrotechnics of irony, lighting up odd aspects of consumption as related to employment and lengthening their shadows. "If the Treasury were to fill old bottles with banknotes, bury them at suitable depths in disused coal mines which are then filled up to the surface with town rubbish, and leave it to private industry...to dig the notes up again," he wrote toward the end of Book 3, "there need be no unemployment." This was hardly different in effect from gold-mining operations, he suggested. He might have mentioned New Deal agencies hiring men to dig holes and fill them up again. "Ancient Egypt was doubly fortunate...in that it possessed *two* activities, namely, pyramid-building as well as the search for precious metals," Keynes wrote, moving through space and time. "The Middle Ages built cathedrals and sang dirges. Two pyramids, two masses for the dead, are twice as good as one..." He qualified: "...but not so for two railroads from London to York."[26] Doubled railroads meant overabundant usefulness and durability; consumption would choke on them. It was a brilliant satire on the contemporary failure of capitalism, but it left out most of space and time. A proper study of modern Egypt or of the India Keynes never saw would find more cause for irony in the general poverty, malnutrition, and foreshortened life spans of their masses. There the capacity to consume remained uncorrupted.

Keynes and his supporters had gotten consumption all wrong. In advanced and advancing societies it did, in fact, do what he said it did—

lag proportionately behind increasing income over the years. It had to do this to provide the funds for a modern economy's increasing investment needs. The consumption lag was a necessity and not an evil as he assumed. He compounded the error by failing to see how much the world's population could consume, not to mention how much more it wanted to consume. Restricting his view to the dismal England of the 1920s and 1930s, he had mistaken the back eddy for the river. He had remained blind to the potentials both of the demand represented by the working classes of Britain (and perforce of other advanced countries), as Harry Johnson pointed out, *and* the demand of other, much poorer regions. Such a demand, to which might be added that of a Western bourgeoisie habituated to the good life and wanting it always better, would force consumption beyond the capacity of any given capital accumulation of any given period, if only given the opportunity. Consumption was not a problem in its weakness, as Keynes and company thought, but in its strength.

In Book 1 Keynes failed to prove his global point about weak effective demand. Book 3 now shows that he also failed to prove that consumption tends toward the stagnation level. That still leaves investment as affected by liquidity preference, the interest rate, and the peculiarities of money, to which he devoted the greater part of his argument. If he could prove that a weakness arose in this area, at least, he would still have succeeded in demonstrating the tendency of the modern economy to fall into stagnation after all.

Notes

1. *CW,* 7: 104.
2. Ibid., 89. It was actually the second sentence of chap. 8, the first referring back to the earlier discussion.
3. Ibid., 30, 31.
4. Ibid., 96–98.
5. Ibid., 97.
6. Frank H. Knight, "Unemployment: And Mr. Keynes's Revolution in Economic Theory," in Hazlitt, ed., *The Critics of Keynesian Economics,* 67-95; discussion of question, pp. 77–78. Originally published in the *Canadian Journal of Economics and Political Science* (February 1937): 100–23.
7. Letters, Arthur C. Pigou to Keynes and response, and Keynes's letter to the other economist, a Mrs. Elizabeth Gilboy, as published in the *Quarterly Journal of Economics, CW,* 14: 271–77.
8. Knight, "Unemployment," 77–78.

9. *CW,* 14: 275.
10. Ibid., 7: 108-10.
11. Ibid., 105.
12. Ibid., 96-106.
13. Letter, 30 August 1936, ibid., 14: 84-86.
14. "The General Theory of Employment, " ibid., 14: 109-23; quotation, p. 120. The article will be discussed below.
15. Ibid., 7: 127, 128; Keynes's discussion of the figures, pp. 101-4, 127-28.
16. John H. Williams, "An Appraisal of Keynesian Economics," in Hazlitt, ed., *The Critics of Keynesian Economics,* 278, 279.
17. Harold Lubell, "Effects of Redistribution of Income on Consumers' Expenditures," *American Economic Review* 37 (March 1947): 157-70; quotations, pp. 157, 161, 163.
18. James S. Duesenberry, *Income, Saving, and the Theory of Consumer Behavior* (Cambridge, MA, 1949), 23-26, 45-46, 111-16.
19. M. J. Farrell, "The New Theories of the Consumption Function," in M. G. Mueller, ed., *Readings in Macroeconomics* (London, 1969), 77-91. Originally in the *Economic Journal* 69 (December 1959): 678-96.
20. Robert Ferber, "Research on Household Behavior," *American Economic Review* 52 (March 1962): 19-63; quotations, pp. 52, 54.
21. Alan J. Blinder, "Distribution Effects and the Aggregate Consumption Function," *Journal of Political Economy* 83 (1975): 447-75; quotations, pp. 448, 472.
22. R. G. Bodkin, "Keynesian Econometric Concepts: Consumption Functions, Investment Functions, and 'The' Multiplier," in Sidney Weintraub, ed., *Modern Economic Thought* (Philadelphia, 1977), 69.
23. V. K. Borooah and D. R. Sharpe, "Aggregate Consumption and the Distribution of Income in the United Kingdom: An Econometric Analysis," *Economic Journal* 96 (June 1986): 449-66; quotations, pp. 449, 463.
24. *CW,* 2: 19-20.
25. In collaboration with Elizabeth S. Johnson, "The Social and Intellectual Origins of The General Theory," in Elizabeth S. Johnson and Harry G. Johnson, *The Shadow of Keynes* (Chicago, 1978), 80-81.
26. *CW,* 7: 129-31.

9

Investment and the Inducement to It

Book 4, suggestively speculating on various economic factors and phenomena, brought two of them into a relationship that could explain how "The Inducement to Invest," as it was entitled, could or could not lead to enough investment fully to employ an economy. One of the two was an approximation of profit, Keynes's "marginal efficiency of capital" (MEC), or expected returns on capital expenditures. He had derived the MEC, as he acknowledged, from Alfred Marshall's "marginal utility of capital" or "marginal net efficiency" and Irving Fisher's more expressive "rate of return over cost," but with the transformingly important difference of being "prospective," "expected," "intended," or otherwise placed in the future.[1] The other major factor was the interest rate as it related itself to the MEC, the interest rate understood as the return on securities issued by enterprises earning the actualized MEC. The calculation seems irreducibly simple and pure: the rational enterprise invested in its productive operations as long as the MEC, expected returns, exceeded the interest rate, the financing costs. But, if the mathematics of it was simple enough, the results, in Keynes's vision of an economy operating with a weak effective demand, was discouragement.

Both the marginal efficiency of capital and the interest rate were troublesome. Although Keynes went on to emphasize other aspects, the MEC had the unique character of being located beyond reach in the always receding future. Devoting the first chapter of Book 4 to it, he introduced it emphatically enough as *prospective yield*: "This involves the whole question of the place of expectation in economic theory."[2] One should be aware that the MEC is not real by definition and can take no effect on the reality one experiences. While such a term refers to a sufficiently real mental or psychological fact, it is not an *economic* fact, although it gives rise to such. Thus, it poses a special difficulty to which one must return later in this study. In Book 4 itself that particular difficulty does not appear. The problem revolves around the interest rate, upon which Keynes would concentrate his revolutionary designs.

Meanwhile, considering the insecurities of the MEC, Keynes launched into what he admitted was "a digression on a different level of abstraction from most of this book" in the next chapter, "The State of Long-Term Expectation." In fact it was Keynes the connoisseur of market probabilities reviewing his real experiences in making his fortune and, perhaps, trying to elude some guilty thoughts stirred up in the process. Recalling the thesis of his *Treatise on Probability,* he suggested that the best decisions are made "not solely" on the basis of "the most probable forecast" but also "depend on the *confidence* with which we make this forecast—on how highly we rate the likelihood of our best forecast turning out wrong." He was doubtless remembering his fortune's dizzying descents and exhilarating flights upward. Here was little theory, much less than Keynes thought he was proffering, and many memories of probabilities and skewed outcomes, their sense guessed at in a fragmentary and impressionistic account. Here is Keynes of the French casinos losing his last franc and, with the appropriate confidence, correcting his system and borrowing a new stake. He had to grant, "The outstanding fact is the extreme precariousness of the basis of knowledge on which our estimates of the prospective yield have to be made." In this situation Keynes found an imbalance of harmful "speculation," that is, "the activity of forecasting the psychology of the market," over constructive "*enterprise*...the activity of forecasting the prospective yield of assets over their whole life." He slipped into peroration: "The social object of skilled investment should be to defeat the dark forces of time and ignorance which envelop our future. The actual, private object of the most skilled investment today is 'to beat the gun,' as the Americans so well express it, to outwit the crowd, and to pass the bad, or depreciating, half-crown to the other fellow." Keynes judged, "In one of the greatest investment markets in the world, namely, New York, the influence of speculation (in the above sense) is enormous." He concluded, "Speculators may do no harm as bubbles on a steady stream of enterprise. But the position is serious when enterprise becomes the bubble on a whirlpool of speculation."[3] The evil, the United States representing the future, seemed clearly to be winning.

This virtuous eloquence traps Keynes in the question: Did he knowingly commit sin? Clearly, the license for the breaking of rules granted to a follower of G. E. Moore did not extend to vulgar monetary aggrandizement. In his own logic, however, Keynes avoided self-incrimination. For he distinguished between the speculator's short-term efforts "to beat the gun," defined at best as sterile and at worst as damaging to the economy, and the "*enterprise* [of] the long-term investor, he who most promotes the public interest." With faith in well-studied, selected companies, such a person "proposes to ignore near-term market fluctuations."[4] In this, we recall, Keynes expressed, as he praised, his own stock-market strategy. It was in 1936, after seeing *The General Theory* through the press, that he went on to double his capital, which included important American investments, and achieve his best year.[5] Engagingly persuasive and good politics, *The General Theory*'s attack on speculation helped to place the book among the more socially conscious writings of the time. If the reader stumbled over Keynes's interest theory as impossible to understand or believe, he could warmly concur in finding a speculator's greed outrageous.

Approaching the interest rate, on which he would invest much more weight and wordage, Keynes began perversely by undercutting it. Like the marginal efficiency of capital, it defeated prudent calculation to a great extent "due to the characteristic of human nature that a large proportion of our positive activities depend on spontaneous optimism rather than on a mathematical expectation." He concluded with a phrase that has become part of contemporary idiom: "Most, probably, of our decisions to do something positive...can only be taken as a result of animal spirits," enterprise being based on little more calculation than devoted to "an expedition to the South Pole."[6] In another viewing, two pages later, considering animal spirits along with more rational factors and qualifying carefully, Keynes saw the interest rate, at best, "exercising, at any rate, in normal circumstances, a great, though not decisive, influence on the rate of investment." Thus, the entrepreneur's or speculator's animal spirits could brush past the careful calculation of the MEC and the difference between it and the interest rate. Keynes was now "somewhat skeptical of the success of a merely monetary policy towards influencing the rate of interest" and expected to see more state intervention in this insecure area.[7] With this he had retrospectively questioned the sense of his long campaign for low interest rates and, in advance, weakened the complex argument, the longest and most important in *The General Theory,* which was constructed upon and around the interest rate.

Immediately turning his back on such negative thoughts, Keynes entered, beginning with the next page, into chapter 13, "The General Theory of the Rate of Interest." He did not dwell on the MEC–interest rate relation but assumed that the reader had taken in its central character. If the volatile MEC was a problem in its uncertainty, the rate of interest was a much greater one in the opposite sense—the *probability* that it was perversely what it should not be, namely, too high. While he had momentarily faltered approaching it, given the irrationality of animal spirits, he was gripped with its significance. Furthermore, he found himself in possession of the theory he had lacked up to this point on the interest-rate issue. He threw himself into his ultimate debate.

As the chapter title announced, reversing the normal procedure, Keynes began with *his* theory instead of the one accepted by the economic science of the day as fundamental and uncontroversial. According to the draft table of contents of mid-1934, he had originally planned to proceed traditionally, with "The Classical Theory of the Rate of Interest" coming first; he changed the order on the next table of contents, dated June 1935.[8] The editors of the *Collected Writings* provide no documented reason or speculation for the change, which, as it will be shown, gave Keynes an extra advantage in challenging the enemy theory. He offered his version of neoclassical interest theory in a long, knotted sentence, declared that by such means "it is impossible to deduce the rate of interest," and consigned it to the next chapter.[9] He then proceeded to a complete statement of his General Theory of the Rate of Interest in the ten pages of chapter 13.

Keynes approached his interest rate through liquidity preference, the degree of an "individual's" desire to retain "liquid control" of his resources. After disputing a lesser point of neoclassical theory, Keynes arrived at a first viewing: "The mere definition of the rate of interest tells us in so many words that the rate of interest is the reward for parting with liquidity for a specified period." In the modest length of some two hundred words the next paragraph gave the essence of the chapter, thus of Keynes's full statement of his interest theory.[10] He would develop other themes around it elsewhere, particularly in the rest of Book 4, but they would derive from this discussion rather than add to it. All of the sense of interest, according to *The General Theory,* rests upon and revolves around the chapter as reducible to the paragraph. In fact, Keynes efficiently condensed much of that paragraph's meaning in its first sentence: "Thus the rate of interest at any time, being the reward for parting with liquidity, is a measure of the unwillingness of those who possess money to part with their liquid control of it." In the next sentence, he again rejected the neoclassical theory in another formulation he made for it: "The rate of interest is not the 'price' which brings into equilibrium the demand for resources to invest with the readiness to abstain from present consumption." Instead, as Keynes put it in the third sentence, "It is the 'price' which equilibrates the desire to hold wealth in the form of cash with the available quantity of cash." Moving—leaping acrobatically, rather—from the second to the third sentence, Keynes made his revolutionary change in interest theory. The neoclassical statement posited the existence of two economic men, the entrepreneur-borrower representing "the demand for resources to invest" and the saver-lender willing "to abstain from present consumption" and so provide the money. Rejecting this, Keynes saw the interest rate being determined by a process of "equilibrat[ing] the desire to hold...cash with the available quantity of cash." Suddenly there is only one economic man present, the man-with-the-money, the "wealth-holder," as Keynes would identify him, making all the determinations about how much of an interest rate to charge and how much money to lend at that rate. The entrepreneur-borrower has vanished.

Another economic agent makes his presence evident. This is the monetary authority, not here named but elsewhere identified in *The General Theory,* who controls the quantity of money and thus affects the lender's decision on amount loaned and interest rate demanded. Somehow the new pair of economic men, the money holder-lender and the monetary authority, together make all the determinations that transfer money from the lender to the absolutely passive borrower, who invisibly but implicitly accepts the terms of the transaction as given.

Nowhere in *The General Theory* does Keynes make it quite clear that he is talking about the lender(s) alone in relation to the liquidity preference, although he does speak, as quoted above, of "those who possess money." Similarly, in a late chapter, he mentions that in the expansive nineteenth century the MEC was sufficiently elevated to provide full employment "with a rate of interest high enough to be psychologically acceptable to *wealth-owners*" (italics added). In both cases it is persons with money, aside from the monetary authority, who seem to have the only determining role; at least the entrepreneurial borrowers are unmentioned. Keynes does go further outside of *The General Theory*. In the *Economic Journal* of June 1937, in his major article defending the book against dangerous criticism, he stated explicitly enough: "The rate of interest on a loan of given quality and maturity has to be established at the level which, in the opinion of those who have the opportunity of choice—i.e., of wealth-holders—equalizes the attractions of holding idle cash and of holding the loan." Keynes continued, "It would be true to say that this by itself does not carry us very far."[11] One could say in return that it carries us very far indeed, since he made it absolutely clear that it is the "wealth-holder," who, in his character as lender, consults his liquidity preference and alone decides, in the light of the quantity of money in the economy, what the interest rate is and how much money he will give up at that price. Keynes knew what he was doing. Thus, in the debate-by-mail with Roy Harrod during his theorizing summer of 1935 (chapter 6 above) Harrod had feebly objected that Keynes was dispensing with supply-and-demand price determination gratuitously, one may recall, while Keynes returned definitively that there were "no such things" as supply-and-demand schedules, that they were "completely bogus." With his General Theory of the Rate of Interest Keynes has taken us right out of the world of supply and demand.

One should, however, remain aware that Keynes often appeared to be on more than one side of some questions. With a casualness that imposed hard work on his interpreters, he often spoke of the "public" or the "individual" in relation to liquidity preference. Inconsistently he may have wanted to keep his "public" integral during certain moments in his reasoning, and not break the aggregate down into lenders and borrowers. For policy purposes perhaps he wanted to concentrate on just two phenomena, the perniciously high liquidity preference shared by *all* members of the public and the power of the monetary authority to alter it, the problem and the solution. In this Keynes would accept the transactions of lenders and borrowers as beyond his policymaker's powers to affect or as representing an inconvenient distraction from the most economical operational mode at just this stage. In this, also, Keynes was reliving his own life: victorious monetary authority of the war and creative entrepreneur (not speculator unless yielding to his sense of guilt) on the currency, commodity, and stock markets. The two Keyneses could solve the problem without help from third parties.

But the economic world makes no sense simplified down to monetary authority and money man. As we have seen, Keynes could not keep to this. Sometimes he translated his "public" into moneyed lender; sometimes, superbly solipsistic, he permitted his "individual" to alternate successfully, like himself, between being lender and borrower, depending upon which it had to be to outsmart the market. However brilliant, these changing images of Keynes's kaleidoscope could not deny the existence of the huge, incessant waves of money, now threatening, now hopeful, now overwhelming, flowing through the money market. As Keynes very well knew, lenders and borrowers play very different roles in relation to money, and he saw them dramatically and hugely as the bulls and bears of America's Wall Street. Of course he knew that lenders *and* borrowers were no more manageable than the floods of money representing their cupidities and fears. He tamed them by enfeebling them or denying their existence.

Indeed, as in his lectures of the fall of 1932 (chapter 6), Keynes insensibly tended to slip past the point where the interest rate was determined and to see it as an established fact and as such the *causa causans,* taking effect on passive investment, savings, income, and consumption. This became acutely evident in his critique of neoclassical interest theory and policy. Retroactively, it can help explain his long interest-rate campaign, his attacks on the rentier mentality for keeping the rate too high, and his contempt for bankers for failing to bring it down. In the mind's eye, given the interest rate and ceteris paribus, one can easily see further changes increasing or decreasing it. Thus, an increase (decrease) in the public's liquidity preference would mean an increase (decrease) in the rate: the more (less) money desired means the higher (lower) price for the use of money. Similarly, the monetary authority can, at least initially, reduce the interest rate by increasing the available stock of money. But this still does not tell us how the *original* determination was made.

Keynes did go on to suggest this scenario: the lender would be inclined to lend when he expected the interest rate to fall because his loan as capitalized in a long-term bond would be worth more, while withholding his funds upon the opposite expectation. Approaching the subject from another direction in chapter 15, "The Psychological and Business Incentives to Liquidity," Keynes speculated vaguely about the psychology of the indeterminate "individual" who was influenced by a monetary authority concerned about the good of the economy. This Keynesian individual would lend or not on the basis of his expectations of the future interest rate. Thus, Keynes concluded for the moment, "It is evident then, that the rate of interest is a highly psychological phenomenon." But then, on the next page, he determined that expectations were greatly influenced by experience. "Representative opinion" would make its estimates "on the basis of past experiences and present expectations of *future* monetary policy." This carried the discussion partly beyond simple psychology: "It might be more accurate, perhaps, to say that the rate of interest is a highly conventional, rather than a highly psychological, phenomenon," Keynes concluded. But then he added, bringing psychology back, "For its actual value is largely governed by the prevailing view as to what its value is expected to be. *Any* level of interest which is accepted with sufficient conviction as *likely* to be durable *will* be durable."[12] Psychology strengthened by convention would provide the invisible support for an interest rate lacking all visible support—all relation to what is happening in the real, *material* economy. This led Dennis Robertson, recurring to Lewis Carroll, to comment in the *Economic Journal* debate: "Thus the rate of interest is what it is because it is expected to become other than it is—the organ which secretes it has been amputated, yet it somehow still exists—a grin without a cat."[13]

Moreover, still trying to grasp this disembodied sense of the interest rate, one finds it all the more elusive when obliged to strip out an important part of ceteris paribus, namely, Keynes's implicit assumption of constant prices. In the real economy, an increase in money quantity (by way of changes either in liquidity preference or monetary policy) will tend to reduce the interest rate only at first. Thus, the increase in the amount of money going into the economy also means higher prices, an effect that reduces the value of money. Consequently, the lenders will demand a premium in the form of a countervailing interest-rate *increase*. Indeed, if we accept neoclassical premises positing frictionless movements in the economy, the money-quantity increase would have no effect on the *real* interest rate and would work itself out entirely on prices of real values. Keynes's exercise is applicable only to the pristine Keynesian model, not to the world we inhabit unless qualified out of recognition.

What is happening to money and interest in the model itself? Keynes gives us an intriguing clue when he speaks of the "demand for cash," which is broken up into his (original) three "divisions of liquidity-preference," as then defined: "(i) the transactions-motive, i.e., the need for cash for the current transaction of personal and business exchanges; (ii) the precautionary-motive, i.e., the desire for security as to the future cash equivalent of a certain proportion of total resources; and (iii) the speculative-motive, i.e., the object of securing profit from knowing better than the market what the future will bring forth."[14] Keynes saw the first two motives as not much affected by the interest rate (note we are continuing with a *given* interest rate) but primarily by income levels. The speculative motive, however, led to the "demand" for cash on the assumption, typical of the mood of the Depression in which *The General Theory* was conceived, that the interest rate was lower than normal and would tend to rise. This was Keynes's famous liquidity trap, when it was more advantageous to hold the cash until that increase had indeed occurred, since the debts, in other words, bonds, would cost less to buy at that future date. Hence, wealth-holders would refuse to provide the necessary financing of productive enterprise. (The general idea is a skull-cracking conception: the point is that if you wanted to buy a long-term bond for income, you would experience the mathematical law that low interest rates mean comparatively expensive bonds and high interest rates mean cheaper bonds. The objective is to buy your bond when the interest rate is high and sell it, thus at a higher price, when the interest rate is at its lowest; in this way you got the most bond for your purchase money initially and the highest capital gains from your eventual sale of that bond.) No one, however, has been able credibly to identify a real liquidity-trap situation, a fact which has not damped the creative curiosity of generations of economists.

Keynes devoted the rest of chapter 13 plus all of chapter 15 to a discussion of liquidity preference so charged with promise and suggestiveness that interpretations form a voluminous literature themselves. His discussion, however, veered away from the logical development of his theory. He said absolutely nothing about how the wealth-holder actually transferred his money (for a price that was by definition too high) to the entrepreneur-borrower. We do not see how the three liquidity motives affect this putative rentier to part with his funds, nor do we see how he imposes his judgment upon the entrepreneur to achieve the lending-borrowing transaction. We are not shown *how* the interest rate is determined. The General Theory of the Rate of Interest stops short with the issueless motivation of one member of the pair of economic agents in question. Keynes dealt with his interest-rate theory as he had with his consumption theory, promising it beforehand, failing to show it in action when he addressed it, and subsequently, as will be evident, reasoning as if he had indeed produced it.

If he was unforthcoming about his own interest theory, Keynes did undertake to explain neoclassical interest theory with the help of Harrod's diagram. Before inspecting that diagram of the competitive theory, one might profitably use the same teaching instrument to make sense of *Keynes*'s theory. If he had left out an explicit statement he provided definitions and pervasive implications. Figure 9.1 presents a diagram constructed upon them:

FIGURE 9.1
Keynes's General Theory of the Rate of Interest

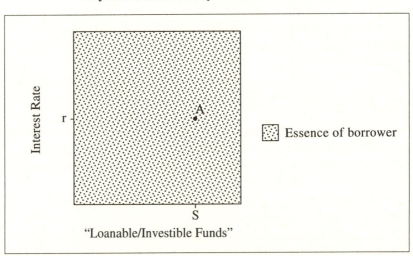

A   Point indicating interest rate and amount of money loaned
r   Interest rate as determined by the lender's liquidity preference
S   Amount of money, as determined by lender, supplied by him to borrower

Granted, this is a most peculiar design. It lacks the characteristic curves of economic science, while the Harrod-Keynes graph will provide no less than six of them. Following Keynes's prescription, this diagram illustrates the action of the wealth-holder fixing upon the interest rate (and the amount of money he will give up) in light of his liquidity preference and the available money quantity. No traditional curve is necessary; a point fully describes his position. The borrower is missing because Keynes passed over him in silence. It is true that the monetary authority plays a role by determining the quantity of money in the economy, but it does not engage in a specific transaction with the given wealth-holder; the total effect of the money quantity is channeled through the thought processes of the latter, who, as Keynes made clear, freely makes his decision after taking cognizance of that determination. The point says it all.

If the entrepreneur-borrower is missing, his function is not, since the money is indeed borrowed to finance the entrepreneurial activity of pursuing the MEC and thereby supplying the economy with real values. Imagine him exploded into subatomic particles penetrating the economy with a given density, equal everywhere, of his essence. That essence of borrower can be seen as covering the entire background of the diagram and, so illustrated, prepared to accept any interest rate and any quantity of funds offered. Thus, *any* location of the point, as determined by the wealth-holder, permits the transaction of lending-borrowing to take place. It is, as has already been conceded, a very peculiar diagram.

For Keynes the problem with a diagram is perhaps that its sense becomes too clear. (We shall see, however, that the diagram he uses to describe neoclassical interest theory is creatively unclear.) While refusing to show or say just how, according to *his* theory, the lending-borrowing transaction takes place, he verbalized a construction that could substitute for it. His phrase, "demand for cash,"[15] would dispense him of the neoclassical supply-and-demand mechanism without requiring wearying argumentation. He attributed that "demand" to the only economic man in sight, the wealth-holding lender. Certainly this economic man wants as much money as he can get or keep, but this is not *demand* in the technical sense as understood in economic science. One might as well speak of the demand of a wheat farmer for wheat or of an automobile manufacturer for automobiles. These economic men represent *supply*. Deciding how much money in his possession he prefers to keep and how much he chooses to lend for interest-rate income, the lender must join farmer and manufacturer as *supplier* to his market. The borrower returns to pay the *given* interest rate, invest the borrowed funds in capital outlay, and go on to produce real values by realizing the marginal efficiency of capital. Hence, he represents the true *demand* for money. Any other interpretation destroys all sense, Keynes's as well as, say, Marshall's, since it is Keynes's model we are discussing. If, however, we defend sense and use it to understand what Keynes as theorist is doing, we see his theory in the act of self-destruction.

Keynes's General Theory of the Rate of Interest has actually conflated two economic systems, the monetary system as operated by the governmental authority or under its supervision and the private market of loanable/investible funds. If we consider the first, we can speak of an "individual's" demand for money vis-à-vis the monetary authority. This individual, however, is not the money-lender but *every* person in the economy who is engaged in all manners of transactions besides lending money. Furthermore, if the individual's demand for money increases (the demand curve moving to the right) with constant money supply, this does not directly affect the interest rate but the price level. The first system expresses itself in the form of monetary inflation and deflation, the second, working itself out in the private money market, on the interest rate. From another perspective, in the first system, money and goods-and-services are exchanged for each other; in the second, money and money debts are exchanged. The systems are completely distinct, although either affects the other. Thus, the secondary effect of an increase in quantity of money in the economy is an increase in the interest rate, ceteris paribus, as lenders, operating in the money market, insist upon compensation for the loss in the value of money. In Keynes's aggregate system of monetary operations and money market, however, the effects are different because he has dispensed with parts of the two systems that are necessary if they are to operate separately, hence the disappearance of the borrower from the money market and of inflation-and-deflation from the monetary system. Another effect is confusion, perhaps in the head of the theorist, certainly in the heads of any readers entering into such theorizing uncritically.

If Keynes's General Theory of the Rate of Interest fails to withstand this testing of its sense, he might nevertheless have found a fatal weakness in the Classical Theory of the Rate of Interest. Indeed, in chapter 14, which is devoted to it, he introduced the enemy theory theory with a definition that expressed its sense comprehensibly and even fairly (after an extravagantly incomprehensible one, however, in chapter 13): "Investment represents the demand for investible resources and saving represents the supply, whilst the rate of interest is the 'price' of investible resources at which the two are equated." A neoclassical economist might question the second "investible resources," but could otherwise find nothing wrong. But Keynes stretches meaning beyond the point of destruction in the next sentence by beginning *and* ending with the interest rate: "The rate of interest necessarily comes to rest under the play of market forces at the point where the amount of investment *at that rate of interest* is equal to the amount of saving *at that rate*" (italics added).[16] He has raced ahead to find his interest rate as given before undertaking to determine it. If the amounts of investment and saving were predicated on a given interest rate, there is no need to wait until the alleged market forces permit it to rest *at that rate.* This is one of too many examples of Keynes's perfect circularity in logic as permitted by the petitio principii.

Before proceeding Keynes makes the extraordinary claim that he could not "discover an explicit account of" the neoclassical interest theory. He does so while quoting a number of entirely explicit definitions over two pages of text and in an eight-page appendix in small print filled with his discoveries.[17] He takes the occasion to quarrel variously and inconsequentially with given definitions among his findings. Oddly, he admits to "perplexity...in Marshall's account of the matter"—not about what Marshall said but because he said it at all. Keynes insists, "'Interest' has really no business to turn up at all in Marshall's *Principles of Economics*—it belongs in another branch of the subject."[18] With his own *General Theory* violating this demand for theoretical purity, he does not attempt to show how a modern economy could be explained without money and interest; a suspicious reader might well think that Keynes had declared irrelevant a discussion he could not refute. Thus, the preliminary skirmish.

Keynes signals the main attack: "This is the point at which definite error creeps into the classical theory." This is when it "again assumes it can...proceed to consider the effect on the rate of interest of (e.g.) a shift in the demand curve for capital, without abating or modifying its assumption as to the amount of the given income out of which the savings [and thus the loans] are to be made." After analyzing the implications a bit further, Keynes concludes, "But this is a nonsense theory."[19] Here he produces his fundamental objection to neoclassical interest theory: it incorrectly assumes constant income in determining *its* interest rate. This is analogous to the fatal error the neoclassical economist

Keynes made in his *Treatise on Money* by assuming constant output, hence constant income. In accepting the fact of his error Keynes was inviting his former comrades-in-theory to admit theirs. One must ask if the new Keynes is right: does neoclassical theory assume constant income and, if so, does that assumption invalidate its interest theory? To right the balance, one must also ask, perhaps too suspiciously, if Keynes is using a conjoint pair of his best rhetorical maneuvers, namely, inserting into his argument another petitio principii and therewith giving the opposing theory an impossible task to perform.

In general terms Keynes was developing the conception, introduced in his theorizing with Roy Harrod, that changes in the level of income would mean changes in the level of savings, hence in the supply of loanable funds going into the money market. These latter changes would play back upon income, causing more changes. The result would be, he argued, continuous motion, with the result that the point of intersection of the supply and demand curves could not be "determinate."[20] As he had done before privately in his letter to Harrod, Keynes was publicly attacking the supply-and-demand theorem, the very glue that holds together the economy according to Walras, his admired Jevons, and his absurd Marshall.

Before going on with Keynes's objection to neoclassical supply-and-demand pricing, one should note his blithe assumption that his own General Theory of the Rate of Interest was impervious to it. But if his theory and neoclassical theory inhabit the same real economic world, the continual income and saving changes would affect his own creation and prevent it from being determinate as well. Indeed, Alvin Hansen, becoming one of Keynes's protective interpreters, did find the General Theory of the Rate of Interest to be indeterminate on its own terms. As we shall see, however, he triumphantly extracted another interpretation out of Keynes's logic to save his proposition and permit it, by a linkage that Keynes himself had not imagined, to achieve its determining function.

Few readers have noted, or, at least, reacted to Keynes's revolutionary operation. One of these few is Frank Knight, who, referring to "wages, the interest rate, and general prices," remarked by way of a footnote in his review of *The General Theory*: "What is mysterious and difficult to state clearly is the manner in which Mr. Keynes sets up an economic system on the basis of assumptions which imply that these variables or variable complexes are either fixed or are determined by other forces than the mutual adjustment of supply and demand, i.e., by 'bargains' or public authority, or 'psychology,' or some other *deus ex machina.*"[21] Certainly Keynes's system needed such *dei* if he had gotten rid of supply and demand.

In mentioning "general prices," Knight makes no exception for Keynes's treatment of nonmonetary values. With this one can as easily agree as disagree. Thus, Book 1, developing its thesis of a failure of effective demand to consume all that production produces, is a complex argument denying the true operation of aggregate supply and demand. That failure implies a failure or falsification of all value and price determination. Yet in the first eighteen chapters that comprise the body of *The General Theory* as pure theory, Keynes made no direct attack on neoclassical price theory, and most of his argument seems to support itself on prices of commodities and services as given in the neoclassical economy of free markets. But then, developing *The General Theory*'s interest theory in chapter 13, he momentarily proceeds to deny it at least partially by remarking, "The market price [of 'debts,' e.g., bonds] will be fixed at the point at which the sales of the 'bears' and the purchases of the 'bulls' are balanced."[22] Here he had permitted the borrowing bears to have equal power with the lending bulls in determining the price of bonds and, necessarily, their interest rates. Similarly, in chapter 16, "Sundry Observations on the Nature of Capital," Keynes sees "the prospective yield" of new investment depending on "the expectation of a *demand* for a specific article at a specific date," (italics added) while both "natural resources" and "assets...command a price according to their scarcity or abundance,"[23] thus supply at least. Keynes's discussion, however, leaves these thoughts incomplete. He had in fact introduced his note on "scarcity and abundance": "I sympathize...with the pre-classical doctrine that everything *is produced by labor*." Here he threatened to debouch into a statement of the labor theory of value, but finished the sentence by accepting the neoclassical price. The revolutionary theorist never changed all of his neoclassical, classical, or preclassical spots.

Yet Keynes does indeed attack neoclassical value and price theory directly and absolutely—in two of the late chapters following chapter 18's summarizing restatement of the pure theory of *The General Theory.* In chapter 20, "The Employment Function," referring to employment (as discussed in Book 1), he unequivocally asserts in part of one paragraph: "[T]he ordinary supply curve for a particular commodity is drawn on some assumption as to the output of industry as a whole and is liable to change if the aggregate output of industry is changed." He had already set the "ordinary demand curve" for that commodity in motion, because it "is drawn on some assumption as to the incomes of members of the public, and has to be redrawn if the incomes change."[24] *Mutatis mutandis* and exception more or less taken, accepting the fact that money and nonmonetary values inhabit the same economic world, Keynes was here restating his fundamental critique of neoclassical *interest* theory in reference to *all* prices. The next chapter, "The Theory of Prices," also rejected supply-and-demand determination of commodity (and service) prices to speculate variously on what does indeed do the determining. Evidently leaning on conceptions of Marshall, who had not completely assimilated marginal utility into his partial-equilibrium analysis, Keynes tried to derive price from costs without reference to demand, but failed to pursue his train of thought to a conclusion. Yet the distractions strewn about in the chapter further defended his position.

As far as nonmonetary values are concerned, the reader is left suspended between the actual model constructed in the first eighteen chapters of *The General Theory*, which lacks this argument denying the workings of supply and demand, and the book itself, which is so equipped but too late to make logical use of it. Beyond *The General Theory* itself, in his 1937 defense, Keynes left that behind and completed the full circle: "If the rate of interest is not determined by saving and investment in the same way in which price is determined by supply and demand, how is it determined?"[25] He went on to set his General Theory of the Rate of Interest in opposition to the supply-and-demand mechanism, which he permitted to determine the prices of all other values. This might suggest that Keynes, while refusing to be locked into one position, accepted the supply-and-demand price determination of goods and services more often than not while rejecting it for his interest rate. One must return to chapter 14, "The Classical Theory of Interest," where Keynes develops his argument explicitly and even, speaking literally, graphically.

About Keynes's general argument against neoclassical interest determination—that income changes cause savings changes and hence permit no determination at all—it would be helpful to illustrate the process with a simple diagram, which is shown in figure 9.2. With a given de-

FIGURE 9.2

Determination of interest rate and money quantity loaned/borrowed with a shifting savings/supply curve

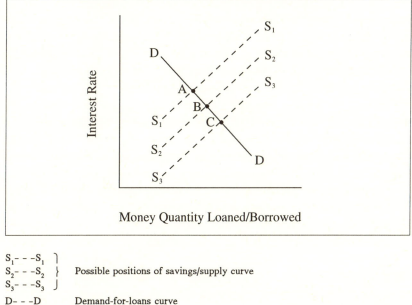

S₁– – –S₁ }
S₂– – –S₂ }   Possible positions of savings/supply curve
S₃– – –S₃ }

D– – -D   Demand-for-loans curve

A, B, C   Possible points where interest rate and money quantity loaned/borrowed are determined

mand for loanable/investible funds, the supply/savings (S–S) curve would be continually shifting in this manner.

The S–S curve would be in continuous motion. But by simple inspection one sees that this motion does not prevent interest-rate determination. At any moment in time the S–S curve intersects with the D–D curve and hence the interest rate is in *continual process of being determined.* Lenders would be willing to lend more or less of their money for lower or higher interest rates, depending on where the intersection is at the moment. To this should be added what everyone knows about any market. The supply curve's movement is not at all remarkable; all supply *and* demand curves are always in motion as buyers and sellers, thus borrowers and lenders, enter and leave the market and as innumerable factors from war to psychology encourage or discourage transactions.

Making a false assumption about the fixed character of such curves, Keynes had gone on to create an objection out of the whole cloth.

Keynes has articulated so many misconceptions about the process of interest and general price determination that they must be corrected as one tries to understand these processes. Thus, about the effects of income changes, one should be aware that the savings change caused by an income change is not simultaneous, but follows it. A person cannot lend out money until he has first received his income. Note, also, that Keynes is inserting another questionable condition into his arguments. While it is true enough that the income level will affect the amount of savings, he has leaped to the assumption—another *petitio principii*—that savings will always remain a *given* and *fixed* proportion of changing income. But that is nonsense. Yet while making no effort to prove the point and without checking his stride, Keynes assumes it. Nevertheless, as he indicates elsewhere in *The General Theory*, savings will react differently to income changes at different moments while also responding to a variety of other factors; one need only recall his pervasive psychological element. This is one of the many stages in *The General Theory* where the readers are required to forget what Keynes had earlier told them. But we should let Keynes make his case, most particularly because he devotes his only diagram to it, which is shown in figure 9.3.[26]

In the diagram, reversing the usual order, Keynes has the vertical axis showing "amount of investment (or saving)," while the horizontal axis shows the interest rate. Upon a simple illustration of price (in this case, interest rate) determination, like that of Harrod's example of German lessons, Keynes has woven too many curves and complications. The X–X curves, however, are not complicated; they represent "investment-demand," that is, the entrepreneurial demand for funds to finance operations. The complexities begin with the four Y curves, which represent the supply of loanable/investible funds going to market but, as Keynes specified, attached to their origins as income translated into savings *and* as affected by the interest rate. As Keynes puts it, "The curve Y_1 relates the amounts saved out of an income Y_1 to various levels of the rate of interest, the curves Y_2, Y_3, etc., being the corresponding curves for levels of income Y_2, Y_3, etc." With this innocent-seeming statement Keynes has inserted a first petitio principii and a fatal complication. He has repeated the statement he made when he first verbalized his definition of neoclassical interest theory. In a diagram purporting to show the deter-

FIGURE 9.3

Keynes's Illustration of Neoclassical Interest-Rate Determination

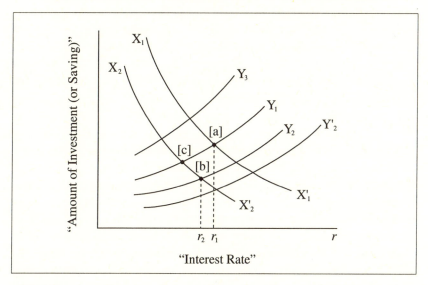

"$X_1 X'_1$ is the first position of the investment-demand schedule, and $X_2 X'_2$ is a second position of this curve."

"The curve Y_1 relates the amounts saved out of an income Y_1 to various levels of the rate of interest, the curves Y_2, Y_3, etc., being the corresponding curves for levels of income Y_2, Y_3, etc."

mination of the interest rate he has begun with *given* interest rates as affecting amounts saved out of given income levels. In this he has forced on the neoclassical economist a series of already determined interest rates that have already taken effect. To permit the logic to work itself out, one must eliminate such violations of sense. The Y curves must be released from their origins in income, protected from given interest rates, and presented as simple supply curves of loanable/investible funds. Conventionally, as in determining the price of German lessons, one can find the interest rate at the XX-Y intersections. But Keynes must be permitted to finish his exercise.

Keynes establishes a first position at intersection *a,* showing interest rate r_1. He then posits a shift in the demand schedule from X_1-X'_1 to X_2-X'_2, the shift indicating that the entrepreneurial borrowers are less eager to borrow. A neoclassical economist would expect that the new interest rate would be indicated at point *c,* where the new demand curve intersects with the Y_1 curve. But Keynes insists that the shift in demand changes income, which changes savings, this latter changing the supply of funds offered the money market. Hence, there must be a new Y curve, but its location is not known. Keynes, however, can find it—by appealing to *his* General Theory of the Rate of Interest! He concludes triumphantly, "If...we introduce the state of liquidity preference and the quantity of money and these between them tell us the rate of interest is r_2, then the whole position becomes determinate." This permits him to arrive at intersection *b*. Disregarding other possible objections, we have already examined Keynes's interest theory and know that it functions without the borrower. Thus, it contradicts the sense of the diagram, where Keynes has drawn two investment-demand curves expressing the borrower's existence and volition. Keynes had no logical right to draw these investment-demand curves, since his own theory denies their existence and its effects: he does not believe in the truth of his own diagrammatic statement. In another sense, he has paused in the middle of explicating the other theory, has arbitrarily asserted that it was false because it conflicted with *his* theory, and has replaced it with a restatement of that theory. Thus, he uses the false promise of his aborted General Theory of the Rate of Interest to annihilate a living and operative one. One notes his debater's skills. He had first established his theory verbally in the previous chapter and then, presuming upon its general acceptance and while graphically erecting the enemy theory with untrue materials, uses the first to give the coup de grâce to the second!

The thesis of Book 4, "The Inducement to Invest," is that while the MEC was dangerously erratic and unpredictable, the interest rate represented a much graver problem. The public's liquidity preference, however expressed specifically, kept the rate too high to permit full employment of men and resources. Keynes's conception challenges the neoclassical theory, which posited a self-correcting situation. According to its reasoning, an underemployed economy would mean underemployed money, and the lenders would permit themselves to be bargained down to an interest rate sufficiently low to absorb the excess funds, at a level assuring full employment. In Keynes's vision, however, liquidity preference and the monetary authority, as Aristotelian or Thomist prime or uncaused causes, determine the interest rate. The lender, influenced by cowardice or greed, or both, and in the absence of an equal opposite number in the person of the borrower, uses his power to evil social effect: he keeps the interest rate always too high to permit the natural economic action, which would close the gap between production and consumption. But we have seen that Keynes is describing a model unrelated to the real economy, that he fails with his refutation of neoclassical interest theory like a schoolboy who neglected to do his homework. He has two arguments. The first one, the argument of indeterminacy, depends on plural petitii principii and the hollow claim that changing income falsifies all efforts to set the interest rate. The second argument is pure petitio principii, Keynes attacking the enemy theory with his interest theory, developed in the previous chapter and accepted as proven. Moreover, when we examine the General Theory of the Rate of Interest, we find ourselves stranded in mid-route. Keynes leads us to the point where the liquidity preference is broken down into the transactions, precautionary motives, and speculative motives—and deserts us there to puzzle ourselves to mental exhaustion with those unfinished materials. We do not *see* how these lead to the determination of the interest rate. Keynes fails both as critic of the old theory and creator of its replacement.

Book 3 has shown that Keynes's consumption theory is an unfulfilled promise, that consumption is fundamentally strong while the modern economy's need for investment increases over time. We now see that his interest theory is similarly evanescent. The two pillars on which *The General Theory* is alleged to stand do not exist.

The blank expressed by Keynes's General Theory of the Rate of Interest has attracted no discoverable efforts to fill it with meaning, while his confusion of curves around neoclassical interest theory has worked like multiple rows of barbed wire to resist penetration. His epigones, so prolific in their exegeses of *The General Theory,* have, to my knowledge, directly examined neither his theory nor his graphical analysis of neoclassical theory.[27] But then no non-Keynesian has attempted much more. Frank Knight did articulate an entirely correct general statement of what Keynes was up to, but he stopped there. Henry Hazlitt, editor of *The Critics of Keynesian Economics,* also wrote a book-length, chapter-by-chapter analysis of *The General Theory* and devoted two chapters to interest theory—blankly.[28] He failed to see that Keynes's theory never got to the actual determination of the interest rate and, while creating his own supply-and-demand diagram of the neoclassical interest theory, simply disregarded Keynes's diagram. His criticism consisted essentially of burying Keynes's treatment under heavy, often irrelevant, quotations from the masters of neoclassical theory. Have the friendly interpreters feared the effects of clarity upon their piety? Or is it possible that friends *and* enemies have joined in failing to understand what Keynes was saying?

With the interest rate, the pure economic argument of Books 3 and 4, thus of the General Theory as a model, is complete. It does not carry us further than did Book 1, where Keynes defined his position. Indeed it is somewhat dependent on that book's round affirmations and skillfully managed logic. In Book 1 Keynes set out with his theory of effective demand to annihilate Say's Law and confidently went on to claim success. He was arguing a general failure of supply and demand to function and the resultant chronic unemployment of men and resources. The detail of the later books attempted to show the failure in terms both of consumption of real values and excessive costs of funds financing productive enterprise. Like the initial abstract statement, the detailed argument required acceptance of arbitrary assertions and extraordinary logic. *The General Theory,* lacking foundations, floats on Keynes's airy imagination.

Notes

1. Keynes's discussion, *CW,* 7: 139–41.
2. Ibid., 135, 138.
3. Ibid., 149, 148, 149, 158, 155, 158–59.
4. Ibid., 157.
5. Table of Keynes's finances, ibid., 12: 11.
6. Ibid., 7: 161, 162.
7. Ibid., 164.
8. Ibid., 13: 423, 525–26.
9. Ibid., 7: 165.
10. Ibid., 167–68.
11. "Alternate Theories of the Rate of Interest," ibid., 14: 201–15; quotation, p. 213.
12. Ibid., 7: 202, 203.
13. Rejoinder to Keynes's article (n. 11 above), *Economic Journal* 47 (September 1937): 433.
14. *CW,* 7: 171, 170. In chap. 15 Keynes divided the transactions motive into two submotives (as developed in the *Treatise on Money*), but then dropped the thought.
15. Thus, Keynes speaks of a "negligible *demand for cash* from the speculative-motive" (italics added) under certain circumstances, ibid., 171.
16. Ibid., 175. Keynes had made use of similar reasoning via the petitio principii in his first reference to neoclassical interest theory in chap. 13; see n. 9, above.
17. Ibid., 175, 175–77, 186–93.
18. Ibid., 189.

19. Ibid., 178–79.
20. Ibid., 181; argument developed, pp. 178–85.
21. Knight, "Unemployment: And Mr. Keynes's Revolution in Economic Theory," in Hazlitt, ed., *The Critics of Keynesian Economics*, nn. 73–74.
22. *CW,* 7: 170.
23. Ibid., 212, 213.
24. Ibid., 281.
25. Ibid., 14: 212.
26. Ibid., 7: 180.
27. Besides Knight's, the most negative critique of Keynes's interest theory I have found was articulated by John Eatwell and Murray Milgate, collaborators of Joan Robinson in her late years, who supported her thesis of a Marxian Keynes. They have adverted to the "crucial weaknesses of *The General Theory,*" referring, inter alia, to "Keynes's unsatisfactory attempts to criticize the internal logic of the [neo]classical theory of interest by means of liquidity-preference theory." This was in their article, "Unemployment and the Market Mechanism," in Eatwell and Milgate, eds., *Keynes's Economics and the Theory of Value and Distribution* (New York, 1983), 260. Their reasoning was part of the general thesis that purely "systematic objective forces," which they saw posited in Keynes's effective demand and Marx's "surplus approach" (p. 278), could accurately describe and explain the objective (and self-evident) failure of the capitalistic economy. As opposed to this they condemned the liquidity-preference theory for being subjective.
28. Henry Hazlitt, *The Failure of the "New Economics": An Analysis of the Keynesian Fallacies* (Lanham, MD, 1983; 1st ed.: 1959).

10

The Close of Keynes's System

"We have now reached the point where we can gather together the threads of our argument," Keynes confidently began chapter 18, "The General Theory of Employment Re-Stated."[1] One might ask why readers should continue with an analysis of that argument if the conclusions already reached here are correct. We have experienced the total failure of *The General Theory* as pure theory. We have, however, also experienced much of its essence as impure theory against a background of knowledge that the book is a major force in world history as the Bible of the Keynesian Revolution. Its impure character compounds crazy ideas, artful and even profound politics and policy-making, and sentimental social philosophizing, that is to say, *The General Theory* has systematized these elements into an operational ideology. One can expect Keynes to fold more pragmatic magic instructively into his summarizing statement.

Keynes had actually completed his exposition of pure economic theory with chapter 14, the second of his chapters on interest, the next three chapters of Book 4 spinning out derivations that added little and changed nothing. Book 1 had proposed the existence of a global gap between supply and effective demand. (Book 2, securing Keynes's argument, had been devoted to definitions, presently to be reviewed here.) More specifically, Books 3 and 4 posited gaps between production and consumption, and between actual and market-clearing interest-rate levels—thus in the real and monetary economies. Yet six more chapters in two more books remain to be traversed. Besides economic factors inessential to the model already constructed, they contain materials permitting Keynes to fit his economics into a larger context: Keynes the historian, political scientist, and social philosopher making policy.

In this last chapter of Book 4 Keynes tried to compress the preceding discussion of consumption and investment into a general scheme confirming the promise of Book 1. According to the scheme, now articulated for the first time, the interaction of the given factors and selected "independent variables" produced the "dependent variables, the volume of employment and the national income (or national dividend)." These last were the factors in distress and the point of Keynes's exercise in the economics of depression. He identified the independent variables as, "in the first instance, the propensity to consume, the schedule of the marginal efficiency of capital, and the rate of interest, though, as we have already seen, these are capable of further analysis." With this qualification Keynes began to complicate the grand simplicity of his summary as he proceeded to develop it. In the first place the given factors "influence our independent variables, but do not completely determine them." He did not, however, make it clear why the given factors should "completely determine," or even partially determine, what he was identifying as "independent variables." If these were determined or even only influenced, how could they be seen as independent? Indeed, he granted they were not, in fact, independent.

Keynes began the next paragraph, "The schedule of the marginal efficiency of capital depends...partly on the given factors and partly on the prospective yield of capital-assets of different kinds; whilst the rate of interest depends partly on the state of liquidity preference...and partly on the quantity of money." With that, the independence of his independent variables was annihilated, and in his next sentence he replaced them, intermittently if not always, with superlatively independent factors: "Thus we can *sometimes* regard our *ultimate independent variables* as consisting of (1) the three fundamental psychological factors, namely the psychological propensity to consume, the psychological attitude to liquidity and the psychological expectation of future yield from capital assets" (italics added). We break off here to note that the psychological element, attributed in common to all of his initially independent variables, virtually transformed them into derivatives of group psychology. The reader was asked to assume that propensity to consume, profit, and interest rate, respectively, were only tenuously related to hunger or need, production, and money. At this point Keynes's economics had become an interlude in psychology, while his simple scheme had turned the corner into Ptolemaic complexity.

Keynes's introduction of the ultimate independent variables with item "(1)" had continued with the items "(2)" and "(3)," which were not psychological, namely, the wage-unit and the quantity of money, the latter as fixed by the monetary authority. These, however, were overwhelmed by the psychology that spilled over into them from his expansive ultimate independent item "(1)." If Keynesian psychology could so dominate consumption, production, and finance, it could surely work its will on wages and money supply, as indeed it had in the form of Keynesian money illusion and hoarding. Keynes did not rest with this. While his more or less independent variables were dominated by subjectivity, they were not necessarily lost to science, if one could competently shift from economics to psychology. Keynes, however, immediately rendered that question moot. In his next sentence, he closed the paragraph, "But these again would be capable of being subjected to further analysis, and are not, so to speak, our ultimate atomic independent elements."[2] And there, Keynes, going on to other thoughts, left his readers transfixed forever.

Keynes offered no explanation of these "ultimate...elements," which exist in *The General Theory* in one sentence but carry the full weight of the whole book. In their "ultimate...atomic" character the independent elements or variables were by definition not to be broken down into subatomic particles of sense; they were to be ingested whole as the collective uncaused cause. Up to this point Keynes had provided a reason, debatable or not, for every thesis. Here he revealed himself as the mystagogue, who, ultimately, demanded an act of faith from all those who would learn from him. To understand one must believe.

Keynes's theory, after having been introduced integrally in terms of a weakness of effective demand, which itself had then been broken down into an inadequacy of consumption and an excess of liquidity preference, plunged beyond them to establish itself upon that set of factors constituting the invisible first cause. The Greeks had posited the Titans as creators of their too familiar Olympians. One blasphemed to repeat the exercise and ask who or what had created the Titans.

In the next sentence and paragraph Keynes's argument based itself on his intuition as informed by experience, the same intuition that provided the foundation of the *Treatise on Probability:* "The division of the determinants of the economic system into two groups of given factors and independent variables is, of course, quite arbitrary from any absolute standpoint." The concluding prepositional phrase, a blur of meaninglessness, could not quite cover Keynes's admission that he was arbitrarily arranging his model economy as it suited him. "The division must be made entirely on the basis of experience," he explained disarmingly, but he was appealing to *his* experience and *his* evaluation of it. He excused himself for any venial errors that might ensue. "In a study so complex as economics, in which we cannot hope to make completely accurate generalizations," the point was to seize upon "the factors whose changes *mainly* determine our *quaesitum.*" Behind his confident opinions was his rich experience as financier of the allies' war effort and constructive private investor. He was returning to his old position of power and decision, renewed, moreover, by his most recent triumphs on Wall Street. "Our final task...might be [*might be?*] to select those variables which can be deliberately controlled or managed by central authority in the kind of system in which we actually live."[3] This was the point: control and management of the selected variables by an experienced and intuitively guided central authority. Keynes put it offhandedly and briefly, almost curtly.

Another important element in Keynes's system was the multiplier. Introduced in his analysis of consumption and the propensity to consume,[4] it was the General Theory's precisely forged central gear, Harry Johnson, however, preferring to call the multiplier "that inexhaustibly versatile mechanical toy."[5] It multiplied as it translated the force of investment, which was mathematically determined by the propensity to consume, into income (and employment). From its central position, tending to dominate them, it connected, directly and indirectly, with the other parts of the General Theory model. Richard Kahn had speculated on a multiplier of 4 in his 1931 article.[6] In *The General Theory* Keynes was more expansive, although appending a qualification: "[I]f the consumption psychology of the community is such that they will choose to consume, e.g., nine-tenths of an increment of income, then the multiplier k is 10; and the total employment caused by (e.g.) increased public works will be 10 times the primary employment provided by the public works themselves, assuming no reduction of investment in other directions."[7] Thus the marvelous multiplier.

As conceded in the qualifying phrase of Keynes's example—"assuming no reduction in other directions"—caveats had to be considered. He was recognizing the crowding-out argument, about which he had debated so unsatisfactorily with Richard Hopkins. Keynes had no better arguments in *The General Theory*. The best he could do was urge the monetary authority to "take steps" to reverse an interest-rate increase into a reduction,[8] a policy easier to articulate than to justify or implement. As Hopkins had mildly proposed in his testimony before the Macmillan Committee, every pound spent on public-works employment tended to reduce private spending by that one pound because of the greater cost of "borrowing" investment funds.[9] The multiplier could not solve the crowding-out problem.

Within the frame of theory the multiplier expressed itself as a complex of the absurd and the impossible. An attempt to translate the theory into policy meant inflation, as Keynes's idea of imposing lower interest rates betrayed. (Kahn himself had fought off such a potential criticism about the inflation danger in his article with an authoritative, but unargued, insult: "extraordinary fatuity.")[10] Another obvious theoretical defect was the fact that the results of a given investment increase would exhaust themselves eventually and the economy would return to the old level, unless new investment funds were pumped in continuously. Yet another problematic aspect lay in the economy's effects on the multiplier, a question that Keynes had not asked. Yet, if it worked, the multiplier meant greater economic activity and increased prices and interest rates, which would react back on it to reduce its effect pari passu. One could be sure of the multiplier only after the fact. Given the statistics of past performance in, say, the last year or quarter, the statistician could conclude that an investment of, say, £80 million had *accompanied* an income figure of £800 million, and that the multiplier was thus 10 as in Keynes's example, with total employment at 10 times the primary employment of a given increment in investment. But the statistician could not show that the £80 million investment had *caused* income to become £800 million. You could not assume that the multiplier would stay at 10 for the next quarter if you again increased investment by a given figure. Multiplier was, alternately, multiplicand.

If it fails as a component of pure theory, the multiplier can, however, be saved by free translation into policy. Its best potential lay in the inflationary effect that Kahn's article strenuously denied and Keynes's book extruded from its model by way of definition. The Depression was a drastic experience of deflation, one should remind oneself, and the cure required a reversal of it, thus inflation or, to use a word that Dennis Robertson seriously articulated, *re*flation. "Inflation" was itself too frightening and could thus weaken the curative effects. The point was to have your inflation without admitting it. If government policy, encouraged to calculate with the multiplier, forced the investment level upward by public works and cheap credit, the result would be increased production and employment. This would mean a salutary inflation or reflation, with consumers and purchase agents for businesses tending to buy now rather than pay higher prices later. The process of recovery would begin. In this way, moreover, the multiplier would outflank, if not defeat, the crowding-out argument.

With the multiplier doing its part, Keynes set the model to work in less than two pages: investment reaching its limits when the marginal efficiency of capital approached "approximate equality with the rate of interest" (as determined by the liquidity preference), the marginal propensity to consume producing the multiplier, and the multiplier times the investment level producing the levels of employment and national income. "If we examine any actual problem along the lines of the above schematism, we shall find it more manageable," Keynes concluded, "and our practical intuition (which can take account of a more detailed complex of facts than can be treated on general principles) will be offered a less intractable material upon which to work."[11] The theorist Keynes had presented the policymaker Keynes with a scheme inviting him to apply his talents.

Pure theory would tell a different story. Harry Johnson has pointed out that Keynes's model is a "system of unidirectional causation," with blithe disregard of the possibility that its parts might choose to reverse or otherwise change direction.[12] The multiplier/multiplicand is one example, but *every* component can do the same. Keynes himself had undercut his "ultimate independent variables," to which he had first given an initiating role, by bringing in his unplumbed "ultimate *atomic* independent elements" (italics added). Even if one forgets the extraordinary admission inherent in their existence, one can derive all manner of effects and directions in the model's workings. Proceeding from the marginal propensity to consume to multiplier to investment level to levels of employment and income, one can also see these last affecting investment level, multiplier (now multiplicand), and marginal propensity to consume, as well as a variety of crisscross effects among these elements. Keynes has accustomed his readers to circular reasoning and random beginnings and endings.

Nor had Keynes, in his brief restatement, provided space for the problem of realizing anticipated results. The difficulty was, as discussed earlier, embedded in his conception of the marginal efficiency of capital as *prospective* yield and generalized throughout *The General Theory* by the ubiquity of expectations as related to the other aggregates. When, for example, the MEC began to get close to the interest-rate level, it was irreducibly the future yield as estimated by the entrepreneur. Keynes accused neoclassical theory of being one equation short of defining economic reality because it had not allowed for output at less than optimum level. But he himself was at least one major equation short, one capable of bridging present and future in the world of *The General Theory*.

Ignoring the element of expectation and condensing out his "practical intuition," Keynes announced abruptly, "The above is a summary of the General Theory," as the opening statement of the final section of the chapter. In its six pages, accepting the above as established, he thereupon characterized the "economic system in which we live" as one of stagnation without being "violently unstable. Indeed it seems capable of remaining in a chronic condition of subnormal activity for a considerable period without any marked tendency either towards recovery or towards complete collapse." His further discussion repeated a few of the familiar arguments of Books 1, 3, and 4, and ended as it began: "We oscillate, avoiding the gravest extremes of fluctuation in employment and in prices in both directions, round an intermediate position appreciably below full employment and appreciably above the minimum employment a decline below which would endanger life."

In his last paragraph, Keynes refused to accept "the mean position thus determined by 'natural' tendencies...[as] therefore...established by laws of necessity." He granted, "The unimpeded rule of the above condition is a fact of observation," but it was "not a necessary principle which cannot be changed."[13] This final note of the restatement of his theory was hardly inspiring, merely negation of negation, in contrast to the book's tone of aggressive and optimistic activism.

Chapter 18 is oddly weak, offhanded, and uncertain about itself and its function in *The General Theory*. With Keynes's great rhetorical skill, it could have been the triumphant, definitive closing of the last buckles of the book's logic. Instead, it falters and declines to its repetitive description of a stagnant economy. It is almost as if Keynes had lost heart and, as in the last pages of his *Treatise on Probability*, was ready to admit that he was less secure about his argument than his declarative sentences had led readers to believe. But he did not retreat nearly so far. The chapter was a holding action that just barely sufficed. The best that could be said for it was that in its brevity it did not recall so much from the foregoing chapters as to bring up their unresolved contradictions and unproven theses.

From *The General Theory*'s depressed level, however, Keynes prepared to swing his philosophical cycle upward. In this he was characteristically making another of his frequent reversals of earlier positions. In 1928 he had given the mathematically and otherwise optimistic talk, "Economic Possibilities for Our Grandchildren." He repeated it plural times into the period of the Great Depression, indeed publishing it in *The Nation* of October 1930. In it, rejecting the moment's "bad attack of economic pessimism," he predicted that the living standard of the "progressive countries" would rise by a multiple of 4 to 8 percent in a century, assuming cooperative facts like a 2-percent annual capital increase and a leveling of world population. He italicized his faith that "in the long run *mankind is solving its economic problem*."[14] He had put such exuberant speculations aside in writing *The General Theory* (which was more in accord with another of his conclusions to the long run, we might recall, namely, that "we are all dead"), but nevertheless, as will be seen below, he refused to let its unhappy logic entrap him after he emerged from it.

Keynes's model of the economy was actually constructed in no more than ten of *The General Theory*'s twenty-four chapters. These are: the three chapters of Book 1 attacking Say's Law and positing effective demand (the first chapter being actually a one-paragraph introductory note); the three chapters of Book 3 on the propensity to consume culminating with the multiplier; and four out of eight chapters of Book 4, those on the marginal efficiency of capital, Keynes's interest theory, his reading of neoclassical interest theory, and chapter 18's concluding statement: 125 out of 389 pages. In the sense of pure theory the rest of the book is definitional, inessential, irrelevant, or a derivative of these ten chapters and 125 pages. Yet, in their exiguity, they had to serve as a lever to overturn all of neoclassical theory.

Keynes was operating with a small number of economic elements, which he further constrained by special conditions. Chapter 18's second paragraph announced a number of elements to be taken "as given." Considering their importance, one might ask why he had failed to introduce them at the beginning of the book, since giving them their due consideration would affect every aspect of his theory. They were: "the existing skill and quantity of available labor, the existing quality and quantity of available equipment, the existing technique, the degree of competition, the tastes and habits of the consumer, the disutility of different intensities of labor and of the activities of supervision and organization, as well as the social structure including the forces... which determine the distribution of the national income."[15] Keynes had left out the capitalistic dynamic of change and growth, and, ignoring Joan Robinson's important *Economics of Imperfect Competition* (1933), failed to consider the economies of scale and the tendency toward monopoly or oligopoly.[16] Earlier, in a definitional chapter, he had also, as discussed below, defined inflation out of his model. Furthermore, while not excluding the trade cycle, the model did not give it enough room to function freely, thus the "oscillat[ion] round an intermediate position." This perhaps reflected the fact that he had not mentioned it in the previous discussion, although he would devote a later, nonessential chapter to it. Keynes had eliminated most of the contemporary characteristics of the West's free-enterprise economy.

Having excised so much, Keynes left it to the reader to reinterpolate enough of the discards in order to conceive of a sufficiently real economy. As Joseph Schumpeter observed in his obituary article on Keynes, "All the phenomena incident to creation and change in this apparatus, that is to say, the phenomena that dominate the capitalistic process are thus excluded from consideration."[17] One is forced to ask if Keynes's model, whatever its inner consistency or elegance, expressed enough of that reality to justify *any* conclusion. Frank Knight thought not: "If one is willing to make assumptions of this sort... one should indeed find little difficulty in revolutionizing economic theory in any manner or in rationalizing any policy which one might find appealing."[18] In a footnote to his obituary article, Schumpeter graciously qualified, "It is really an injustice to Keynes's achievement to reduce it to the bare bones of its logical structure and then to reason as if these bones were all." In regard to theory, Schumpeter, devoting most of his discussion to Keynes the applied economist and policymaker, had to admit that the bones were indeed all: "What a *cordon bleu* to make a sauce out of such scanty material!" He concluded, "The first condition for simplicity of a model is, of course, simplicity of the vision which it is to implement. And simplicity of vision is in part a matter of genius and in part a matter of willingness to pay the price in terms of factors that have to be left out of the picture."[19]

How much had indeed been left out! The reader is not offered a single view of the production process, nor does he find the producer selling his product to a visible customer, not a word directly on production or exchange. If the reader contemplates Keynes's "individual" contemplating action under the impulsion of the transactions, precautionary, and speculative motives, he does not see him actually parting with his money or even clinging to it. Labor, unobserved at work, is either unemployed or in the act of refusing its services as defense against money-wage cuts. Speculators, uselessly or harmfully, buy and sell nominal values unrelated to the real economy, although some entrepreneurs of money investment make the necessary minimum of useful placements. Keynes's model is a pattern of solipsistic monads connected chiefly by the suggestiveness of his superimposed, often contradictory discussion.

Keynes's definitions, to which the four chapters of Book 2 are devoted, are a hugely important part of his system. From his work schedule it can be seen that they came after his ideational breakthroughs of the first three years and served to connect the various parts of his economic model to each other. Donald Moggridge has mentioned "the inordinate care [Keynes] took over the definitional chapters of *The General Theory* during 1934–1935," adding, "[f]or in the papers one finds evidence of much more redrafting in these sections than elsewhere." Loyally, Moggridge explained this as characteristic of "a mind that attempted to get to the fundamental bases of an argument or a system."[20] But the policymaker dominated the theorist in Keynes. As master of the petitio principii, he was clearly using his definitions as he used his given elements in chapter 18, not to get to the bottom of an idea, but to advance his argument-and-policy as far as possible. As he had made clear to Hawtrey, Harrod, and Robertson, he was perfectly sure of the rightness of his basic conception and the futility of plunging any deeper into it. In the end he may have advanced it further than he wanted.

Chapter 4, "The Choice of Units," presented the wage-unit as possibly the most important definition in the book. Keynes introduced it in the innocuous and ambiguous form of "the money-wage [which]...we shall call the wage-unit." In *The General Theory*, this "money-wage" was established as the standard of all values, with the remuneration of ordinary labor at one unit, compared with two units for skilled work, and the various rewards, exorbitant and resistant to measurement, of the speculator.[21] Since all prices were expressed in wage-units, they all moved together and were, in effect, constant. In this way, not breathing the word "inflation," Keynes had constructed an inflation-proof model. To the extent that they kept to the model, he and his followers could undertake radical adjustments of a given economy uninhibited by fear that inflation would falsify their projections.

Keynes provided the example for such policy-making in the widely discursive chapter 22 on the trade cycle, when he proposed action to increase British output in order to eliminate a deficiency he put at 15 percent. Believing it unlikely that "the existing propensity to consume" could ever provide full employment, he recommended action to increase consumption from an index of 90 to 100 and net investment from 10 to 15. But then he thought to improve the situation by giving consumption an extra increase at the cost of the full increase of investment, bringing consumption beyond 100 to 103 and investment short of 15 to 12. He discussed all these manipulations with not a word addressed to the possibility—the certainty—of price increases.[22] Keynes's feelings about inflation expressed themselves most freely in his five-page encomium of the "strange, unduly neglected prophet Silvio Gesell (1862–1930)." Incidentally taking the occasion to reduce a rival stature by another few cubits, Keynes would "believe that the future will learn more from the spirit of Gesell than from that of Marx." To combat the tyranny of the interest rate Gesell conceived of "stamped money," a national currency that had to be revalidated periodically by the purchase of stamps. While conceding certain practical defects, Keynes insisted, "The idea behind stamped money is sound."[23] It was not sound at all but clever-crazy, a prescription for an inflationary bonfire as holders of a currency steadily losing its value hurried to rid themselves of it. The publicist had momentarily overcome the economist in Keynes.

In the early 1960s, licensed by Keynes's silence on its dangers and creating imaginative derivatives of his conceptions, economists launched the American economy toward a proper Keynesian inflation. President John F. Kennedy's Council of Economic Advisers employed the conception of the "implicit surplus" or, more revealingly, the "full-employment surplus," which could be a deficit just as easily. When Kennedy

entered office in 1961, his economic advisers argued that if excess unemployment, the total figure being then at 6.8 percent, were eliminated,
the nation's output would rise at an annual rate of $50 billion and the
budgetary deficit of $3.8 billion would be transformed into a $10-billion
surplus. Thus, the actual governmental budget, despite the deficit, could
be seen as restrictive and deflationary—having the effect of a governmental surplus taking money out of the economy.[24] While this reasoning
was not entirely wrong, it expressed itself, as Keynes did in his calculations of the 1930s, with figures standing immovably and misleadingly
for real values. In any event, while reducing unemployment gratifyingly
enough at first, this conception led to uninhibited expansionist policy
and the long march of rising prices. Keynes's theoretical suppression of
inflation had become a great inflation generator—and the terms "implicit surplus" and "full-employment surplus" have since been relegated
to the Museum of Economic Fossils.

If the wage-unit remained unobtrusive, Keynes wrestled overtly and
long with the definitions of saving and investment, devoting a chapter
and a half to them. Even Richard Kahn, as recounted here, had disagreed with him during the theorizing period. Further considerations
failed to eliminate Keynes's differences with Kahn and many others,
including himself, on saving and investment. Section 2 of chapter 6 had
begun confidently, "Amidst the welter of divergent usages of terms it is
agreeable to discover one fixed point.... *[S]aving* means the excess of
income over expenditure on consumption." Bringing in "investment,"
Keynes then asserted, "These two amounts are necessarily equal, since
each of them is equal to the excess of income over consumption." Almost exactly as Kahn had summarized them for him, Keynes then laid
down the verbal equations:

Income = value of output = consumption + investment.
Saving = income - consumption.
Therefore, saving = investment.

Yet he introduced the proposition by saying, "[T]he amount of saving
is an outcome of the collective behavior of individual consumers and
the amount of investment of the collective behavior of individual entrepreneurs."[25] How could these two sets of actions by different groups of
economic agents always achieve and maintain perfect equality? Indeed,
much of the sense of *The General Theory*'s argument depended on the

distinction between them, emphasizing the buoyant aspects of increased investment and, contrariwise, the depressive defects of increased saving. Keynes granted himself another definitional chapter, "The Meaning of Saving and Investment Further Considered," to explain.

Having rejected Kahn's insistence that they were indeed different things, Keynes began by asserting that "for the community as a whole," saving and investment were "merely different aspects of the same thing," thus an identity as well as an equality. He recalled to the reader that he was giving up the scheme of his *Treatise on Money*, when he had used "special definitions of these terms on which they are not necessarily equal." He now firmly declared that any apparent inequality in saving and in investment was "an optical illusion," which could be "reconcil[ed]" with the "apparent 'free-will' of the individual to save what he chooses" by the fact that "saving...like spending [was] a two-sided affair." Keynes could argue, "Every...attempt to save more by reducing consumption will so affect incomes that the attempt necessarily defeats itself." Symmetrically, "It is, of course, just as impossible for the community as a whole to save *less* than the amount of current investment, since the attempt to do so will necessarily raise incomes to a level at which the sums that individuals choose to save add up to a figure exactly equal to the amount of investment."[26] As Keynes described it, the system might well achieve equality of investment and saving at a certain stage, but only after emerging from an inequality that, however temporary, seemed real enough and that, in passing, had annihilated the claimed identity. Each succeeding strophe of the argument confounded matters more: as distant, pure abstractions saving and investment were equal, indeed identical, but when Keynes began to fill them with the stuff of reality, they began to pull apart from each other. Seven chapters later, "The Classical Theory of Interest," Keynes achieved their complete separation.

Developing his system's interest theory, Keynes had made the inequality of saving and investment a necessary premise. First he suggested that the income level influenced the level of savings, a proposition that no one would oppose. Thus, he mentioned, "the readiness to save out of given levels of income." But *The General Theory*'s one diagram required the assumption that all amounts saved were *given proportions* of income at whatever levels considered. Keynes then concluded, "[T]he level of income must be the factor which brings the amount saved to equality with the amount invested."[27] Saving and investment were not *inherently* equal, *but had to be made equal* by adjustments in the income level. Yet, while this view of unequal saving and investment was essential to the mechanism of *The General Theory* model, Keynes lapsed again in one of the later chapters, and apropos of a view he contested, remarked: "This implies that saving and investment can be unequal, and has, therefore, no meaning unless these terms have been defined in some special sense."[28] Like the persons of the Trinity, saving and investment could be seen in their separateness *and* in their character as "different aspects of the same thing." Religion lives more comfortably with such contradictions than does economic science.

Keynes made the dynamics of his system dependent on the separateness of saving and investment. In his revealing article "Alternative Theories of the Rate of Interest" of 1937 he insisted, "[I]t is not the rate of interest, but the level of incomes which ensures equality between saving and investment." That conception had, however, threatened to break an essential bond holding the system together even as he was in the act of constructing it: "But the result... was to leave the rate of interest in the air. If the rate of interest is not determined by saving and investment in the same way in which price is determined by supply and demand, how is it determined?"[29] This led to his thesis, as he had put it in his letter to Roy Harrod about his theorizing (chapter 6), that the liquidity preference of the wealth-holders, replacing the supply-demand interaction, was the determining factor. The letter had then, we recall, brought in his definition of the marginal efficiency of capital as the ultimate factor "link[ing] up one thing with another."[30] Thus, enlisting helpful definitions and absolute contradictions in his service, Keynes achieved, in his mind, the close of his system.

This sense of an ultimate and all-validating linkage of such selected factors as saving, investment, income level, liquidity preference, interest rate, marginal efficiency of capital, propensity to consume, and multiplier was, however, clearer in Keynes's mind than in *The General Theory*. Following the all-embracing abstraction of his theory of effective demand, he would feel obliged to make plural efforts to strengthen the logic of his model, the first having been the completion of his interest theory as set beside his consumption theory, and the second, chapter 18's restatement of the whole theory. There remained the different terrain of Book 5, "Money-Wages and Prices," and Book 6, "Short Notes Suggested by the General Theory," on which to try again.

Strictly speaking, Keynes had eliminated the need for his chapter 21, "The Theory of Prices," the last of Book 5 and the last to address his model's pure theory. The General Theory had finessed the problem, since it operated with constant prices based on its wage-unit as a unit of value. The chapter is an inconclusive disquisition on prices, essentially the remains of thoughts relating to the economic world of the *Treatise on Money* and failing to fit into the new model. While avoiding fundamental questions on its stated subject, Keynes filled it with other matters, one of them the application of mathematics to such *General Theory* materials as wage-units, effective demand, income velocity, and liquidity factors. In it, expressing his long-held view of mathematics in economics and again undercutting his own thesis, he deprecated, "I do not myself attach much value to manipulations of this kind."[31] As monetary economist he then contributed a final, *italicized* insight on money: "*For the importance of money essentially flows from its being a link between the present and the future.*"[32] Nonsense! The importance of money flows from its being able to buy something. Many other things, from bonds to imagination perform as present-to-future links. In the chapter introducing the marginal efficiency of capital, Keynes wrote, "It is by reason of the existence of durable equipment that the economic future is linked to the present."[33] The oracular Keynes invites belief in nothing much or anything at all.

A related digression deserves brief note, namely, chapter 17, "The Essential Properties of Interest and Money," which immediately precedes Keynes's restatement of chapter 18. Chapter 17 associates the interest rate with the "forward" prices of commodities as fixed by "futures" contracts. Keynes would have a "wheat-rate of interest, a copper-rate of interest, a house-rate of interest, even a steel plant-rate of interest," and also a "land-rate of interest," thus "own-rates of interest" as against the "money-rate of interest."[34] Keynes evidently got the idea from a review article in the *Economic Journal* by Piero Sraffa, who was operating as his auxiliary in his post-*Treatise on Money* debate with Friedrich von Hayek. In 1932, examining a collection of Hayek's lectures on money and capital, Sraffa found in it the same muddle Keynes had seen in his *Prices and Production* (chapter 4) and was inspired to speculate that "there might be...as many 'natural' rates of interest as there are commodities."[35] Sraffa's talent for scholastic reasoning matched his patron's; Keynes could join him in an exercise that was not only an exquisitely false use of analogy but one that contradicted his basic theses on money and interest. Indeed, misled by Sraffa, he permitted *The General Theory*'s chapter 17 to deny those essential properties of interest and money it promised to discuss, particularly the liquidity that *The General Theory* emphasizes. The essential property of money, again, lies in its character as an instrument for *buying,* thus as a uniquely *liquid* representative of all values. In that sense it is not just another commodity. In a rational (and stable) order the future price of money is always less than the present price by the magnitude of the interest rate; the future price of a commodity, given storage and maintenance costs, can reasonably be more (exception taken for seasonal factors, etc.). As Keynes the commodity speculator well knew, a futures contract is a wager between persons making two different predictions of the future price of a commodity. Here, his paralogic does not assist *The General Theory*'s persuasions. Rather it detracts from its argument as a *monetary* theory of employment.

Book 6, Keynes's last movement toward his general conclusion, begins as another reactionary return to the *Treatise on Money.* Its opening chapter 22, "Notes on the Trade Cycle" (not *credit* cycle, as he had preferred earlier), describes it as an affair of a three- to five-year up-and-down regularity incompatible with the permanent stagnation of the General Theory as a model.[36] Keynes fails to wrench the chapter back on course, but chapter 23, the penultimate and longest, swings fluently and unerringly into the right direction. It also has more unity than it promises with its helter-skelter title, "Notes on Mercantilism, the Usury Laws, Stamped Money, and Theories of Under-Consumption." Its politics provides the unity. In the *Treatise* Keynes had been sympathetic to "the army of heretics and cranks," as one might remember, but cautiously assigned it to "an entirely different terrain."[37] Now he cast compunction aside, found fellow revolutionaries among them, and organized them into his New Model Army. Sweeping over "several millenniums," he added the ancients and the medieval theologians as well as the early mercantilists to his forces. Besides the Malthus of effective demand, he officered the army with the talents of Stanley Jevons (imaginatively viewing sunspots as trade-cycle generators after applying himself to the rigors of marginal utility), stamped-money Gesell, and underconsumption Hobson, inter alia, "who, following their intuitions, have preferred to see the truth obscurely rather than to maintain error."[38] Keynes sent the elderly Hobson a fresh copy of *The General Theory,* responding to his congratulations with a note reasserting his own ascendancy but granting, "I am ashamed how blind I was for many years to your essential contention as to the insufficiency of effective demand."[39] So joining the cranks' ranks and putting himself at their head, Keynes achieved, on his final attempt, this one pragmatic and political rather than theoretical, by force of numbers and on the strength of his authority, the close of his system.

Chapter 24, the final chapter, drew upon Keynes's social philosophy to shore up this political solution of his problems in economic theory. "Concluding Notes on the Social Philosophy Towards which the General Theory Might Lead" would have been more accurately expressed as "Concluding Notes on the Social Philosophy on which the General Theory is Based." For Keynes's social philosophy was the petitio principii of all those petitii principii encountered in the book, Keynes having again and again arrived triumphantly at his starting point, number 6 Harvey Road. He had found it such a totally satisfactory beginning that retaining all the presuppositions noted by Roy Harrod,[40] he saw no sense in changing his address, a living and unmoving pole for all of his years, both parents surviving him and living on into their high nineties there. Although adjustments from Marshallian to Keynesian economics had been necessary, Keynes never had any difficulty in keeping his economic views comfortably within the matrix of his social philosophy as taught by John Neville and particularly Florence Ada Keynes, and as reinforced in his mind by his experience of the tragedies of the world beyond Cambridge. The neoclassical Maynard Keynes, predestined Liberal, had emphasized the Liberal Party's concern for the unfortunate somewhat more, perhaps, than its policy did; the ultimate Keynes, if no longer a little Liberal, had found any other party unthinkable. When he had begun calling himself a democratic socialist, he was to make his liberalism more or less socialistic. *The General Theory* was Keynes's *Tract on Socialist Reform (of a Liberal England)*.

"The outstanding faults of the economic society in which we live are its failure to provide for full employment and its arbitrary and inequitable distribution of wealth and incomes," Keynes began the chapter.[41] In one sentence this was its most important and comprehensive statement of a social philosophy, although it had mixed into it a substantial amount of economics. A few other social-philosophical statements followed, all interwoven with more economics, but still it was this terse expression of social philosophy that dominated the economics. While the social philosophy determined the argument, Keynes had provided it with little substance. Full employment, designated as the prime objective, remained a vague conception clarified neither in the book nor in his other writings. Elizabeth and Harry Johnson have called Keynes's emphasis on it, relating that emphasis to his narrow views on consumption, an "extremely crude definition of the economic requirements of the good society, which left out a host of desiderata, including equality of opportunity, social mobility...and a much more interesting life for all."[42]

Certainly Keynes, contemplating the failure to achieve anything close to full employment at the time, made no effort in *The General Theory* to separate out the economic factuality of unemployment from the personal distress it caused, nor to consider each in terms appropriate to its character. As for the "inequitable distribution of wealth and incomes," it was a moral statement condemning economic injustice in the form of an unfair—"inequitable," not unequal—division of material goods. Keynes was assuming that most persons would charitably agree with him and again made no effort to argue his point. It would be unkind, but not necessarily irrelevant, to refer to the income and capital gains of the City magnate John Maynard Keynes in 1936. Continually veering between the social and the economic, the swings away from either preventing much discussion of each, Keynes then added a few more undeveloped statements, the sense of which was: "[T]here is social and psychological justification for significant inequalities of incomes and wealth, but not for such large disparities as exist today"; money-making inspired "valuable human activities [and] canalized...dangerous human proclivities...into comparatively harmless channels"; "a somewhat comprehensive socialization of investment," thus "central controls necessary to ensure full employment will, of course, involve a large extension of the traditional functions of government [although] there will still remain a wide field for the exercise of private initiative and responsibility"; and if all nations acted this way they would be peaceable since with full employment they would not be so dangerously competitive with each other.[43] Associated with such sociological observations were these familiar Keynesian economic motifs: the situation required a lower rate of interest to encourage investment and consumption, and discourage excessive saving; it "would mean the euthanasia of the rentier" as capital scarcity would be eliminated. It would also mean the end of the unworkable combination of a domestic laissez-faire system and the

international gold standard, which had caused the intense and dangerous international competition of the past.[44]

In the end this social philosophy, insistent upon the deep peace and
security of the womb of Harvey Road, had required the economics of a
crank. All economic pain and inequity would be eliminated. Competition would be a bloodless game played by the few sharing the entrepreneurial animal spirits. The lower classes, provided with jobs and money
illusion, would contentedly carry out the work appropriate to their sta-
tion, and an expert, public-spirited mandarinate would make the adjustments necessary to keep the system operating with fairness and efficiency,
while, beyond the pale, other nations would do their best to emulate
Great Britain's example of civilized progress.

"Is the fulfillment of these ideas a visionary hope?" Keynes had begun the final, page-long section 5. He was willing to grant that at the
moment people demanded "a more fundamental prognosis." It was a
half-concession that all he could give was the restricted diagnosis of an
economist and social philosopher, and not the gratuitous profundity of
an unqualified philosopher licensed to think the unthinkable. But then,
feeling capable enough in his own character, he could celebrate his future conquest, surely comparable to the triumphs of the Inquisition and
David Ricardo: "The ideas of economists and political philosophers,
both when they are right and when they are wrong, are more powerful
than is commonly understood. Indeed the world is ruled by little else."[45]
He had gotten to power rather quickly, social philosophy having failed
to detain him very long. More than a decade previously, asking "Am I a
Liberal?" at the Liberal Summer School of 1925 (chapter 3 above), along
with his doubts on his own party character, he had proposed more contradictions, thus a "regime...controlling and directing economic forces
in the interests of social justice." Daringly, he had imagined the resolution of "sex questions," specifying birth control, contraceptives, marriage laws, and "treatment of sexual offenses and abnormalities."[46] Now,
with his free socialism and social controls, he was again denying all
contradiction and conflict. Hardly visionary, his ideas, except for the
implications of "sex questions," were a jejune arrangement of two-
dimensional overlapping paper cutouts in a pretty but muddled pattern.

Politics and power now validated Keynes's social philosophy, whatever weaknesses a pedant might find in it. Armed with his complex of
ideas, Keynes would supersede the mere administrators of power: "Prac-

tical men, who believe themselves to be quite exempt from any intellectual influences, are usually the slaves of some defunct economist." He put it lyrically: "Madmen in the authority, who hear voices in the air, are distilling their frenzy from some academic scribbler of a few years back." He could end, "But soon or late, it is ideas, not vested interests, which are dangerous for good or evil."[47] Economist and social philosopher—ideologue—Keynes could tranquilly await confirmation of *The General Theory*'s theses.

Redundantly, Keynes again brought his system to a close. It had not been the system as social philosophy; there simply was not enough to his social ideas. Instinctively correct, combining the qualities of practical man and skilled theoretical and applied economist, Keynes achieved a second political resolution of *The General Theory*. The social philosophy had been nevertheless valuable. Blessing and disguising the irreducible crudity of the power politics, leading away from the failure of the economics, it invited his readers to join his New Model Army.

Notes

1. *CW*, 7: 245.
2. Ibid., section 1, pp. 245–47; quotations, passim.
3. Ibid., 247.
4. Chap. 10, "The Marginal Propensity to Consume and the Multiplier," ibid., 113–31.
5. Harry G. Johnson, "*The General Theory* after 25 Years," in Natalie Marshall, ed., *Keynes: Updated or Outdated?* (Lexington, MA: 1970), 39–49; quotation, p. 43.
6. Richard F. Kahn, "The Relation of Home Investment to Unemployment," *Economic Journal* 41 (June 1931): 191–93.
7. *CW*, 7: 116–17.
8. Ibid., 119–20.
9. Ibid., 20: 166–79.
10. Kahn, "The Relation of Home Investment," 178.
11. *CW*, 7, section 2, pp. 247–49; quotation, p. 249.
12. Johnson, "*The General Theory* after 25 Years," 36.
13. *CW*, 7, section 3, pp. 249–54; quotations, pp. 249, 254.
14. Keynes, "Economic Possibilities for Our Grandchildren," as published in *The Nation*, 11 and 18 October 1930, ibid., 9: 321–32; mathematical argument, p. 326; quotations, pp. 321, 326, 325.
15. *CW*, 7: 245.
16. Joan Robinson, *The Economics of Imperfect Competition* (London, 1933). Thus, "We see on every side a drift towards monopolization..." (p. 307), and "[W]hen there are economies of large-scale industry the optimum distribution of resources is not achieved" (p. 316).
17. Joseph A. Schumpeter, *Ten Great Economists* (London, 1952), 282.

18. Frank H. Knight, "Unemployment: And Mr. Keynes's Revolution in Economic Theory," in Hazlitt, ed., *The Critics of Keynesian Economics,* 92.
19. Schumpeter, *Ten Great Economists,* n. on p. 281, pp. 281–82.
20. Donald E. Moggridge, "Keynes: The Economist" (mimeograph of lecture, Keynes College, University of Kent, 10 November 1972), p. 8; endnote 31. Much of this lecture was further developed in his Modern Masters biography of Keynes but the note on definitions was not in the book.
21. *CW,* 7: 41.
22. Discussion, ibid., 324–26.
23. Commentary on Gesell, ibid., 353–58; quotations, pp. 353, 355, 357.
24. Account in Thomas F. Dernburg and Duncan M. McDougall, *Macroeconomics* (New York, 1972), 409–10.
25. *CW,* 7: 61, 63.
26. Ibid., chap. 7, pp. 74–85; quotations, pp. 74, 81, 84.
27. Ibid., 179.
28. Ibid., 328.
29. Ibid., 14: 212.
30. Letter, 30 August 1936, ibid., 84–86; quotation, p. 85.
31. Mathematical discussion, ibid., 7: 304–6; quotation, p. 305.
32. Ibid., 293.
33. Ibid., 146.
34. Ibid., 223, 241.
35. Piero Sraffa, "Dr. Hayek on Money and Capital," *Economic Journal* 42 (March 1932): 42–53; the "muddle," pp. 52–53; quotation, p. 49.
36. *CW,* 7: 317.
37. Ibid., 6: 193.
38. Ibid., 7: 371.
39. Hobson's letters, 3 and 10 February, and Keynes's letter, 10 February 1936, ibid., 29: 208–11; quotation, p. 211.
40. Harrod, *The Life,* 4, 183.
41. *CW,* 7: 372.
42. Elizabeth and Harry Johnson, "The Social and Intellectual Origins of *The General Theory,*" in Johnson and Johnson, *The Shadow of Keynes,* 79.
43. *CW,* 7: 374, 378, 379–80, 381–83.
44. Ibid., 376, 382.
45. Ibid., 383.
46. Ibid., 9: 295–306; quotations, pp. 305, 302, 303, respectively.
47. Continuing in section 5, ibid., 7: 383, 384.

11

Defense

Published on 4 February 1936, *The General Theory* raised the abundant dust Keynes had told Roy Harrod he wanted. Some three months later Keynes cheerfully wrote one of those unpersuaded seniors, "I have not made very good progress amongst the seniors of the subject." In fact, he had made none at all, the established economists having unanimously rejected its major contentions. He continued more accurately, "[B]ut, apart from that, the book is, I am told, making great and rapid progress in London and Oxford as well as Cambridge."[1] The progress was represented by the opinions of laymen who appreciated an economist attacking the Depression with more than adjurations to let nature take its course, and by the younger economists and students, who agreed with him on action and who would be the commanding seniors soon.

Keynes's combative intentions were part of a long-pondered strategy, as he had indicated to Harrod. Other expressions of his emphasized the value of controversy in getting heard and understood. In a discarded fragment of a preface written in 1934 he asked rhetorically whether he should follow the pacific example of Marshall and Pigou or "go at it hammer and tongs?" Defining his attitude as "equivocal," he forthwith requested "forgiveness" for future aggressions.[2] Without equivocation the published preface intended "much controversy."[3] The point was, as Austin Robinson later put it, "to force his fellow economists to decide whether *in toto* they were for or *in toto* against."[4] Actually, as Keynes's response to Dennis Robertson's rejection of either extreme showed, he defined those who were not totally for as being totally against.

Validating his position with the same intuition that had produced his general theory of probability, Keynes proceeded against those declaring themselves reluctant to agree. In the preface fragment he had stipulated

The General Theory's "technical incompleteness" while demanding that his readers nevertheless associate their intuition holistically with his belief that "[a]n economic writer requires from his reader much good will... and a large measure of cooperation." It was too easy for an opponent to raise "a thousand futile, but verbally legitimate objections." It might well be the case that "his head is so filled with contrary notions that he cannot catch the clues to your thought."[5] Thus, Keynes had attacked Friedrich von Hayek as incapable of good will and cooperative intuition in regard to the *Treatise on Money*. Shifting his secure intuitions to *The General Theory*, Keynes prepared to deal similarly with newer opponents.

In 1938, writing to Harrod about Harrod's address, "The Scope and Method of Economics," Keynes later generalized such specifics on intuition into an epistemology of economic science (and necessarily the other social sciences). He argued that Harrod's talk had failed "to repel sufficiently firmly attempts...to turn economics into a pseudo-natural science," and insisted that "economics is essentially a moral science and not a natural science. That is to say, it employs introspection and judgments of value."[6] In relation to these thoughts, Keynes conveyed to Harrod his opposition to the pioneering work in econometrics of Jan Tinbergen, for which Tinbergen would receive the Nobel Prize in Economics in 1969. While the natural sciences could work with quantitative methods, "In economics that is not the case and [as Tinbergen was doing] to convert a model into a quantitative formula is to destroy its usefulness as an instrument of thought." Keynes explained, "It is as though the fall of the apple to the ground depended on the apple's motives, on whether it is worth while falling to the ground, and whether the ground wanted the apple to fall, and on mistaken calculations on the part of the apple as to how far it was from the center of the earth."[7] This is an often quoted passage, widely unexamined and seductively imaginative. Indulging again in a false analogy, Keynes was correcting reality as well as science. Apples and the ground do not think; the apple's fall is directed by the laws of physics. Economics and all other social sciences assume that human subjects do think and indeed establish themselves as sciences by constructing laws consistent with that assumption. If Keynes had had his way econometrics would have been smothered in its cradle. The same fate would later have befallen the mathematical applications of his own General Theory.

Keynes could more easily defend the products of his intuition by employing the "Cambridge didactic style," which Marshall had developed, as identified by the American economist, Lawrence E. Fouraker. "Having satisfied themselves [of the truth of a proposition] they employed a curious device," Fouraker explained, referring to Keynes as well as Marshall. "Instead of leading the reader through the intricate analytical processes that their minds had recently traversed, they would provide a short cut...whose purpose was to eliminate consideration of the difficult problem they had faced and solved."[8] Or, as Keynes himself described Marshall (and perforce himself) at work, "The difficulties are concealed...a pregnant and original judgment is dressed up with a platitude."[9] If the Cambridge didactic style spared readers the strain of resolving given difficulties, it also spared them from understanding what they had been taught.

With such defenses activated, Keynes commenced to resist the range of private and public criticism of his theses. Permitting *The General Theory*'s proportions to shape the debate, his opponents concentrated on his interest theory while neglecting consumption and otherwise losing themselves in odd points expressing Keynes's emphases or appealing to their own individual expertise. In the immediacy of the post-publication response no one had the time or mental speed to assimilate the crisscross effects of so many novelties from money illusion to "own-rates of interest" and seize the whole. Even Dennis Robertson, with his early exposure to Keynes's ideas, did not quite achieve it, and he had the best chance, having fenced with Keynes privately before participating in the two published debates. No one, Keynes included, did justice to *The General Theory*. His theses pervading economic thought, this has remained true today.

The two major debates took place in the two centers of Anglo-Saxon economics, in Keynes's *Economic Journal* from March 1937 to June 1938 and in the *Quarterly Journal of Economics* of Harvard, in that other Cambridge, in the issues of November 1936 and February 1937. The American exercise ended with Keynes's important statement, "The General Theory of Employment," a month before the *Economic Journal* carried its first article. The significance of the *QJE* encounter, in which Robertson joined with three Americans against Keynes, can be better appreciated if one first experiences the more complex set of interchanges at home. That statement, furthermore, provides a logical, if not temporal, climax to his general defense of his general theory.

Among the preliminaries to these debates, one of the first hostile reviews was written by Hubert Henderson, now a research fellow at Oxford, who further extended his swing away from his old patron's ideas. In *The Spectator* of 14 February 1936, agreeing with Keynes on at least one point, he found the book an attempted revolution against neoclassical theory. Henderson went on to denounce Keynes's interest theory, which Robertson, Ralph Hawtrey, and Arthur Pigou, among his fellow economists, also rejected. Henderson, moreover, came to Cambridge in May to repeat his arguments at a meeting of the undergraduate economics society. "I was astonished at the violence of his emotion...he thinks it a poisonous book," Maynard reported to Lydia the next day. "He came off badly in the debate with Joan [Robinson] and Alexander [Richard Kahn] and myself barking round him."[10] Robertson, who chaired the meeting, once again disagreed with Keynes, writing Henderson, "Of course I think you had much the best of it."[11] Henderson then pursued Keynes with closely argued "notes," locating his position on interest: "The essential issue is whether you can make the rate of interest more or less what you like by manipulating the quantity of money, or whether it is governed by the fundamental factors of the demand curve and supply curve of savings."[12] Keynes was willing to admit "extra complications" but still refused to budge from any part of "my theory.... The rate of interest still depends on the interaction of liquidity preference and the quantity of money." He challenged Henderson to produce a defensible "orthodox" interest theory.[13] Henderson responded with a standard exposition of the supply-demand intersection as interest determinant: "Behind the demand curve is the productivity of capital for investment; behind the supply curve is the disposition and ability to save."[14] Keynes made off with Henderson's argument: "I do not quarrel with your last sentence beginning, 'Behind the demand curve'—but this sentence would be a good opening...leading up to my theory, not to one leading up to the [neo]classical theory."[15] Henderson's reply was a waste of time.[16]

The publication of *The General Theory* set Maynard and Dennis to reviewing their older arguments and their sorely tried friendship. After a long silence, in September 1936, Dennis wrote that he had spent "a lot of time this summer on the said book." Unhappily, "It's no use pretending I like it much better." He was conscious of a "sort of tabu which has arisen between us" and wondered if it "can profitably be removed."[17] Maynard had written, "I don't, dear Dennis, feel differently, and we must try to come to closer touch again," but he was as "cocksure" as ever about "arguments which are for me of painfully practical importance."[18] Three months later, immovable as ever, Maynard returned to the personal while associating Dennis with his new ideas: "I do feel that there is not a great deal that is fundamental which divides us." He insisted, "I certainly date all my emancipation from the discussions between us which preceded your *Banking Policy and the Price Level.*" Dennis was himself no longer "classical or orthodox. But you won't slough your skins like a good snake!"[19] On 29 December 1936, Dennis replied, "With each new skin you are apt to put on a pair of blinders." Feelingly, enclosing detailed notes on *The General Theory,* he reported having "gone through real intellectual torment," only to conclude that Maynard had produced nothing really original, "rather a rearrangement...of existing pieces."[20] With that their correspondence halted until the next August.

Three other readers, unencumbered by close relations with Keynes, can be seen as representing much of the profession's general resistance. In a major review Arthur Pigou, with whom Dennis had said he agreed,[21] rejected the multiplier, found the interest theory generally inconsistent and the own rate of interest "confused and confusing," and attributed the book's lack of clarity to other confusions. With damning appreciation he concluded, "We have watched an artist firing arrows at the moon."[22] The most thorough negative criticism, smarting with exasperation and laced with sarcasm, was pronounced by Frank Knight, who found "examples of confusion" in more than a half-dozen passages. Approaching one of his examples through institutional functions, he interpreted with sustained sarcasm: "In the capital market, saving has no influence on the interest rate, while on the other side demand is similarly without effect on price.... The theory of interest is the most difficult part of the whole construction to take seriously." Knight cut through to Keynes's policy: "[T]he entire work [was] built around, and built to support, Mr. Keynes's conception of inflation as the cure for depression and unemployment." Resignedly, he concluded, "With this general position, I happen to be in sympathy.... But I had hopes of learning more about the problems involved."[23] Alvin Hansen, who would become a leading Keynesian convert and maker of converts, dismissed *The General Theory* but as a strategist, like Keynes, of *political* economy. One could almost trace the line of his future retreat in the review itself. Forgetting his strategist's caution, however, Hansen achieved a perfection of false prophecy in calling the book "more a symptom of economic trends [than] a landmark in the sense that it lays a foundation for a 'new economics.'" The interest theory was "wholly inadequate" and the price theory, highly questionable. He agreed with Keynes on the "underemployment equilibrium," but the one theory he himself had evolved attributed it to the stabilization, "if not, indeed, decline," of population.[24] The persisting unemployment and his students' response to *The General Theory* would prompt his second opinion. Meanwhile, Keynes had to break through the homogeneous block of negative opinion expressed in such reviews.

In defense, always ready to go over into attack, Keynes employed a flexible strategy adjusting itself economically to need. In dealing with Henderson he had adopted a laissez-faire attitude as far as the considerable public reached by *The Spectator* was concerned, but, as we have seen, resisted him aggressively within the supportive university family as his home base. His colleague Pigou, however, had his formidable capacities and *his* following in that para-incestuous family. In Maynard's September 1936 letter to Dennis, he had found Pigou's review "something about which the less said the better.... [I]t is no use whistling a new tune to an organ-grinder."[25] With Dennis or perhaps himself relaying it further in Cambridge, that would have to do. As for Hansen, although the probabilities were against it, Keynes could successfully leave those arguments to be eroded in the course of time. Knight's general barrage might, like that of the practiced artillery of a World War I army corps, threaten to annihilate, but it had been fired in an outlying front, in a Canadian journal of economics. The editor had respectfully and conspiratorially offered Keynes or Kahn "as much space...as we gave Professor Knight."[26] Keynes told him he felt no need to react to Knight's "passionate expiring cries"; it was just another wearying case where, repeating his general and well-exercised explanation, "our minds have not met."[27] Keynes could better orchestrate his rebuttals in the strategically important *Economic Journal* and *Quarterly Journal of Economics*.

Early in March 1937, having felt unwell for some weeks, Maynard took Lydia to Cannes for a week's holiday. Upon his return, unrestored, he presently submitted to an examination by his medical uncle, but on 16 May, before the diagnosis was complete, suffered a major heart attack in the form of a thrombosis of the coronary artery. He would be a cardiac invalid for the remaining nine years of his life. Except for the first year of this new existence, he would refuse to act like one, although Lydia, rationing his time and expelling overstaying guests and colleagues, did her best to protect him from his fatal compulsion to do too much of the labor of his many personae. Limited to two hours of work a day for an extended period, he did reduce his business activities. He withdrew as chairman and board member of the National Mutual Life Assurance Society, but it was partly because the acting chairman had reversed his investment policy and only after his speech at the company's annual meeting in February 1938. He also began to relinquish his bursar's duties to Richard Kahn, but he remained active in the Council of the Royal Economic Society, the meetings being held for a time in his Gordon Square residence. He would remain a Cambridge lecturer (but he had long since reduced his lectures to eight annually), editor of the *Economic Journal* (at least he had Austin Robinson as assistant editor), director of the Provincial Insurance Company, and speculator. In the last character he composedly saw half of his half-million pounds of net assets lost in 1937, but, persisting, made good most of those losses in the next years. In 1940 he joined the Consultative Council of the Chancellor of the Exchequer after bombarding government and nation with memoranda and other writings on wartime economic policy, including a book on combating inflation (a subject unaddressed, as we have seen, by *The General Theory*), and, the same year, could not resist an invitation to enter the Governing Board of Eton, where he enjoyably undertook aggressions in the name of a bolder financial policy. From 1941 to 1946, engaged in financial matters culminating with negotiations on the Bretton Woods agreements and a postwar American loan, he made six exhausting, and thus doubly dangerous, wartime trips to the United States.

Besides contending with attacks on various theses of his *General Theory,* Keynes found himself defending its originality against implications that the Stockholm school of economists had anticipated or paralleled those theses. One might have read that sense in the two-part article, "Some Notes on the Stockholm Theory of Savings and Investment," which he published in the *Economic Journal* of March and June 1937 as its initial expression of the debate.[28] The author, Bertil Ohlin (also leader of Sweden's Liberal party), pointed out an amazing congruence between the Stockholm *ex ante* and *ex post,* and Keynes's expected or planned as opposed to real economic factors. Another important similarity was the concentration on the investment-saving relation and the interest rate, but this clearly went back to the great Knut Wicksell, as we have seen in Keynes's case, while the contemporary Swedish emphasis needs no explanation. Beyond that, however, any significant similarity was absent. Sweden did undertake public works as early as 1932, but not on the basis of the Stockholm school's ideas.[29] In his article, speaking for his colleagues as well, Ohlin rejected Keynes's liquidity-preference theory of the rate of interest and the policy of financing an investment increase by credit expansion, thus half of *The General Theory*'s theory (the *Economic Journal* debate ignored consumption) and the expansive policy that could break the deflationary stasis. But then Ohlin had accurately noted "striking differences" as well as "surprising similarities."[30] Keynes and Ohlin concentrated on the differences.

On liquidity preference, Ohlin, bringing the other debaters with him, specified, "The rate of interest is simply the price of credit."[31] The others were Dennis Robertson and, in a minor role, Ralph Hawtrey. Cheerily, Keynes prepared to resist: "I am very glad that you have been able to put down in a way I can understand the rate of interest as established by the demand and supply for credit.... I...consider it fundamental heresy."[32] His first public response to Ohlin (and the others) was the article, "Alternative Theories of the Rate of Interest," evidently written before his heart attack and published the next month in the *Economic Journal* of June.[33] Referring also to Robertson's *QJE* review and the critique going into Hawtrey's *Capital and Unemployment* (1937), Keynes would render all past, present, and future objections to his interest theory irrelevant and nugatory. He developed an entirely new argument, although *The General Theory* had, in a negative way, prepared it by "mak[ing] the rate of interest to depend...on the demand and supply of money," as he put it now. "The alternative theory held...by Professor Ohlin... Mr. Robertson...and probably by many others, makes it to depend, put briefly, on the demand and supply of *credit*."[34] He meant *money*; his opponents meant *credit*. In making this point he meant all the difference in the world. In one way *The General Theory* supported his new argument.

Chapter 13, "The General Theory of the Rate of Interest," uses the words "money" and "cash" many times and "credit" *never*. Yet it does make numerous mentions of "debts" and "bonds," which, of course, are synonyms for "credit." Furthermore, the book's chapter 15, "The Psychological and Business Incentives to Liquidity," says flatly, "The banking system and the monetary authority are dealers in money and debts."[35] In another passage, which can be located both in and out of *The General Theory,* specifically in a long footnote on the book's first and second proofs but then dropped, Keynes wrote, "It is equality between the demand and supply of loans of money, i.e., of debts, which is brought about by the rate of interest."[36] All these expressions by Keynes himself would seem to agree with Robertson, who in the next issue of the *Economic Journal* insisted that when Keynes set his own theorem to functioning, he was positing banking systems with credit as a central element.[37] "Money" and "credit," as Robertson and Keynes himself have shown, are both necessary to express the idea of transferring money from lender to borrower. It is difficult to see Keynes's money-credit dialectic as anything but a rhetorical maneuver to cover his syllogistic tracks with confusion. Forcing his opponents to restructure their rebuttals, it deflected the debate away from the logic he had employed in *The General Theory*'s chapters on interest theory.

As introduced with his money-credit distinction, Keynes's strategy was to seize the initiative with his first article and generate new glosses on his original theses or entirely new contentions. To an extent his overconscientious opponents found themselves starting Keynesian hares and chasing them in all directions instead of building consecutive arguments of their own. Ohlin, it is true, introduced *his* hare in the form of the *ex ante–ex post* dichotomy, but then Keynes pursued it in ways the Stockholm economist would find surprising.

On Keynes's initiative, money-credit joined *ex ante–ex post* and a third dialectic, that of a *stock* as opposed to a *flow* of money. About the latter he now proposed that the economy's money total was the stock, part of which became a flow in the form of active investment funds. Related to this he would develop another novel idea, that of *finance* as one more liquidity motive to be added to the transactions, precautionary motives, and speculative motives formalized in the book. Exhibiting his genius for creative syllogizing, these terms linked up variously with each other in an intricate series of combinations.

With the aid of finance, which remains yet to be elucidated, Keynes then proceeded to elaborate on the stock-flow distinction. He found his opponents confused between "credit in the sense of 'finance'" and "credit in the sense of saving." He explained that the first, forming a revolving fund for continued use, had to do with the *flow* of investment funds, while "saving can be used once only. It relates to the net addition to the *stock* of actual assets" (italics added).[38] The idea had a lively afterlife (which an appendix to this chapter will trace). Besides being related to the stock-flow dialectic, "finance" was also inseparably associated with the *ex ante* state. After arranging the money-credit distinction, Keynes proceeded to another "possible source of confusion." He explained, "An investment *decision* (Professor Ohlin's investment *ex ante*) may sometimes involve a temporary demand for money before it is carried out." Therefore, "planned investment—i.e., investment *ex ante*—may have to secure its 'financial provision' *before* the investment takes place"— thus the "finance" motive.[39]

Here one is wise to pause to take stock. (One might note in passing that Keynes has made a conditional statement with "may" but his argument proceeds as if "may" became "must.") In the first place the initial three liquidity motives clearly belong to the wealth-holder, while the finance motive is the concern of the entrepreneurial "borrower" planning, as Keynes described it, a new investment expenditure. Keynes never explained how the new motive associated itself with the others. Leaving that problem unsolved and addressing the entrepreneur's situation alone, one must now ask why he should need "finance" for investment, that is, capital outlay, "*before*," to repeat Keynes's words, "the investment is carried out." If the entrepreneur were rational, he would not have planned the investment until receiving assurance of the "financial provision," and he can comfortably wait until the future moment when he must disburse the money. Keynes pressed on. Finance, he insisted, "may be regarded as lying halfway, so to speak, between the active and the inactive balances."[40] What is conceivable as the halfway point between the active and the inactive? His precautionary interjection, so to speak, signaled that Keynes required the reader's forbearance: he was arriving at a favorite location, the excluded middle.

Keynes complicated the confusions in "The *'Ex-Ante'* Theory of the Rate of Interest," his second article of the debate, published in the *Economic Journal* of December 1937. The article is noteworthy for its elevation of finance as "the coping stone of the liquidity theory of the rate of interest."[41] With that, the transactions, precautionary motives, and speculative motives constituting the original liquidity preference were transcended in the process of becoming familiar elements in economic thinking. The afterthought, however, did not win general adherence,

Keynes himself withdrawing into ambivalence, while most of his interpreters were content to take the unamended *General Theory* as canon.[42]

While distracting his opponents, Keynes's novelties also permitted him further to divide up the economy into noninteracting sectors. Referring to the capital market, inter alia, Frank Knight protested this segregating effect in *The General Theory*, where it was not nearly so explicit as in the post hoc debate. In his first *Economic Journal* article, Keynes, while failing to explain its origins, had gone on to argue that "'finance' has nothing to do with saving."[43] (One might recall the distress of the student Robert B. Bryce at Keynes's analogous rejection of a relation between saving and the rate of interest discussed in chapter 6.) With this and other assertions he created a mysteriously fragmented set of economic arrangements beyond any understanding. Adding elaborations in his second article, he created a magical black box in which finance invisibly carried out the unnecessary function of financing outlays during a period *before* they had to be made. These black-box operations permitted Keynes to attack a favorite bête noire, the bankers.

Keynes was conceiving of a situation in which a "higher scale of planned activity increases...the demand for liquidity." In his reasoning saving could do nothing to satisfy that demand: "If there is no change in the liquidity position, the public can save *ex ante* and *ex post* and *ex* anything until they are blue in the face, without alleviating the problem in the least." Yet, if the saving is real, the increased amount saved means more liquidity by definition. The banks could then be passing on that greater amount of funds without altering their (to Keynes) excessive caution. Keynes, however, refused to permit that to happen. "For 'finance' is essentially a revolving fund," he insisted. He had not told the reader how it was constituted, but now he gave the bankers the power to manage that revolving fund. The failure to provide the needed liquidity was due to them: "The banks hold the key position in the transition from a lower to a higher scale of activity." Keynes went on to accuse the bankers of probable dereliction of duty: "If they refuse to relax, the growing congestion of the short-term loan market or of the new issue market, as the case may be, will inhibit the improvement, no matter how thrifty the public purpose to be out of their future incomes."[44] Thus Keynes's "finance" and more confusion.

The rhetorical value of Keynes's December 1937 article can be suggested by the rebuttal he evoked from Robertson in the June 1938 *Eco-*

nomic Journal. Entering deeply into Keynes's reasoning, he accurately showed that Keynes had given three different accounts "as to what is the process by which...the illiquidity taken on itself by the banking system if the provision of 'finance' is canceled."[45] In the process of seizing upon these inconsistencies, however, Robertson had lost himself in the great black hole of Keynesian "finance" and wandered further away from a more meaningful rebuttal. He also provided the occasion, in that same June 1938 issue, for Keynes's ultimate defense (see below) in the debate.[46]

As shown here in the previous chapter, Keynes's General Theory of the Rate of Interest had produced its interest rate without reference to the entrepreneurial "borrower." Is this writer correct in finding the absence of the borrower and his demand so important that he dismisses Keynes's interest theory as nonsense? Why had Keynes's three opponents, who also objected to that theory, failed to make an issue of that significant omission? Actually, two of them did indeed remark on the absence of demand in his interest determination, but, attempting to do justice to all of his arguments, neglected to establish a sense of proportion appropriate to the whole debate. The September 1937 issue carried three rejoinders to Keynes's first article. Hawtrey, however, continued his private disagreement with Keynes and concentrated on his inconsistent attribution of identity, equality, and nonequality of investment and saving, among other delicti, and failed to address interest-rate determination. Ohlin, for his part, again went over the *ex ante–ex post* issue, but did move on to say that the "willingness to borrow" was also essential in the process. Similarly, Robertson, permitting himself to be thrown on the defensive, argued that, contrary to Keynes's claim, there was nothing circular in seeing that the "demand curve for loanable funds can exercise a direct influence on the rate of interest."[47] He would do much better in later expressions, but it would be too late. In this crucial question Keynes-as-debater had been fortunate in Keynes-as-editor's choice of debating opponents.

Supporting himself upon the aggressive theses of his articles of June and December 1937, and beginning fluently with a reply to Robertson's *mise au point* of the June 1938 issue, Keynes could conclude the debate triumphantly in that same issue. In his first sentence he coolly denied the self-evident and gave himself the victory: "Now that we have got away from the idea of the rate of interest being dependent on saving and

have reached the idea of its being in some sense a monetary phenomenon, the remaining difference of opinion cannot be fundamental and
agreement should be within reach." Most of the "outstanding confusion" was due to the fact that he still meant *money* while his interlocu-
tors went on translating him to mean *credit*. He taunted Robertson: "Yet
what I am trying to say is extremely simple and need put no soul into
torment." The announced agreement began to disappear with Keynes's
mention of it, and Robertson's "very bold confusion" became a part of
his "outstanding confusion" and was succeeded by his "incorrigible confusion." Keynes ended, "Until Mr. Robertson understands that, he will
not grasp what I am driving at, however carefully I attempt to re-word
it."[48] Thus the ultimate argument of the debate: insult. In concentrating
on Robertson, moreover, Keynes had rhetorically shrunk all his opponents into one intimately known, vulnerable figure. Respecting the other
opponents the personal insult logically obtained as well.

The private debate of Maynard and Dennis, continuing on parallel
lines with their public expressions, meanwhile matched them with instructive counterpoint. Maynard was still insisting that "the strictly intellectual differences between us are probably very small indeed at
bottom," as he put it to Dennis in a letter of 6 December 1937. "But I am
trying all the time to disentangle myself, whilst you are trying to keep
entangled. You are, so to speak, bent on creeping back into your mother's
womb; whilst I am shaking myself like a dog on dry land."[49] On New
Year's Day 1938, Dennis returned, triumphing over Maynard's dominating pride with his own humble sensitivity,

> By way of varying your picturesque metaphors, may I suggest that I—managing to
> keep throughout in touch with all the elements of the problem in a dim and fum-
> bling way—have been a sort of glow worm, whose feeble glimmer lands on all the
> objects in its neighborhood: while you, with your far more powerful intellect, have
> been a lighthouse casting a far more penetrating, but sometimes fatally distorting,
> beam on one object after another in succession.[50]

In "The Hedgehog and the Fox," his great essay on Leo Tolstoy, Isaiah
Berlin would use different metaphors to categorize the same paired types
of thinkers, quoting a Greek poet, "'The fox knows many things but the
hedgehog knows one big thing.'"[51]

In one sense—in one blow—Keynes had already defeated his opponents of the *Economic Journal* before the battle was joined. He had
already employed an argument of total annihilation in the *Quarterly*

Journal of Economics. He did not, however, repeat it in the *Economic Journal,* where his logic, assisted by his complex confusions and ad hominem suggestions, had been effective enough, even though it had been limited essentially to interest-rate theory. The *QJE* action of general annihilation, like a radioactive cloud, would descend upon all naysayers in due time.

Perhaps the four *QJE* critics had earned this fate by the greater severity of their collective testing of *The General Theory.* In this debate Dennis Robertson had achieved more telling arguments than he would in the *Economic Journal,* while all three American disputants and their criticisms were formidable. The major review, which was more prominently displayed and longer than the others, was written by Jacob Viner, a highly respected member (like Frank Knight) of the Chicago school and a learned historian of economic thought. The two other Americans were the Harvard professors Wassily W. Leontief, creator of input-output economics and a future Nobel laureate (1973), and Frank W. Taussig, an expert on international trade, particularly tariffs. A scattering of arguments by Leontief and Taussig strewed a general skepticism over Keynes's theses, while Viner and Robertson attacked major specifics.

It would be redundant to repeat objections made by others as well and already discussed here, and futile, furthermore, since Keynes would not respond to any of them.[52] Of the lesser reviews, Taussig's rejected the idea of satiated consumption and (capital) investment, while Leontief demanded statistical proof of the money illusion. Viner, also attacking Keynes's consumption and its inverse of saving, remarked on the difference between individual and corporate savers. He went on to object to the "breakneck speed" of Keynes's argumentation, the "unbelievable complexity" of his definitions, and to contest the validity of his involuntary unemployment, hoarding, and liquidity preference. Like Frank Knight, he saw the policy value of Keynes's prescription of inflation, but also the danger: his theory "point[ed] obviously to the superiority of inflationary remedies for unemployment over money-wage reductions." But, Viner continued, "In a world organized in accordance with Keynes's specifications there would be a constant race between the printing press and the business agents of the trade unions."[53] Robertson uncannily seconded many of Viner's criticisms. Thus, in an exquisitely apt term, he saw *The General Theory* with Kahn's multiplier producing "engineered reflation." He went on to refract a variant of Keynes's claim that they were closer to agreement on theory than he would admit. Sympathetic to Keynes's attack on the current blight of deflation but demurring on pure theory, on "high matters of judgment and policy...I am, I think, more nearly in agreement with Mr. Keynes than the reader of these notes might suppose!"[54] Together, the four commentaries presented a firmly interlocking negation.

In the first three pages of his defense, entitled "The General Theory of Employment," Keynes followed his lesser strategy of agreement, concession, and ambiguity. Thus, he granted to Viner that his involuntary unemployment was "particularly open to criticism." He added, "I already feel myself in a position to make improvements." He went on to transform his book before their eyes: "I am more attached to the comparatively simple fundamental ideas which underlie my theory than to the particular forms in which I have embodied them." With that he made any given part of his General Theory disappear whenever credibly challenged. Humbly for the moment, he would accept aid in correcting his own betrayals-in-translation of his sometimes ineffable ideas: "If the simple basic ideas can become familiar and acceptable, time and experience and the collaboration of a number of minds will discover the best way of expressing them." He was suggesting that the objections of his critics were due to his own failure to make himself clear. He would therefore prefer to use the space to "[try] to re-express some of these ideas [rather than engage] in detailed controversy which might prove barren." And so, in three pages, Keynes dispensed himself from responding to any objection at all. He used the remaining dozen pages to reaffirm his position as given—but with an argument that was essentially new, although well prepared in the draft of *The General Theory* and his other writings. The argument was uncertainty.

Calling his probability studies to his aid, Keynes rejected the claims of the "calculus of probability" and associated neoclassical economics with it in a common ban: "Thus the fact that our knowledge of the future is fluctuating, vague and uncertain, renders wealth a peculiarly unsuitable subject for the methods of the classical economic theory." He proceeded to a tour of such uncertainties as "the prospect of a European war...the price of copper and the rate of interest twenty years hence...or the position of private wealth owners in the social system in 1970." Echoing the *Treatise on Probability*'s categorization of certain probabilities as measurable and others as incorrigibly immeasurable, he concluded, "About these matters there is no scientific basis on which to form any calculable probability whatever." He went on also to suggest the dangers emanating from "the whirlpool of speculation" of *The General Theory*'s chapter 12, "The State of Long-Term Expectation": "All these pretty polite techniques, made for a well-paneled boardroom and a nicely regulated market, are liable to collapse." He repeated, "I accuse the classical economic theory of being itself one of these pretty polite techniques which tries to deal with the present by abstracting from the fact that we know very little about the future."[55] As if no one had taken exception to them, Keynes then summarized *The General Theory*'s major theses as correcting the neoclassical failings. The uncertain vitiated all rationality in neoclassical theory, QED.

Keynes did not try to show how his theory's unexceptionable components went on to defeat the uncertainty invalidating neoclassical theory. Becoming a terrorist-in-theory, he acted like the selfless young terrorists who achieved the assassinations of Czar Alexander II in 1881 and Prime Minister Rajiv Gandhi in 1991. The terrorists, choosing to assure the success of their missions, blew themselves up with czar and prime minister. For if uncertainty were so pervasive that the neoclassicals had no basis for any conclusion, the same laws condemned Keynes's theory to the same annihilation. Hence, uncertainty, as Robertson had argued, shattered the ability of the multiplier to remain constant and productive of calculable results: you could not predict the effects of a given increase in investment. It also shook the stability Keynes attributed to the consumption function, which might consume everything and demand more, or consume next to nothing and initiate an ultimate depression. It even called into question any confidence that the liquidity preference would persist in demanding excessively high interest rates. In sum it destroyed the intricate workmanship and precise movements of the various moving parts of the General Theory. Keynes's uncertainty had annulled economic theory and the sense of economic policy.

If one resists Keynes's hypnotic effects and steps out of his thought system, one can easily question every Keynesian thesis on uncertainty. Thus, he was falsifying the history of economic theory by attributing to classical or neoclassical economics a failure to address it. Uncertainty was a central concern to a Ricardo or Malthus studying the post-1815 depression, the innumerable students of cycles, the marginalist Jevons pondering fluctuations as far as the sun, Marshall with his concern for working-class victims of free enterprise, Pigou on unemployment, and the neoclassicals Keynes and Robertson, inter alia, on prices and the trade or credit cycle. With all its errors neoclassical economics was dedicated to the study of uncertainty as the economics of socialism and Keynesianism, each in its own way, were committed to a willed certainty, with which, as a principle of order and justice, they chose to replace what they saw as the unmanageably and impermissibly uncertain. Pigou had seen Keynes firing arrows at the moon. But he was making practical sense. Providing an example to his followers, he was using a weapon of desperation if all persuasions failed.

Keynes had defended *The General Theory* with perfect success. Of course, as we have seen, the book's internal defenses helped enormously. Beyond that, his most important arguments had elegantly overleaped the limits of reason, thus, in the *Economic Journal,* the destruction of meaning in interest theory through the separation of money and credit, the division of the same money into a stock and a flow, the silent denial of the existence of the demand curve for investment funds, and, in the *QJE* debate, the uncertainty that annihilated all rebuttals to the book's theory. In the first he had entangled and trussed thinking into paralysis; in the second he had wiped it out. Now the younger economists of the capitalist world, having choked on the Depression as they absorbed their economics and willing to spit out as much as necessary of the latter if they could only defend humanity against the former, were ready for their new leader and his new economics. Keynes was canceling out and reversing his "not...very good progress amongst the seniors of the subject."

Appendix: Stock and Flow

In his *Years of High Theory,* the most imaginative, indeed rhapsodic, interpretation of Keynes's theory, G. L. S. Shackle found "effortless power" in his stock-and-flow conception and developed it well beyond his suggestiveness in the *Economic Journal* debate. Shackle proposed to identify the flow with the supply curve of loanable/investible funds seeking "borrowers." He argued that the existence of a large stock of money overhanging the market annihilated the ability of supply and demand to determine the price—Keynes's interest rate—of those funds.[56] In this way Shackle set another argument besides Keynes's of *The Gen-*

eral Theory to support his attack on neoclassical interest-rate determination (where Keynes had income changes vitiating the process). But Keynes never used the stock-and-flow distinction in this sense.

Shackle's argument suffers from a mortal flaw. For if an economist were to draw a supply curve to represent the flow, he thereby swore that his curve expressed *all* the influences upon it. Surely anyone bringing money to the money market would be powerfully affected by the knowledge that much more of the same was threatening to compete with his funds seeking borrowers; the supply curve, by its location and slope, would have to express all this. For Shackle to claim, after sharing his mind's eye vision with his reader, that there was still another influence on the supply curve was to commit double-counting and falsification of the sense of a diagram. Nevertheless, on Shackle's example, if not on Keynes's, the stock-and-flow conception has been used in this fashion to strengthen *The General Theory*'s argument. In any case, while trying to attack neoclassical interest theory, this does nothing to rehabilitate Keynes's General Theory of the Rate of Interest, with its denial of the role of the entrepreneurial borrower in interest-rate determination.

Notes

1. Letter, 20 May 1936, *CW*, 29: 213-14; quotation, p. 213. The correspondent was Professor H. O. Meredith, Apostle and economist, of Queen's University, Belfast.
2. Preface fragment, ibid., 14: 469-71; quotations, pp. 469, 471.
3. Ibid., 7: v.
4. E. A. G. Robinson, "John Maynard Keynes," *Economic Journal* 57 (March 1947): 40.
5. *CW*, 14: 470.
6. Letter, 4 July 1938, ibid., 295-97; quotation, p. 297.
7. In a second letter, 16 July 1938, ibid., 299-301; quotation p. 300.
8. Lawrence E. Fouraker, "The Cambridge Didactic Style," *Journal of Political Economy* 46 (February 1958): 65-73; quotation, p. 66.
9. Keynes, *CW*, 10 *(Essays in Biography)*: 212.
10. Letter, 3 May 1936, ibid., 29: 218.
11. Letter, 21 June 1936, quoted, Skidelsky, *JMK*, 2: 587.
12. The "notes," *CW*, 29: 219-20; quotation, p. 220.
13. Letter, 28 May 1936, ibid., 221-24; quotations, pp. 221, 221-22, 224, 223, respectively.
14. Letter, 4 June 1936, ibid., 224-26; quotation, p. 226.
15. Letter, 11 June 1936, ibid., 226-29; quotation, p. 228.
16. Letter, 18 June 1936, ibid., 229-31.
17. Letter dated 28(?) September 1936, ibid., 163.
18. The letter to Robertson, dated 20(?) September 1936, ibid., 14: 87-88. While this letter is dated earlier than Robertson's (above) it seems to be a response to it.

19. Letter, 13 December 1936, ibid., 89–95; quotations, pp. 89, 94–95.

20. Letter and notes, ibid., 95–100; quotations, p. 95.

21. In his letter to Keynes of 28(?) September 1936 (n. 17, above).

22. Arthur C. Pigou, review of *The General Theory*, in *John Maynard Keynes: Critical Assessments*, ed. John Cunningham Wood (Canberra and London, 1983), 2: 18–31; quotations, pp. 25, 30. From *Economica* 3 (May 1936): 115–32.

23. Frank H. Knight, "Unemployment: And Mr. Keynes's Revolution in Economic Theory," in Hazlitt, ed., *The Critics of Keynesian Economics*, 67–95. The "confusions," nn. 72 (twice), 73, 75; pp. 76, 77, 80. The quotations, pp. 81, 94, 95. From *The Canadian Journal of Economics and Political Science* (February 1937): 110–23.

24. Alvin H. Hansen, "Mr. Keynes on Underemployment Equilibrium," in *JMK: Critical Assessments*, 2: 71–84; quotations, p. 83, n. 84, pp. 73, 81, 80; discussion of price, p. 73. From Alvin H. Hansen, *Journal of Political Economy* 44 (October 1936): 667–86.

25. In the Keynes letter dated 20(?) September 1936 (n. 18, above), *CW,* 14: 87.

26. V. W. Bladen, letter, 1 March 1937, *CW,* 29: 217.

27. Letter, 13 March 1937, ibid., 217–18.

28. Bertil Ohlin, "Some Notes on the Stockholm Theory of Savings and Investment," *Economic Journal* 47, part 1 (March 1937): 53–69; 47, part 2 (June 1937): 221–40.

29. See Don Patinkin, "The Stockholm School," in his *Anticipations of the* General Theory*?*, 36–57, especially pp. 39–40.

30. Ohlin, "Some Notes," part 1, pp. 53, 68–69.

31. Ibid., part 2, p. 221.

32. Letter to Ohlin, 3 February 1937, *CW,* 14: 185–86; quotation, p. 185.

33. Ibid., 201–15.

34. Ibid., 202.

35. Ibid., 7: 205.

36. Ibid., 14: n. 479.

37. Robertson's rejoinder, "Alternative Theories of the Rate of Interest: Three Rejoinders," *Economic Journal* 47 (September 1937): 428–36. The other rejoinders were by Ohlin, ibid., 422–27; and Hawtrey, pp. 436–43. See below for more on the rejoinder.

38. Keynes, "Alternative Theories," *CW,* 14: 209. Similar thoughts in Keynes's other statements, ibid., 219–20, 230, 232–33.

39. Ibid., 207.

40. Ibid., 208–9.

41. Ibid., 215–23; quotation, p. 220.

42. In correspondence with a Stanford University economist, Keynes responded to a criticism of his arguments (letter, E. S. Shaw to Keynes, 29 March 1938, ibid., 29: 276–79) by asserting that finance did *not* "make any significant change in my previous theory." Rather, "I described it as 'the coping stone' mainly because... it provided a bridge between my way of talking and the way of [Ohlin, Robertson, et al.]" (Keynes to Shaw, 13 April 1938, ibid., 281–82; quotations, p. 282).

43. In "Alternative Theories," ibid., 14: 209.

44. In "The *'Ex–Ante'* Theory," ibid., 221, 222, 219, 222, respectively.

45. "Note," *Economic Journal* (June 1938), ibid., 227–29; quotation, p. 228.

46. Robertson was permitted a brief note on one point (to which Keynes briefly replied), *Economic Journal* 48 (September 1938): 555–56. The interchange can be called a postscript signifying too little to require examination.

47. "Alternative Theories...Three Rejoinders," *Economic Journal* 47 (September 1937): 422-43; quotations, pp. 427, 431.
48. "Mr. Keynes 'Finance,'" *CW,* 14: 229-33; quotations, pp. 229, 231, 232, 233.
49. Ibid., 29: 164-65; quotation, p. 165.
50. Letter, ibid., 166-68; quotation, pp. 166-67.
51. As reprinted with additions in *Russian Thinkers* (New York, 1978), 22-81; quotation, p. 22.
52. The four reviews, *Quarterly Journal of Economics* 51 (November 1936): 168-203. Viner's is reprinted in Hazlitt, ed., *The Critics of Keynesian Economics*, 46-65.
53. Hazlitt, ed., *The Critics of Keynesian Economics*, 47, 49.
54. *Quarterly Journal of Economics* 51 (November 1936): 174, 168.
55. *CW,* 14: 109-23; quotations, pp. 110, 111, 112, 113-14, 115.
56. Various expressions of G. L. S. Shackle's argument, *The Years of High Theory* (Cambridge, 1967), 145, 147, 154-57, 239-41.

12

Conquest

Had *The General Theory* been written by a lecturer at Manchester University or Ohio State University, it would most probably not have been published, or if miraculously published, reviewed with easy imperviousness and otherwise not read. Keynes made the most of his personal connections. Of course, as the very model of a great achiever, he had always innocently and naturally done so. His instinctive, incessant actions had constructed a great factory of personal persuasion.

The friendships and associations going back to childhood were always helpful. To them one must add all the newer relations spun out of his activities. Austin Robinson has emphasized his personal influence through his Political Economy Club and his lectures. Through the club, founded, one may recall in 1909, during his early days as lecturer, "Keynes knew intimately...all the best of each generation of Cambridge economists." As a result, "we insensibly acquired certain elements in Keynes's own approach." The intellectual intimacies of the club built upon Keynes's annual set of eight lectures: "Each year he gave us the development of his ideas to date." The audience included "the third-year undergraduates to whom the course was officially addressed...the whole body of research students, at least half of the members of the faculty, a visiting professor from America, Australia, or where you will, and on occasion a few spies...from London, Oxford, or elsewhere." In this way Keynes nurtured his ideas and his following together. "Gradually year by year the essential features of *The General Theory* emerged. Thus...Cambridge at least knew fairly well what to expect." Furthermore, as assisted by their spies, so did London, Oxford, and Cambridge, Massachusetts.

"[S]ubsequent discussion was conducted very much in the atmosphere of the revivalist meeting: 'Brother are you saved?'" Indeed, "The first to be saved seemed to include not only the pure in heart, but a large admixture of the empty of head."[1] The process was indefinitely extensible. G. L. S. Shackle, requiring direct contact with neither Keynes nor *The General Theory,* was converted into exalted Keynesianism at an ad hoc joint seminar relaying the new ideas to students of Cambridge University and the London School of Economics in October 1935. He brought to the seminar "a mind already, for personal intellectual reasons, desperately needing new illumination.... We heard first a paper by Mrs. Joan Robinson, and no other discourse has ever released upon my mind so staggering and thrilling a flood of light. At last I understood." Shackle tore up the dreary dissertation he had been writing under Friedrich von Hayek. He went on to read Richard Kahn: "I saw the flash of each bomb as it exploded."[2]

Robinson found among the "sinners...many whose intellectual honesty forbade them to commit themselves...without a very thorough process of sifting." Others objected to what they saw as "exaggerations or misrepresentations.... The following years provided a most illuminating example of the processes and psychology of conversion, as economists...all over the world adjusted their thinking to the new set of ideas that Keynes had put before them, some going the whole way with him, some even dashing ahead of him."[3] The equitable justice of his memoir suggests that Robinson, while seeing his wife dashing ahead of Keynes, had lagged far behind her and considerably behind Keynes.

Joseph Schumpeter observed the process of American conversion at Harvard, where the students, already apprised of the new doctrine, had to await copies of *The General Theory* to see what Keynes really said. Some of them were so eager that they ordered copies directly from England. Keynes had created a "Keynesian school" as a "sociological entity...a group that professes allegiance to One Master and One Doctrine, and has its inner circle, its propagandists, its watchwords, its esoteric and its popular doctrine." The only other examples in the history of economic thought were the Physiocrats and the Marxists.[4] Schumpeter's observations indicate that the United States was very close behind Britain in seizing upon Keynes's "new economics."

Keynes had been moving almost simultaneously into the environs of *The General Theory* and the councils of the United States. His personal contacts included two acquaintances of the Paris Peace Conference: Walter Lippmann, since 1931 the most influential American columnist, and Felix Frankfurter, then a professor at Harvard Law School, both progressive-minded supporters of President Franklin Delano Roosevelt and his New Deal. Although they would later fall away into skepticism, if not classical conservatism, they now sought to enlist Keynes's brains to improve the intellection behind the New Deal. In early 1933, as the American reform and recovery program gathered momentum, Keynes's article series in the London *Times*, "The Means to Prosperity," encouraged it with its explicit advocacy of expansionary public works accompanied by the implicit advocacy of deficit-spending. The series was published as a pamphlet in the United States in April (following publication in England), the pamphlet incorporating Keynes's separate article, published on 1 April in the *New Statesman*, on the multiplier. Contributing with his presence to the conversion process there, as mentioned briefly above (chapter 5), Keynes visited the United States in 1931, bearing suggestions leading to these major components of *The General Theory*, and, in 1934, expounding the book's virtually complete theses.

It was only natural that an American foundation should have invited the resourceful Keynes to participate in its 1931 conference in Chicago on the Depression. Typical of his multiplex activities, he had to launch himself into an intense burst of work on the Macmillan Committee report to get off in time.[5] In June, turning to American circumstances, he gave three lectures under the heading, "An Economic Analysis of Unemployment," to a select group of economists. While still referring back to the *Treatise on Money*, he extended his proposals to such preoccupations of *The General Theory* as the false equilibrium of an economy at less than full employment and the urgent need for public investments uninhibited by budget-balancing considerations. On 1 July, he then introduced the no less appropriate discussion, "Is it Possible for Governments and Central Banks to do Anything on Purpose to Remedy Unemployment?"[6] He never quite recognized the fact consciously, but Wall Street had superseded the City as the center of his financial imagination, hence his close examination of the American stock market in the *Treatise on Money* and the substantial American public utility holdings he built up in the 1930s. Roosevelt's election victory and the swift commencement of the New Deal in the "Hundred Days," from 9 March to 16 June 1933, could be seen excitingly to validate Keynes's own efforts with the British economy. One need only recall his urgent advice to

Prime Minister MacDonald in 1929 to lead a united action against the economic crisis and his intensive work on the Economic Advisory Council and the Macmillan Committee: Keynes had imagined the New Deal three years and more in advance. Now the United States presented itself as a grander canvas on which to paint the economic future.

In a sort of way, Keynes fell in love with the creator of the New Deal. They would meet on his next American visit, but before then he responded with enthusiastic approval to Roosevelt's effective annihilation of the World Economic Conference, held in London in mid-1933. Yet it had aimed at the major Keynesian objective of currency stabilization. The American lightning bolt of 3 July, rejecting any agreement to that end, illuminated another solution to the problem of monetary disorder. The headline to Keynes's reaction, published in *The Daily Mail*, was "President Roosevelt is Magnificently Right." Doubtless also agreeing with Roosevelt's reference to the "old fetishes of so-called international bankers," Keynes could appreciate his masterful style of dispensing with absurdly conceived puzzles: "It is a long time since a statesman has cut through the cobwebs as boldly as the president of the United States." Although Keynes had hoped for British advantage, the decisiveness and superior potentials of Roosevelt's stroke captured his enthusiastic assent.[7] The president, who had already devalued the dollar, was following Keynes's alternate strategy of shameless autarchic action. In the long run it would be better for Britain and the world if the greatest economic power, without waiting for impossible international agreement, would rebuild its economy behind defenses erected by the necessary national egoism. Meanwhile, as a beneficent Trojan horse, Keynes could penetrate those defenses to conquer the United States from within.

Guided by Lippmann, who had lunched with him in London during the failed conference, and more particularly by Frankfurter, providentially in England later in 1933, Keynes found a way to approach Roosevelt with his advice personally and publicly. On 6 December, as a guest of Keynes's at the Founder's Feast at King's College, Frankfurter, then a visiting professor at Oxford, worked out with him a scheme to apply his influence on the president. Keynes would write Roosevelt an open letter to be published in *The New York Times* of 31 December. Frankfurter, presumably to disarm the president, was to make sure that he received a private copy beforehand. "You have made yourself the trustee for those in every country who seek to mend the evils of our condition by rea-

soned experiment within the framework of the existing social system,"
Keynes superbly established. He proceeded to heap a mass of advice
upon Roosevelt. The economic part was excellent, thus "I put in the
forefront...a large volume of loan expenditure." Yet he was tactless
enough to refer to some of the counsel the president was getting from
his trusted advisers as "crack-brained and queer."[8] While suggesting the
incompatibility of the two men, the open letter offered Roosevelt something much more important than good advice, powerful, if incomplete,
theoretical support for policies that affronted orthodox economic science.

A few months later Keynes was able to follow up his epistolary approach to Roosevelt with a personal encounter arranged by Frankfurter
and Secretary of Labor Frances Perkins. As it happened, providing the
occasion for many other fruitful contacts as well, Columbia University
invited Keynes to New York to receive an honorary degree. He had an
interview with the president in the White House from 5:15 P.M. to 6:15
P.M. on Monday, 28 May 1934. Convinced that hands revealed character
and that he could read them, Keynes found Roosevelt's "disappointing," rather like those of a businessman, as he pejoratively recorded in
his notes, while he told Mrs. Perkins that he had "supposed the president
was more literate, economically speaking." Roosevelt, for his part, complained to her that Keynes "left a whole rigmarole of figures. He must
be a mathematician rather than a political economist."[9] Both men had
found each other baffling, although Roosevelt, always the politician,
wrote Frankfurter, "I had a grand talk with K[eynes] and liked him immensely."[10] Clearly, Keynes had thrust more gratuitous and incomprehensible advice upon a leader who understood only politics well, but
how well! Indeed it was through the political that Roosevelt, instinctively responsive to reality and feelings, dealt with the economy indirectly but not badly at all. The president, who worked tolerantly with
many difficult types, could dispense himself of coming to an understanding with this strangely numerate English academic, while Keynes
would continue to appreciate his courage and skills in addressing his
unbounded responsibilities. The affair was regularized as a happy marriage of convenience.

During a three-week visit in New York and Washington, from 15 May
to 8 June 1934, Keynes saw a great range of influential persons in
academia, finance, and government. He gave instructive talks to a group

of government officials and a gaggle of senators. At a meeting of the American Political Economy Club, whose members included the leaders of the profession, he expatiated upon *The General Theory*'s effective demand and the multiplier, with special application to the United States.[11] It is not recorded that the economists understood him better than did the bureaucrats or the senators.

Before returning home, Keynes, who could not leave well enough alone, fired another open letter at Roosevelt, this one authoritatively entitled, "Agenda for the President," and published in the *New York Times* and the London *Times*. In the face of growing fears at the size of the government's deficit it correctly and vainly warned against a slackening of expenditures, but the recession of 1937–38 and all of *The General Theory* would be needed to reinforce its persuasions.[12] After that the war would dominate economic questions.

The General Theory moved inexorably on to its conquest of Britain and the United States more or less simultaneously. Although he helped it along from his elevated but less than prepotent position, Keynes, who had many other things to do, was no longer necessary to Keynesianism. Early during the war James Meade of the Circus joined the Economic Section of the War Cabinet Offices, successor to the old Economic Advisory Council and the Committee of Economic Information, and developed the accounting framework for the nation's 1941 budget. In this the criteria were shifted from budgetary balance to a balance of the economy as a whole, "really a revolution in public finance," Keynes thought.[13] A greater one, in which Meade was also instrumental, was worked by the White Paper *Employment Policy* of May 1944, which began, "This Government accepts as one of their primary aims...the maintenance of a high and stable level of employment after the war."[14] Paired with the Beveridge Plan, Keynesian policy would revolutionize British economy and society. In the United States, Keynesian converts, who included a few free spirits among businessmen as well as economists and government officials, began to draft an employment measure in 1943. The result was the Employment Act of 1946, which dropped the phrase, "full employment," as the result of opposition from those who feared it meant inflation. Nevertheless, it announced the government's commitment "to promote maximum employment, production, and purchasing power," and created the Council of Economic Advisers to advise the president to that end.[15] Other advanced nations were taking similar measures.

Supporting such explicit political and administrative measures was the process of conversion, as Austin Robinson and Joseph Schumpeter described it during the nascent stage. *The General Theory* was too difficult a work, even for economists, to achieve its effects on its own. While Joan Robinson and Richard Kahn were important, they added little that was new. Three others were absolutely essential in translating it appropriately for their fellows and converting them: Alvin H. Hansen and Paul A. Samuelson in the United States and the Englishman John R. Hicks. Two of the three, Hicks and Samuelson, never quite became complete Keynesians, while Hansen, originally negative to Keynes, remained a special case. Moreover, Hicks virtually repudiated his major contribution to the Keynesian revolution, while Samuelson was careful to keep his distance from the quickly and totally converted. If Hansen soon presented the bland face of easy belief, part of his capability as statesman-in-chief of the American Keynesian revolution derived affirmatively from his taste for empirics and negatively from his tone deafness to theory; once he got the motor running smoothly he did not much care how or why. What Hicks later said of himself was true of the others: "I was... 'converted,' or rather, I may claim, I converted myself."[16] Three missionaries concealing doubt on their persons.

With the work of Hansen and Samuelson, Keynesianism shifted its operational center from England to the United States.[17] It was only pursuing Keynes's movement toward the more powerful economy, its more numerous human resources, and its greater openness to new ideas. Keynes and the United States triumphed together.

Hicks used the general equilibrium system of Léon Walras as his own theoretical framework, a conception to which Keynes's thesis of disequilibrium was antithetical, but that did not disturb him. A score of years younger than Keynes, at the time a fellow at Gonville and Caius College, Cambridge, his mind and imagination could easily stretch to appreciate that senior's theorizing as well as the power of his position. Reviewing *The General Theory* for the *Economic Journal* of June 1936, he asked himself whether he should accept Keynes's claim of a revolution in economic theory or rather find "a pleasing degree of continuity and tradition." Virtuously, he proposed to "consider the new theory on its own merits." Actually, he wrote a statesmanlike article that found *The General Theory* revolutionary in parts and only seemingly revolutionary in others, with its "technique...on the whole, conservative."[18] A mild response from Keynes, who did not address Hicks's major criticism, nevertheless persuaded Hicks, "I have got to beat some retreats."[19]

Hicks, however, cast his views much further, but in the same direction, in his famous, and indeed revolutionary, "Mr. Keynes and the 'Classics': A Suggested Interpretation." Originally a research paper and published the next year, it endeavored to express the core sense of the General Theory in the IS-LM ("SI-LL," as he less aptly called it) diagram. In the article Hicks went on to develop his theme of a conception rooted in the conservative tradition that somehow achieved a remarkably radical effect. He composed three equations to express the neoclassical theory Keynes thought he had overthrown and another set of three for Keynes's theory. He found a neoclassical predecessor to Keynes in the unremarkable and barely precedent Frederick Lavington (1881-1927), who, in a pre-Keynesian reversal, found, as Hicks put it, "The demand for money depends on the rate of interest! The stage is set for Mr. Keynes."[20] Yet, as the Hicks quotation shows, Lavington said nothing about determining the interest rate but inquired into the effect of an already determined rate on demand. If Hicks's finding of revolutionary or semi-revolutionary thought in Lavington's case is surprising, so is Keynes's reaction to this new interpretation. For Keynes had responded equably and trivially to Hick's new gloss, although it would strip his theory of some of its revolutionary allure, thus: "I found it interesting and really have next to nothing to say by way of criticism." His greatest objection was his sense that Hicks had been unfair to the neoclassical view.[21] Figure 12.1 shows the IS-LM diagram as constructed out of the three equations translating the article's translation of *The General Theory* (and as refined by Hansen).

Hicks used two curves that approximated simple supply and demand curves. The LM curve illustrates the "money" part of the economy; the IS curve, the "real" part. More specifically, the LM curve expresses the "demand" for money (in the way Keynes conceived it) by showing how much money would be held at the various interest rates. An individual would retain less and pay out more into the economy as the interest rate increased because the higher interest rates gave him higher returns on his money; thus, the curve rises from left to right. At any point on the curve the individual's demand for money would be equal to the supply of money provided by the monetary authority: he would be in equilibrium in relation to money. An interest-rate change would mean a rise or

FIGURE 12.1
The IS–LM (Hicks-Hansen) Diagram

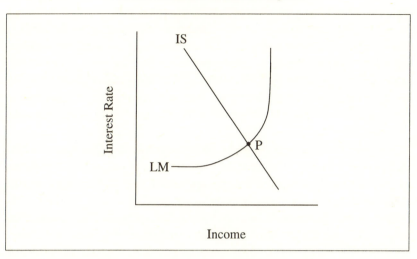

IS Investment-saving curve showing equality of investment and saving at various interest rates.

LM Money supply-money demand curve showing equality of money supply and demand at various interest rates.

P "Equilibrium" point, where both investment-saving and money supply-money demand relations are at an "equilibrium" which *excludes* labor supply. Thus there could be massive unemployment with economy at point P; this could be illustrated by locating the labor-supply figure at any point to the right of P.

a fall in the individual's position on the LM curve. Symmetrically, the IS curve, leaning in the opposite direction, shows the equilibrium and equality of investment and saving at the various interest rates: at any point on that curve investment and saving are in balance and equal to each other. Since investment (business outlay) tends to increase as the interest cost decreases, the IS curve portrays increasing business activity as one goes from left to right. In that movement income increases in step with increased investment. Or, as Hicks put it, "The curve IS...show[s] the relation between income and interest which must be maintained in order to make saving equal to investment." Thus money supply and money demand, and investment and saving, in relation to interest and income.

Hicks could then bring his version of the Keynesian system to a close. "Income and the rate of interest are now determined together at P, the point of intersection of the curves [LM] and IS. They are determined together, just as price and output are determined together in the modern theory of demand and supply."[22] Given this order of things economic, the whole system, comprising both money and real values, is in equilibrium. Yet Keynes began and ended the logic of the General Theory model with the thesis of a systemic *dis*equilibrium. This begins to suggest the problems that the IS–LM diagram creates along with its extraordinarily deft solution.

Restricting this examination to the barest essentials, one can too easily see other exceptions to be taken. One of the odd characteristics of the IS–LM economy was the strict separation of its LM "money" and IS "real" sectors, which relate to each other only indirectly by *their* relation to the (given) interest rate. Suggestive of a process of barter, saving somehow is translated into investment without the agency of money; similarly, the money of the LM curve seems to have intrinsic value unsullied by contact with the real values of the goods and services in the IS curve. By this Hicks was replicating Keynes's own refusal to register the many side effects and contrary directions taken by the factors in his model, whose movements he chose to limit to the unidirectional. Similarly, Hicks did not denote those intervals when Keynes's investment and saving were simply unequal or when they were identical and incapable of determining an equilibrium point. Similarly again, his diagram dealt with the planned, prospective, expected, or *ex ante* aspects of investment and saving by not registering them as well: investment and saving were trapped in the actual state only. Hicks's diagram only extended the galactic distance between reality and Keynes's model.

The IS curve, furthermore, expresses an unwanted solution to the core problems, as Keynes saw them, of stagnation and unemployment. Keynes had posited a quasi-equilibrium with the economy oscillating around a point below the desirable level. Hicks did indeed express this by allowing that his diagram's "equilibrium" did not include employment, that point P of the IS–LM intersection could be anywhere to the left of the point signifying full employment, the gap signifying the endemic unemployment of Keynes's system. But, since investment was equal to saving along its entire length, this would mean that all savings had been used up as business outlay, with the rest of production necessarily devoted to satisfying consumption: a full-employment economy! The Hicksian equilibrium was only too perfect.

Interest was also a problem, since it was present only after it was determined—exogenously, as the economist says, washing his hands of responsibility for it. In this way Hicks avoided the whole problem of interest and its determination, which joins with the propensity to consume in forming the two pillars of the General Theory's logical construction.

Of course Keynes had not accepted the article and diagram as fair but rather as useful statements. A strategist on a more elevated terrain, he could use this Oxford-trained outsider arriving from the London School of Economics only the year before (and to depart for Manchester University in 1938) to help transmit his message, however garbled, to the benighted. Keynes did not need to waste his time on such details. True converts, referring back to *The General Theory* itself, could make the necessary corrections. After all, Keynes was not responsible for any given interpreter's errors. As for Hicks's denial of the theory's revolutionary character, the Keynesian revolution, helped by his verbal and graphic translations, was moving along nicely.

The IS–LM diagram had its considerable values. For good and ill it did communicate a fair amount of *The General Theory*'s sense without torturing the reader as the book did. The student could almost immediately begin to think in terms of the economic system's real enough aggregates, investment, saving, income, and the rest. It was exhilarating to be lifted up to a position overlooking the entire economy and equipped with the levers capable of managing those aggregates. The Great Depression made acceptance of Keynes's new economics almost a moral imperative.

The Hicks-Hansen diagram became a prime instrument of indoctrination. Students could be assigned to manipulate the aggregates according to the carefully designed patterns. They could, for example, be given problems of this kind: The government wants to increase the national income by 20 percent; what happens when it (a) increases the money supply, (b) increases spending financed by taxation, or (c) increases spending financed by borrowing? They could then use simple algebra to calculate the various magnitudes and, wielding colored pencils, plot variations of the IS–LM relationships. But they are being led further and further away from the total economic reality. If they were trained to think in terms of given magnitudes, they were also being trained not to think of others, and even more important, not to think for themselves at all. They must simply pursue the pattern as given. Thus, since the diagram says nothing about prices, none of the students' manipulations could have inflationary effects, and so they are being indoctrinated into making false calculations that can have damaging results. In fact, economists trained in this way were recommending actions that produced more and more inflation into the 1970s, when its all too real magnitude brought a corrective, if painful, disillusionment with programmed Keynesianism.

Hicks himself expressed substantial doubts at an Oxford conference held in his honor in 1972, projecting a brilliant image of *The General Theory* (and his own related role) in the economists' culture:

> The Keynesian revolution was not just a revolution in economic theory. Keynes was a prophet, or propagandist; there were many audiences to which he was addressing himself. He was selling his policy to politicians and public, by *Essays in Persuasion* and by newspaper articles galore. *The General Theory* was his way of selling his policy to professional economists. It is tailored, most skillfully tailored, to their habit of mind.... It provides a model on which professional economists can comfortably perform their accustomed tricks. Haven't they just? With SI-LL [IS-LM] I myself fell into the trap.[23]

In Alvin Hansen's first review of *The General Theory,* despite his general rejection, he had credited it with "warn[ing]...of the danger of reasoning based on assumptions which no longer fit the facts of economic life." In a more positive sense, hollowing out his dismissal of it as "wholly inadequate," he found that "Keynes's interest theory contains promising suggestions" that might lead to "an improved theoretical apparatus."[24] In his second review, published in the triumphal essay collection *The New Economics* (1947),[25] he found that its theoretical apparatus needed essentially no improvement. Uttering a graceful mea culpa, he suggested that the difficulty of understanding Keynes proved his originality: "Witness, for example the first reviews (including my own)." The eventual converts had experienced a "rebirth."[26] A series of Hansen's increasingly Keynesian writings smoothly connected the two reviews. His total conversion was celebrated in his *Fiscal Policy and Business Cycles* (1941), which drew upon "prolonged discussions" with younger faculty members and graduate students, including John Kenneth Galbraith, R. V. Gilbert, Walter Salant, Paul Sweezy, and Paul Samuelson, all more or less Keynesian. Among these younger economists Galbraith recorded their prior conversion in his memoir, "How Keynes Came to America": "The old economics was taught by day. But in the evening...almost everyone in the Harvard community discussed Keynes."[27] In 1953, his vision further deepened by Hicks's perspective, Hansen produced his *Guide to Keynes,* which guided readers to an admiring understanding of *The General Theory* unencumbered with the book's contradictions. Using, renaming, and popularizing Hicks's diagram, he deftly finessed the interest-theory problem. This was part of a strategy of convicting Keynes of venial errors only to see him solve the problems created by his solutions on a higher level of theoretical and pragmatic effectiveness. Hence, Keynes had correctly found the neoclassical interest rate indeterminate because of income variations, but failed to see that his own theory was guilty of the same failing. In Hansen's reasoning, referring to the IS-LM diagram, Keynes had, in effect, said that the neoclassicals had produced not an interest rate but an IS (thus investment-saving) curve, with a different interest rate for any point on the curve. But Keynes failed to see that all he got by his liquidity-preference theory was, symmetrically, an LM (money demand–money supply) curve, with similarly indeterminate results. Now Hansen could conclude that the IS-LM diagram was itself the solution, since the intersection of the two curves produced the point P expressing the so determined, hence determinate, interest rate. QED, elegantly.[28]

This marvelous resolution raises Keynes's interest theory to a higher level of imaginative theorizing. But, since it began with nonsense, it can only compound the nonsense. The diagram had not *determined* the point P as the interest rate. On the contrary the interest rate was found exogenously, thus off stage, in a process Keynes never explained, with the "lender" somehow imposing his liquidity-preference judgment on the entrepreneurial "borrower." Inserted in the diagram, in a classic Keynesian reversal, this interest rate determined the point where the IS and LM curves met. Hicks had not inquired how Keynes had got it; had he done so, he would have been forced to reject it because it denied the supply-and-demand bargaining relation (which he still accepted as a believer in the Walrasian equilibrium) that determines price. Hicks had achieved a magical diagram that elided Keynes's problem; Hansen had achieved a verbal translation of the diagram that similarly elided the same problem. Keynes had learned and demonstrated that magic is often more persuasive and better politics than an economic theory attempting to describe rebarbative reality.

Much like Keynes, the converted Hansen was converting distinguished visitors from Washington and the business community as well as his students in his famous Harvard seminar. He was also associated variously with influential organizations, thus the Federal Reserve Board, the Economic Advisory Council of the National Industrial Conference Board, and the Committee for Economic Development, this last a remarkably open-minded, minority business group founded to further Keynesian principles. In the United States, as in Britain, the Keynesian virus spread healthily through the students and faculties of the universities and the key personnel of government.

In the circumstances Paul Samuelson, a brilliant theorist, was content to direct his own theorizing into another area and translate the Hicks-Hansen Keynesian translation as found into the textbook language of his *Economics*. The first edition appeared in 1948 and the most recent, the fourteenth, in 1992. In his obituary, "Lord Keynes and *The General Theory*," Samuelson himself had defined the role of a textbook in forming opinion: "Keynesian analysis has begun to filter down into the elementary textbooks;...once an idea gets into these, however bad, it becomes practically immortal."

Unlike Hansen, who achieved an unmarked surface of easy belief, Samuelson could not forbear suggesting that he knew too much to be fitted completely into the Keynesian mold. In the obituary itself he confessed and explained his early resistance to *The General Theory* by a catalogue of its deficiencies: "It abounds in mare's nests and confusions: involuntary unemployment, wage-units, the equality of savings and investments, the timing of the multiplier, interaction of marginal efficiency upon the rate of interest, forced savings, own rates of interest, and many others." The multiplier, for example, "often seems like nothing but a cheapjack way of getting something for nothing and appears to carry with it a spurious numerical accuracy." Samuelson summed the parts: "In it the Keynesian system stands out indistinctly, as if the author were hardly aware of its existence or cognizant of its properties." Only now, perhaps guided by Hansen's leap of faith, was the epiphany vouchsafed: "When it is finally mastered, we find its analysis to be obvious and at the same time new."[29] Samuelson won his Nobel prize in 1970 for work that assumed the presence, which Keynes denied, of equilibrium and Say's Law in the economy. (So did Hicks, two years later, also for work based on the same assumptions.) Samuelson's obituary of Keynes abounded in mare's nests and confusions.

Samuelson's *Economics* is a hospitable Keynesian house of many friendly mansions.[30] It was the first economics textbook with multiple colors. As time and editions went on, it gained more and more pied graphs and other illustrations, while the text added extended appendices on policy matters and, discussed with tolerance and sympathy, competitive theories like Marxian economics. It has become a rich education in responsible, aware citizenship in modern economic society. With 4 million copies sold by the 1990s, its success has called up many competitors in a lucrative market, but virtually all textbooks tell the same Keynesian story. As successful a conqueror, Keynes takes rank besides the Inquisition and David Ricardo.

The textbooks alternate between macroeconomic sections with their aggregates of investment, saving, income, and so on, like well-trained circus elephants obediently gyrating to Keynes's commands; and microeconomic sections under the sway of the law of supply and demand as developed within the frame of Say's Law and the marginalists' theory, the sum of these latter as organized into equilibrium systems by Marshall and Walras. The textbook structure seems to incorporate the dominant "neoclassical synthesis," which Samuelson claimed to have invented in his *Economics*. In this instance as bold as Keynes in his assertions, Samuelson would have his textbook achieving that synthesis in the sense that Keynesian macroeconomics produces the full employment needed to permit the microeconomics of neoclassical theory to come into its own.[31] This sweeping statement brushes past the fact that *The General Theory* and neoclassical economics disagree with each other absolutely on Say's Law, the law of supply and demand, and the conception of equilibrium. Samuelson (and his imitators) had simply put two contradictory theories between one pair of book covers.

Samuelson could not avoid Keynes's contradictions but skillfully blurred them by ambiguities and reversals of meaning in the Keynesian manner. One example is the account of interest-rate determination. Thus, the Keynesian macroeconomic part of the fourteenth edition of *Economics* offers a diagram entitled "The Money Market" actually showing the monetary system providing money to the public, while the text and the legend suggest Keynes's conflation of money market and monetary system. The legend makes the flat neoclassical statement, "Demand and supply of money determine the interest rate." But, although the diagram shows it, the text contradicts both diagram and legend by taking the interest rate as given and charging it with the determining: "At higher interest rates, people and businesses shift more of their assets to higher-yield assets and away from low-yield or no-yield money."[32] The microeconomic part presents a different compound of contradictions. Here the text has the interest rate determined by the intersection of the supply of and demand for funds in the money market, as shown by the diagrams illustrating the short- and the long-run situations. The legend of one of the microeconomic diagrams, however, strews confusion on the subject by reversing cause and effect and declaring, "As pictured here, the supply of wealth is responsive to higher interest rates." Nevertheless, the text's discussion in the section, "Capital, Interest, and Profits," runs along the traditional microeconomic lines with supply and demand determining the interest rate as explained by the great Irving Fisher.[33] Other textbooks (a half-dozen of which this writer has examined) replicate these contradictions between their macroeconomic and microeconomic parts variously but with similar confusions. As buffered by these confusions, the textbooks record the views of the winner and his allies in the war of theory *à outrance*.

After Keynes's death on 21 April 1946 one last action helped secure the victory of his liquidity preference over the loanable funds, that is, supply-and-demand, theory of interest determination. His champions were the redoubtable Joan Robinson and the ingenious Richard Kahn; the enemy was Dennis Robertson, who made up now for his diffidence in his debate with Keynes. In the article, "Mr. Keynes and the Rate of Interest," published in 1940, he reaffirmed his position clearly and absolutely.[34] Keynes correctly found it politic to rest on his self-proclaimed victory in the *Quarterly Journal of Economics* and the *Economic Journal,* and on his steadily ascending dignity. (Among other distinctions, on 18 September 1941 he accepted a directorship of the Bank of England, replacing his late friend, Josiah Stamp, killed by a bomb; in June of the next year he was raised to a peerage as Baron Keynes of Tilton.) Mrs. Robinson and Kahn continued the war in their lectures and supervisions, Mrs. Robinson eventually committing herself to print in the April 1951 issue of *Econometrica.* Her article, "The Rate of Interest," was a perfect nonresponse. It began, "The most important influences upon interest rates...are social, legal, and institutional." This permitted her to lose the interest rate among miscellaneous noneconomic factors. Thereupon, following Keynes, she took it as given and irrelevantly devoted the rest of the essay to studying its effects.[35] This aggressive defense led to a newer development not foreseen in Keynes's prophecies but taking its point of departure from his thought. He had left his followers trapped in a dilemma. If one abstracted from the sticky wages of the British economy and the General Theory as a model, Keynesian theory tended to lose its revolutionary élan and slip back into the neoclassical mode. His anarchistic essay, "The General Theory of Employment," could save it from so mediocre a fate, but only, as Joan Robinson would demonstrate, at the price of plunging ahead into the Marxian anarchy of post-Keynesianism.

Becoming more Marxian than Keynesian, Joan Robinson led the way with *An Essay on Marxian Economics* (1942), which, overriding Keynes's disdain for Marx, sought to reconcile Keynesianism with Marxism. She then proceeded to her thoroughly Marxian *Accumulation of Capital* (1956). The other post-Keynesians more or less in agreement, she denied the existence of economic laws *en soi,* except perhaps those graven on stone tablets by Marx, thus empowering politically correct economists to establish new laws guaranteeing economic security and social justice. She was not able to win or organize many supporters in Britain, and, like mainstream Keynesianism, post-Keynesianism established its center in the United States, with the *Journal of Post Keynesian Economics* as its organ. It has not, however, advanced beyond Keynes to announce any new theses. One indication is the theoretical trajectory of the prominent American post-Keynesian Hyman P. Minsky, who published a tract for the times misleadingly entitled *John Maynard Keynes* in 1975. In Marxian idiom, asserting that the Keynesian "revolution was aborted," he vaguely advocated thorough government intervention in an economy threatened by the apocalypse Marx had predicted. Two years later he confessed, "The construction of a new theory is difficult."[36] Post-Keynesian thought remains transfixed at that point.

Robert W. Clower, managing editor of the *American Economic Review* in the mid-1980s, and his erstwhile pupil, Axel Leijunhufvud, established themselves vanishingly in the space between Keynesians and post-Keynesians. Expanding on Clower's views emphasizing uncertainty, Leijunhufvud published the 400-page *Keynesian Economics and the Economics of Keynes* (1968),[37] which landed amongst the economists' fraternity like a large but damp firecracker that failed to justify the early attention given it. The distinction made in the title constituting its most important statement, it argued credibly enough that mainstream

Keynesianism had distanced itself from the more revolutionary conceptions of *The General Theory,* particularly as specified in Keynes's "General Theory of Employment." Leijunhufvud did not, however, propose any advance on Clower's first thoughts, and Clower himself had retrograde second thoughts. In a series of elegant and allusive essays, Clower had pursued Minsky's ideas and teased out a variant of Keynes's effective demand, but later repudiated it and disowned models developed from it by others as "'monsters'...whose paternity I admitted but whose character I deplored." He retreated to a "well-focused research program" within the frame of the Walrasian system.[38] If Joan Robinson had gone all the way back to Marxism, Clower was content to settle down with the neoclassicals.

What would Keynes have thought of the range of interpreters and interpretations of his theory? He has the last word. He gave it in the form of a paper published posthumously in the *Economic Journal,* which he had read to his Political Economy Club on 2 February 1946, two and a half months before he died. Harry Johnson, who was present, thought that Keynes displayed "extreme rudeness" toward Joan Robinson and had the "perhaps erroneous impression" that the point of the paper's criticism "was aimed partly at her."[39] Keynes, after discussing Britain's payments problem vis-à-vis the American economy, slipped into a valedictory mood and added a pendant: "I find myself moved...to remind contemporary economists that the classical teaching embodied some permanent truths of great significance." Britain's situation was not so desperate: "There are in these matters deep undercurrents at work, natural forces, we may well call them, or even the invisible hand, which are operating towards equilibrium." Equilibrium: Keynes turned to it as if it had always been a friendly power in his world. The United States, he went on, "will discover ways of life which...must tend toward, and not away from, external equilibrium."

Abruptly, Keynes moved on to another, related thought: "It shows how much modernist stuff, gone wrong and turned sour and silly, is circulating in our system, also incongruously mixed, it seems, with age-old poisons." He carefully qualified: "I must not be misunderstood. I do not suppose that the classical medicine will work by itself." He quoted from a speech he had recently made in the House of Lords: "'Here is an attempt to use what we have learnt from modern experience and modern analysis, not to defeat, but to implement the wisdom of Adam Smith.'"[40]

Keynes had never quite let go of the "classical" essence; he would never repudiate his radical constructions. If that left vast ambiguities, it also granted full freedom to those who came after him to contribute not an imitation of his initiatives, but work as original and challenging.

Notes

1. E. A. G. Robinson. "John Maynard Keynes," *Economic Journal* 57 (March 1947): 1-68; quotations, pp. 27, 40, 41.
2. G. L. S. Shackle, *The Nature of Economic Thought* (Cambridge, 1966), 53.
3. Robinson, "John Maynard Keynes," 41.
4. Joseph A. Schumpeter, *Ten Great Economists* (London, 1952), 287-88.
5. As Keynes wrote to Richard Kahn, 14 May 1931, *CW,* 20: 310.
6. Lectures and discussion, ibid., 13: 343-67; ibid., 20: 529-44.
7. Roosevelt quoted, editorial note, ibid., 21: 273; Keynes's article, pp. 273-79; headline and quotation, p. 273.
8. Editorial note, ibid., 289; Skidelsky, *JMK,* 2: 492; Moggridge, *MK,* 580-81; letter, *New York Times,* 31 December 1933, *CW,* 21: 289-97; quotations, pp. 289, 296, 290.
9. Keynes's notes quoted, Harrod, *The Life,* 20; Frances Perkins, *The Roosevelt I Knew* (New York, 1946), p. 225.
10. Excerpt, letter, 11 June 1934, quoted in Harrod, *The Life,* 448. Other accounts of Keynes's U.S. visit, Skidelsky *JMK,* 2: 504-9; Moggridge, *MK,* 581-83.
11. Editorial notes, *CW,* 21: 320-21; ibid., 13: 456; Keynes's talk to economists, ibid., 457-68.
12. Ibid., 21: 322-29. Keynes attempted two more letters in 1938 but got a cool reply to the first and evidently none to the second; the letters, ibid., 434-39, 440.
13. Letter to his mother, 4 April 1941, ibid., 22: 353-54; quotation, p. 353; see also Moggridge, *MK,* 642-48.
14. Quoted, Moggridge, *MK,* 714.
15. Robert Lekachman, *The Age of Keynes* (New York, 1966), 153-75; quotation from Employment Act, p. 171.
16. John R. Hicks, *The Crisis in Keynesian Economics* (New York, 1974), 2.
17. See John Kenneth Galbraith, "How Keynes Came to America," in *A Contemporary Guide to Economics Peace and Laughter* (Boston, 1971), 43-59. A later Galbraith account with other details, *A Life in Our Times* (Boston, 1981), 61-91.
18. John R. Hicks, "Mr. Keynes's Theory of Employment," *Collected Essays on Economic Theory,* Vol. 2: *Money, Interest and Wages* (Cambridge, MA, 1982), 84-99; quotations, pp. 84, 99. From *Economic Journal* 46 (June 1936): 238-53.
19. Keynes to Hicks, 31 August, and Hicks's reply, 2 September 1936, *CW,* 14: 72, 72-74; quotation, p. 72.
20. In Hicks, *Collected Essays,* Vol. 2, 101-15; quotation, p. 106. From *Econometrica* 5 (April 1937): 147-59.
21. Letter, Keynes to Hicks, 13 March 1937, *CW,* 14: 79-81; quotation, p. 79.
22. Hicks, "Mr. Keynes and the Classics," *Collected Essays,* Vol. 2, 108, 109.
23. Hicks, "Recollections and Documents" (paper at conference, Merton College, Oxford, 3-4 July 1972), *Economica* 40 (February 1973): 1-11; quotation, p. 11.

24. Cited here in chap. 11, Hansen, "Mr. Keynes on Underemployment Equilibrium," in Wood, ed., *JMK: Critical Assessments,* 2: 83.
25. Ed. Seymour Harris, New York.
26. Alvin H. Hansen, "The General Theory"; also in M. G. Mueller, ed. *Readings in Macroeconomics,* 16–23; quotations, p. 23.
27. Alvin H. Hansen, *Fiscal Policy and Business Cycles* (New York, 1941), viii; Galbraith, "How Keynes Came to America," 49.
28. Discussion, Alvin H. Hansen, *A Guide to Keynes* (New York, 1953), pp. 140–53.
29. Paul A. Samuelson, "Lord Keynes and *The General Theory,*" in Wood, ed., *JMK: Critical Assessments,* 2: 190–202; quotations, pp. 191–92, 193, 200, 193, respectively. From *Econometrica* 14 (July 1946): 187–200.
30. References here to Paul A. Samuelson and William D. Nordhaus, *Economics,* 14th ed. (New York, 1992). Nordhaus recently joined Samuelson as collaborator.
31. Mark Blaug, *Great Economists Since Keynes* (New York, 1988), 215.
32. Diagram, Samuelson and Nordhaus, *Economics,* 537; text, ibid., 536–37.
33. Ibid., 275.
34. Dennis H. Robertson, *Essays in Monetary Theory* (London, 1940), 1–38.
35. Joan Robinson, *The Rate of Interest and Other Essays* (London, 1952), 3–30; quotation, p. 3.
36. Hyman P. Minsky, *John Maynard Keynes* (New York, 1975), v. Also, Hyman P. Minsky, "The Financial Instability Hypothesis," in Wood, ed., *JMK: Critical Assessments,* 4: 282–92; quotation, p. 290. From *Nebraska Journal of Economics and Business* 16 (Winter 1977): 5–16.
37. Axel Leijunhufvud, *Keynesian Economics...,* subtitled *A Study in Monetary Theory* (New York, 1968).
38. In Robert W. Clower, *Money and Markets: Essays by Robert W. Clower,* ed. Donald Walker (Cambridge, 1984); motif of uncertainty, "Keynes and the Classics: A Dynamical Perspective" (1960 article), 21–26; the "dual-decision hypothesis" as variant on effective demand, "The Keynesian Counter-Revolution: A Theoretical Appraisal" (1965 article), pp. 34–58; the "'monsters'" and "well-focused research program" (p. 267), "Afterward" (1980 paper), pp. 259–72.
39. Harry G. Johnson, "The Shadow of Keynes," in Johnson and Johnson, *The Shadow of Keynes,* n. 159.
40. John Maynard Keynes, "The Balance of Payments of the United States," *CW,* 27: 427–46; quotations, pp. 444, 445. From *Economic Journal* 56 (June 1946): 172–87; quotations, pp. 185, 186.

Epilogue: Sic et Non

In 1941 Friedrich von Hayek rigorously and rightly accused Keynes of "a betrayal of the main duty of the economist."[1] Keynes, as Hayek protested, had violated the laws of responsible thinking in economic science, a capital professional crime. He had traversed the length of neoclassical theory, a self-disciplined way of addressing the hard and sometimes cruel problems of economy and economic choice, and ruthlessly broken or bent every one of its fundamental components: Say's equality of supply and demand, supply-and-demand determination of the price of real values *and* money, the irreducible nature of scarcity, the illimitable nature of demand, the ubiquity of the margin, and equilibrium as defender of the economy against centrifugal forces. He turned a science into a shambles and went on to invite dreamers and demagogues, himself foremost, to transform the shambles into the model of a self-indulgent utopia: a stationary state (to appropriate a conception used by the classical John Stuart Mill) of sufficient capital, satiated demand, and, as Harry Johnson saw it, the peaceful coexistence of a well-rewarded ruling elite and an obediently satisfied substratum of fully, if modestly, employed inferiors. Other demagogues, accepting Keynes's invitation but overbidding him, could insert growth and envy into their utopias, and make them increasingly wealthy and dangerously dynamic.

An attentive reading of *The General Theory* registers a high sum of a remarkable variety of instances of paralogic: the unidirectional character of its model, the hidden tenets of the petitio principii, the false analogies, the irrelevant proof of the ignoratio elenchi, the pars pro toto and the related exclusion of vast economic sectors like production and all too common conditions like inflation, the elimination of essential economic agents like the entrepreneur-borrower in interest-rate determination, the qualified argument that loses its qualified character in the succeeding pages, the false attribution of given meanings to the opposing theory (which are thereupon elegantly refuted), the absolute self-

contradictions as in the identity/equality/inequality of saving and investment, the too easy shifting of economic factors between the actual and
the *ex ante*/intended/expected/prospective mode, the double character
of liquidity preference as desire for liquidity and for too much of it, the
false statement of the one diagram in the book (on the neoclassical interest theory), the superior reality of Keynes's money illusion, the reversal
of cause and effect (thus interest rate determining investment), the frequent occupation of the excluded middle, the noncommunication between the theoretical and the empirical or historical, the easy,
unprofessional condemnation of such economic agents as rentiers and
bankers, and the requirement that numerous theses be accepted without
proof. Keynes is the greatest confidence man in economic science since
Marx.

One jewel-like example of the blight Keynes cast on *thinking* was
contributed in a speech by John Anderson, a former chancellor of the
exchequer, in October 1945. He was commenting on the policy of his
Labour successor, Hugh Dalton, who had reduced short-term interest
rates as part of a Keynesian expansive policy. With World War II just
over, demand high, and shortages throughout the economy, it was, as
Keynes might have said, a crazy policy, but he could not undo his too
successful persuasions. Anderson, speaking for the Opposition in the
budget debate, was remarkably gracious and forbearing: "I do not hesi-
tate to say that if I had been in [Dalton's] position, I should have done
what he has done." Anderson went on to give the House of Commons a
Keynesian lecture: "The whole problem of interest rates is a fascinating
one. Interest rates, as I understand the position, do not respond fully to
the ordinary economic laws of supply and demand. There is what may
be called a psychological factor."[2] Keynes's long campaign for low interest rates had achieved mindless acceptance. One can easily imagine
that one of his epigones had been skillfully briefing Anderson. With
Conservative, as well as Labour, opinion so persuaded, Dalton went on
leading British finances (some of the money provided by Keynes's loan
negotiations) deeper into deficit until late 1947, when Stafford Cripps
succeeded him and instituted his famous austerity program. Theoretical
nonsense cast aside, the government permitted interest rates to rise to
more appropriate levels.

It is not surprising that John Hicks, appalled at what he had helped
Keynes create, distanced himself from it in a series of lectures given in

April 1973 and published under the title *The Crisis in Keynesian Economics.*[3] At the time he was properly concerned with accelerating inflation and what he had come to see as *The General Theory*'s rationalization of inflation-generating policies, hence *The Crisis.*... In 1980 Daniel Bell and Irving Kristol, editors of the neoconservative quarterly *The Public Interest,* devoted an entire issue to what they also agreed was a crisis. They published the articles making up that issue as the book *The Crisis in Economic Theory* the next year. They meant *Keynesian* theory, as their introduction made clear: "Keynes's own ideas have become the orthodoxy of academic economists and politicians, with the dissenters now regarding them as the *mortmain* that must be lifted if economic theory is to rise to the tasks of the day."[4] Most of the contributions, which represented the range of economic opinion, agreed, if they agreed on little else. One article announced "The Dissolution of the Keynesian Consensus,"[5] but like the others, could not suggest how to dislodge its *mortmain.* The problem lay in the combination of *The General Theory*'s paralogic with what was seen, by the 1970s and before that decade's inflationary burst, as the long success of Keynesian policy, with such exemplars of conservatism as Richard Milhous Nixon calling themselves Keynesians. Hicks had found economists as vulnerable as the pragmatists of politics to Keynes's miraculous ideation. They seemed unable to think their way out of it. The noneconomist Irving Kristol reviewed all the contributions, found economics "at something like an impasse," and concluded with "The Bedrock Truths of Economics," which turned out to be a summary of the neoclassical verities.[6]

Later in the 1980s, another article collection, published by the (British) Institute of Economic Affairs under the title *Keynes's* General Theory: *50 Years On,* found the condition of its subject even more critical. One contributor, expressing the majority opinion, saw *The General Theory* as a sphinx that "stares down on us after fifty years and we read into it what we will." He added, as unappreciative of history as of the book, "One hundred years on I expect it will be lost in the oblivion of history."[7]

Another expression of the crisis in theory is the existence of the rational expectations school, also called "the new classical economics." In the Bell-Kristol compendium one of its proponents rejected Keynesian ideas as "fundamentally wrong" but could not quite specify why.[8] Without going to the root of Keynesian error, the rational-expectations view, originating early in the 1960s, argues that economic agents rationally anticipate Keynesian macroeconomic policies and, in so doing, radically reduce or destroy their effectiveness.[9] If, for example, the government adopts an expansive policy meant to reduce unemployment, lenders, expecting more inflation, will demand higher interest rates on their loans and thus counterbalance the government's action. This makes sense, and, in fact, explains the failure of given macroeconomic measures in the past, but the sense consists of a significant qualification of a theory, hardly something that could be called a free-standing theory itself. The best value of this new thinking, as Kristol's commentary suggests, has been to reaffirm the usable truths in the old neoclassical economics.

Symmetrically, it has remained for Friedrich von Hayek, as long-enduring exponent of the older theory, to suggest an accommodation with post-neoclassical views. In 1974, while beginning to adjust his thought, he remained adamant on Keynes's "responsibility for current worldwide inflation." As he put it to British newspaper readers, "What we are experiencing are simply the economic consequences of Lord Keynes."[10] In a 1975 lecture, however, Hayek was fair enough to say that he had been wrong and Keynes right about dealing with the Depression. "I did then believe that a short process of deflation might break [the] rigidity of money wages...and that in this way we could restore a determination of relative wages by the market," he told a conference on monetary problems in Rome. "But I no longer believe that it is...possible to achieve this in this manner." He had been wrong to give the task to the free market.[11] With a sense of its limitations readjusting its advice, neoclassical economics, as Kristol argued, has much to say to the present and future ages.

No one, certainly not Keynes, has refuted any one of the fundamental theses of neoclassical economic theory. The law of supply and demand worked as inexorably under Stalin as it did under Gladstone or Coolidge. The Soviet Russian official prices might deny it, but the actions of humans expressed it in queues, shortages, premiums valued more than money, and time expended in purchasing or seeking to purchase. The one difficulty in neoclassical economics is that it cannot isolate the economy from society and polity. The economist is always talking society and politics when he applies his pure theory to the real world. We have seen that Keynes realized this and tried consciously to shuttle between economics and politics, the latter including the social *and* psychosocial factors.

The Great Depression misleadingly validated *The General Theory*. It should be repeated here: the book's pure theory is pure nonsense. But it was great politics. *The Economic Consequences of the Peace* was better economics; indeed, it can explain the Depression while *The General Theory* cannot. The earlier work correctly argued that the political-economic errors of the peace compounded the economic distortions of the war itself, that the result would be terrific economic disorder leading to economic and political breakdown. It was these factors that prepared the disaster of the 1930s as assisted by a few others: the huge new economic power of the United States combined with its international economic and political irresponsibility, Britain's continuing relative decline along with the depleting effort to maintain its old primacy, the disappearance of Russia as a market and a collegial nation, and the Balkanization of Central Europe. As Keynes had warned, the interconnected international debt had a particularly nefarious effect. The leading nations were strung between the monstrously wealthy American and the dangerously vulnerable German economies, the first sucking in war-debt payments, the last straining to pay increasing reparation sums, until the Hoover Moratorium of 1931 halted the insanity—too late!

The United States had made matters all the worse by sterilizing much of the money inflow rather than letting it increase American prices and so classically shift the terms of trade more to the advantage of the other, poorer nations. The American inflation thus failed to appear in the monetary system but erupted into the stock market. "[T]he position is serious when enterprise becomes the bubble on a whirlpool of speculation" (*The General Theory*, p. 159). The Crash annihilated the normal defenses: the United States had no unemployment insurance, pension system, and the other elements of a social safety net. In its history of abrupt declines, the American economy, unemployment befalling a quarter of the work force, suffered its greatest disaster. Meanwhile, the dominant economic thinking was rigidly subservient to neoclassical principles, as Hayek admitted in his case, and blind, or nearly so, to the effects of governmental policies on the economy. The other major nations, relativized into economic dwarfs by the colossal bulk of the United States, were dragged down with it. One example of their vulnerability, as worsened by the reparation situation, was the great unemployment figure in Germany. With more than a third of the insured workers out of work, it was the greatest proportion among the major nations and threatened to bankrupt the national unemployment-insurance system. The problem of unemployment payments paralyzed the Weimar Republic, turned it into a semi-dictatorship, and set it up for the Nazi takeover. The domino effect among nations, meanwhile, was intensified by generalized economic nationalism, the American Smoot-Hawley Tariff of 1930, superimposed on the excessive height of earlier American tariffs, in the lead and closely followed by the German policy of severe restrictions on imports. Keynes had been unforgivably right about such economic, and *their* political, consequences.

It has been shown here how the neoclassical Keynes practiced his theorizing upon Britain's depression of the 1920s, how he failed with the *Treatise on Money* and how, given a second chance, got it right—in the sense of *political* economy—on his second try. Constrained by his training, limiting himself to the old Marshallian and Wicksellian materials, he made it both too difficult and too easy for himself. The General Theory as a model worked so well because there was so little to it, some parts saved from the wreck of the neoclassical *Treatise on Money,* and others borrowed from Hobson and other cranks. All the simple mechanism had to do was to express a global economic leakage that appeared more specifically in weak consumption and investment. A crucial characteristic of the model, as important as any active part of its machinery, was its inability to express inflation. Hayek was right: to the extent that it was heeded, *The General Theory* manufactured inflation while denying its existence. All sensible economists in that period of destructive deflation agreed that inflation was indeed the cure, Dennis Robertson, as noted above (chapter 11), defining the book's message as "engineered reflation." Only the political Keynes found the formula to win inflation's benefits without its disadvantages—in the short run.

Keynes had justified the right policy with false arguments. There was no endemic weakness of consumption and investment, simply a short-run decline resulting, as sketched here, from perversities of the political economy. Yet beneath this layer of falsity was a true sense of deeper economic phenomena—of the fundamental political economy.

The great political value of *The General Theory* was demonstrated in one important way during the Cold War. Approaching the end of World War II, economists were predicting huge unemployment and the possibility of severe depression. Meanwhile, as recounted here, Keynes's ideas had seized the leadership of the Western nations. The result was double: planning and substantive action in shifting from wartime to peacetime

without significant unemployment and the confidence to do it while com-
peting with the threat represented by Soviet Russia and *its* confidence in
having mastered the economic problem. The Western leadership, its
morale wounded by the Great Depression, would have been under heavy
handicap without the hope Keynes had promised. In this case the psychology was more important than the substance: it is irrelevant that the
feared unemployment never came, chiefly because of the great shortages and the resultant high demand, and only secondarily because of the
early Keynesian policies.

Keynes was aware, as other economists were not, of the government's
growing *economic* importance. *The General Theory* is also his reaction
to that. Before he began writing it, his almost immediate response to the
crisis was to recommend the creation of an economic general staff. Correctly calling himself a "democratic socialist," he understood that the
government had the responsibility to take the initiative aggressively and
manage the economy, nothing less than that. His intense, furiously frustrating work on the Economic Advisory Council and the Macmillan
Committee in 1929-31 expressed his thought accurately. Although he
failed to articulate it in the book, he had got the sense of the massive
shift toward governmental involvement in the structure of an advanced
economy.

In *The General Theory,* however, Keynes gave away the best arguments for his "democratic socialism," the two big things neoclassical
orthodoxy could not quite appreciate but which silently influenced his
thinking. One he simply did not mention while he explicitly excluded
the other. The first was the economic importance of government itself.
The process was well enough under way at the time of the book; today—to make his case contemporary—more than one third of the American Gross Domestic Product and more than half of Britain's (and, e.g.,
Sweden's), are taken in taxes by those governments and poured back as
expenditures. Government is the biggest business in any modern
economy, but its economic operations do not obey the economic laws.
Alone, economic theory is helpless. The other big thing was the growth
of the great corporations, but in the restatement of his theory, as quoted
here earlier, Keynes had stipulated, "We take as given...the existing
quality and quantity of available equipment, the existing techniques, the
degree of competition," and many other things.[12] This was to deny what
he knew very well, and as emphasized by Joan Robinson's book on

imperfect competition, that economies of scale, giving the advantage to these increasingly larger firms, were transforming economy, society, polity. Keynes had been responding to this development in the 1920s when he nominated the Bank of England as one of the coordinating agencies. One reason for the government's increasing magnitude was its need to control the trusts (today's conglomerates and multinational corporations) if they were not to control it. Democratic government and free (although somewhat decreasingly free) enterprise are cooperating in building the socialism of the future, although to this day government and society in the advanced countries refuse to be conscious of it.

The general principle of this unobtrusive socialism of the future, and perforce of the present and lengthening past, was institutionalized in the Keynesian British White Paper *Employment Policy* of 1944, the U.S. Employment Act of 1946, and similar actions by other nations, as noted here in the previous chapter. Within that frame and so a commitment to maintaining socially desirable employment levels, thus accepting general responsibility for governmental leadership of the economy, innumerable specific measures have piled up a mass of socialistic instances, which themselves have formed precedents for more action in that sense. Departing office, President Dwight D. Eisenhower, a prime figure in it, warned of the military-industrial complex, a nationwide interweaving of governmental and private enterprise in another dynamic socialist pattern. During the Depression, taking their depositors' money with them, 5,000 of the nation's 24,000 banks had failed. It was agreed that nothing of the sort would happen again, thus the Federal Deposit Insurance Corporation. In the same sense, toward the end of the century, actions going well beyond that were taken at the taxpayers' expense to prevent a general collapse of the savings-and-loan institutions. Similarly, a consensus thought that the Lockheed Corporation was too essential an element in national defense (and too great an employer) to be permitted to go bankrupt, while the demise of the Chrysler Corporation would have meant a general weakening of American industry and unbearable regional unemployment: the U.S. government suspended the inexorable laws of economic survival and helped save both.

In another economic action, the terrific inequality in medical care has combined with magical, but extravagantly expensive, technical improvements, dialysis machines and equipment used in neonatal medicine, for example, to drive the United States, like other advanced countries, toward a more or less governmentally managed medical system, hence socialized or socialistic or quasi-socialist medicine, linguistic specification becoming a waste of energy. Nor is it necessary for congress to legislate and presidency to execute explicitly in this sense. Any substantial private firm makes its major decisions conditioned on the government's attitude: our political leaders are effortlessly socialist.

Superficially viewed, other phenomena prominent in the twentieth century's waning years might seem to reverse, some spectacularly so, this Keynesian-socialist direction: the privatization movement in the advanced countries, the colossal implosion of the Soviet variant of socialism with *its* privatization actions, and, leading the Asiatic rimlands, the overwhelming success of Japanese capitalism. Closer examination, however, establishes the proper proportions of capitalism-and-socialism according to Keynes. Indeed, with the aid of such phenomena, one can further develop his general theory of political economy to comprehend both the somewhat capitalistic and the former Soviet worlds.

We might remind ourselves of Keynes's last words in his posthumous article on the "permanent truth [of] the classical teaching," specifically the "invisible hand" and the other enduring ideas of Adam Smith (chapter 12). Together with Keynes's socialistic pronouncements, this statement throws a loop of understanding and support over virtually all major constructive actions upon the world economy to this day.

In the 1980s the parallel governments of Margaret Thatcher and Ronald Reagan proclaimed pristine capitalistic principles and led their countries deeper into socialism. Neither leader could effectively reduce their social-welfare establishments. Perhaps Mrs. Thatcher's most substantive economic action was to snatch back from the Trades Union Congress the governmental power it had usurped; this was to restore the leadership over the economy to a properly elected government so that it could carry on with socialism. The handing over of a few nationalized enterprises to private ownership has weighed little in the balance. Somewhat similarly, Ronald Reagan broke the imprudent air controllers union and reduced labor power with the help of other self-defeating union actions, but his administration, vastly expanding the military-industrial complex, made government a bigger business than ever. His espousal of deregulation has had modest effect; indeed the eventual result in the air transportation industry, during the succeeding administrations of the Republican Bush and the Democrat Clinton, has been to kill off the weaker firms and produce greater monopolization, hence a more pressing need for governmental management, hence the full circle back toward a socialistic variant. Exhausted, these conservative Anglo-American efforts were succeeded by a general renunciation of their mild rigors. Socialism inched ever forward.

The self-destruction of Soviet-style socialism functioned comfortably in the Keynesian sense. Keynes had detested Marxism as the conversion of reactionary utopian ideas into a ferocious religion; and found life in Soviet Russia a horror. His democratic socialism demanded precisely that feedback of private opinion which the Soviet Russian leaders excluded from their system and so brought about that process of self-destruction. In one way or another most of the new leaders in the whole ex-Soviet region have tried to create a more or less democratic socialism, one consistent with free enterprise. The various resistances to privatization have included many objective factors, particularly the threat of unemployment, as well as the subjective and inevitably declining efforts of unregenerate Communists. Also among the objective factors are those that are impelling the advanced non-Soviet world toward *its* democratic socialism, ultimately the need to *govern* the economy according to the principles of democracy and efficiency. In a Keynesian sense the two worlds, absent, perhaps, Red China and other dictatorial regimes, converge. And even China has blunted its hard edges with peripheral capitalist practices and increasing economic dependence on trade with the United States, Japan, and other theoretically hostile states.

Another indication of socialism's persistence and ubiquity, assisted by reverberating international effects, is the case of Japan as a conquering capitalistic economy. While that success has been generated by the great entrepreneurship of its business leaders, the close relations between business and government have permitted the detailed planning of economic action in a substantially pansocialistic, pan-Keynesian manner. (Japan has read Keynes as closely as the Western nations.) Joint operations have been institutionalized by the creation of the notorious MITI, the Ministry of International Trade and Industry, which sponsors cooperation among private firms, in other words, the creation of monopolistic operations to improve efficiency and win competitive advantages in international trade. Defending itself against such practices, the United States has, in fact, emulated them. Thus, it set up a governmental program to combine the efforts of several computer-chip manufacturers and so protect the country's position in computer production generally. More broadly, the old Bureau of Standards has been transformed into the National Institute of Standards and Technology, uncannily in MITI's image, with the announced objective of promoting advanced technology in industry generally. The United States has found one more route to socialism.

And so our own mostly neoclassical world is moving into socialism following the mostly neoclassical Keynes. If it is not the socialism of Marxian fanatics, it is also not the socialism of gentler reformers. It will disappoint both, who joined in dreaming of a completely just society. The real socialism of the future will retain too many of the realities the old socialists thought to eliminate, the great inequalities, deeply ingrained or random injustice, discrimination, irreducible insecurity, the wretched layers and patches of poverty, and, of course, inflation: real socialism in an intractably real world.

Although his own impressionistic speculations did not reach so far, Keynes permitted himself to be instructed by Friedrich von Hayek's *Road to Freedom* (1944) on the threat to liberty and efficiency of any socialist solution. He read it on his way to America for the Bretton Woods negotiations and, on 28 June 1944, took the time to write Hayek from Atlantic City: "[I]t is a grand book." He made the precision: "You will not expect me to accept quite all the economic dicta in it." Against Hayek's strictures he defended the need for planning but, once again recurring to the Mooreian good, hoped that persons who "wholly share your moral position" would resist socialism's negative aspects. In sum, "morally and philosophically I find myself in agreement with virtually the whole of it; and not only in agreement with, but in a deeply moved agreement."[13]

The threat in socialism is still with us. Normally the leaders of any socialist state will move toward total power, the goal that Soviet communism approximately achieved before losing all, and the general inefficiency of a command economy. In the old Soviet Union the governmental and the money power were fused and wielded integrally by the masters of the party-state. In the democratic nations today, with their still vital, still somewhat free enterprise, the people with money have comparatively little power, while the political and administrative personnel are similarly deficient in money. If this leads to corruption, as private wealth tries to buy economic advantage from the needy people in government, it also makes either group a check on the other's drive for more money or power. A democratic socialism will tend to lose such a guarantee without vigorous counteraction. The gradual nature of the process, however, gives such a society time to counter the governmental thrust by appropriately resistant measures. The passage of the Freedom of Information Act is one example of giving private persons and groups the legal power to oppose political and bureaucratic tyranny; it can serve as a model for other measures seeking the same end. Granted, this defensive scenario is less than inspiring, but history teaches us that total and permanent safety is one of the greatest utopian delusions. Keynes, student of Edmund Burke and defender of a nongolden mean, would instinctively know how to act if he found himself at a given point in socialism's creep toward tyranny. While enjoying his first editions and the rest of his multiple interests, he would conjure up models of political economy to keep society tolerably democratic and efficient. He would remain a revolutionary within the establishment.

Notes

1. Friedrich von Hayek, "The Economics of Abundance," excerpt from *The Pure Theory of Capital* (1941), in Hazlitt, ed., *The Critics of Keynesian Economics*, 129.
2. Debate, 24 October 1945, quoted, J. C. R. Dow, *The Management of the British Economy 1945–1960* (Cambridge, 1970; 1st ed., 1964), n. 225.
3. John R. Hicks, *The Crisis in Keynesian Economics* (New York, 1974), thus, "The view which emerges...is more radical than 'full employment without inflation'; it is nothing less than...inflation does not matter" (p. 61).
4. Daniel Bell and Irving Kristol, eds., *The Crisis in Economic Theory* (New York, 1981), vii.
5. James W. Dean, "The Dissolution of the Keynesian Consensus," in ibid., 19–34.
6. Irving Kristol, "Rationalism in Economics," in ibid., 201–18; quotations, p. 217.
7. Michael Beenstock, "*The General Theory,* Secular Stagnation, and the World Economy," in *Keynes's* General Theory: *Fifty Years On,* ed. John Burton (London, 1986), 121–35; quotations, pp. 121, 135.
   Keynes's latter-day defenders have shown increasing embarrassment in dealing with crisis and critics. Two recent major biographies, both quasi-official and both gratefully cited here, have expressed, each in its own way, the difficulty in sheltering *The General Theory* from criticism. In his 941-page work, subtitled *An Economist's Biography,* Donald E. Moggridge, managing editor of the Keynes *Collected Writings,* dispenses with any analysis of it, although he analyzes the *Treatise on Probability* at length and the *Treatise on Money* briefly. In his book *John Maynard Keynes,* Vol. 2: *The Economist as Saviour 1920–1937* (731 pp.), Robert Skidelsky devotes one long chapter and part of another to it, but his dis-

cussion, pursuing the suggestion of the title, proposes the transcending of economics: "Just as Keynes was more—and perhaps less—than an economist, so *The General Theory* is both more and less than a book of economics" (p. 538). In this perspective, "The fundamental unity between Keynes's liquidity-preference theory of interest and the rest of his ideas...lies at the instinctive, or visionary, level" (p. 563). If Moggridge says nothing about the sense of *The General Theory,* Skidelsky removes it from testing by reality.

8. Mark H. Willes, "'Rational Expectations' as a Counter-Revolution," Bell and Kristol, eds., *The Crisis in Economic Theory,* 81-96; quotation, p. 81.

9. See, for example, G. K. Shaw, *Rational Expectations* (New York, 1984). In his *Keynesian Economics: The Permanent Revolution* (Aldershot, 1988), however, Shaw saw the "new Keynesian economics" of the 1980s as effectively restoring Keynesianism. N. Gregory Mankiw and David Romer, eds., *New Keynesian Economics* (Cambridge, MA, 1991), claim that their collaborators have "refuted" the theses of rational expectations (introduction, p. 15). But, like rational expectations, the new Keynesian economics has neglected to examine Keynes's *theory* and concentrates on contemporary policy issues.

10. "Inflation's Path to Unemployment," *Daily Telegraph* (London), 15, 16 October 1974, in Friedrich A. Hayek, *New Studies in Philosophy, Politics, Economics, and the History of Ideas* (Chicago, 1978), 192-96; quotations, p. 192. See also "The Campaign Against Keynesian Inflation," in Hayek, *New Studies,* 191-231.

11. Ibid., 206.

12. *CW,* 7: 245.

13. Letter, ibid., 27: 385-88; quotations, pp. 385, 387, 385.

Bibliography

Archival Sources

Public Record Office, London

Cabinet. Conclusions of the meetings of the Cabinet, 7 October 1929–16 December 1931. Vols. 62–69.

Committee on Finance and Industry. Discussions, 20 February–21 March 1930. T 200/4.

———. Discussions, 23 October–11 November 1930. T 200/5.

———. Discussions, 20 November–5 December 1930. T 200/6.

Economic Advisory Council. Memoranda by the staff, 1930–35. CAB 53/14.

———. Memoranda, April 1930–April 1934. Series H, CAB/10–13.

———. Minutes of meetings, 17 February 1930–1 May 1930. CAB 58/2.

———. Notes, December 1929. CAB 58/15.

———. Committee on Economic Information. Meetings, 15 September 1931–4 July 1939. CAB 58/17.

———. Committee on Economic Information. Memoranda, 14 September 1931–8 May 1933. CAB 58/18.

Treasury Class List. Papers of Sir Richard Hopkins. T 175.

———. Papers of Sir Otto Niemeyer. T 176.

———. Papers of Sir Frederick Phillips. T 177.

Published Sources

The Collected Writings of John Maynard Keynes, 30 vols., ed. Sir Austin Robinson and Donald E. Moggridge. London: Published for the Royal Economic Society by Macmillan, 1971–89.

Volume	Title
I	*Indian Currency and Finance*
II	*The Economic Consequences of the Peace*
III	*A Revision of the Treaty*
IV	*A Tract on Monetary Reform*
V	*A Treatise on Money, 1: The Pure Theory of Money*
VI	*A Treatise on Money, 2: The Applied Theory of Money*
VII	*The General Theory of Employment, Interest and Money*
VIII	*A Treatise on Probability*
IX	*Essays in Persuasion*
X	*Essays in Biography*
XI	*Economic Articles and Correspondence: Academic*
XII	*Economic Articles and Correspondence: Investment and Editorial*
XIII	*The General Theory and After:* Part I, *Preparation*
XIV	*The General Theory and After:* Part II, *Defence and Development*
XV	*Activities 1906–14: India and Cambridge*
XVI	*Activities 1914–19: The Treasury and Versailles*
XVII	*Activities 1920–22: Treaty Revision and Reconstruction*
XVIII	*Activities 1922–32: The End of Reparations*
XIX	*Activities 1922–29:* 2 Vols., *The Return to Gold and Industrial Policy, I and II*
XX	*Activities 1929–31: Rethinking Employment and Unemployment Policies*
XXI	*Activities 1931–39: World Crises and Policies in Britain and America*
XXII	*Activities 1939–45: Internal War Finance*
XXIII	*Activities 1940–43: External War Finance*
XXIV	*Activities 1944–46: The Transition to Peace*
XXV	*Activities 1940–44: Shaping the Post-War World: The Clearing Union*
XXVI	*Activities 1941–46: Shaping the Post-War World: Bretton Woods and Reparations*
XXVII	*Activities 1940–46: Shaping the Post-War World: Employment and Commodities*
XXVIII	*Social, Political and Literary Writings*
XXIX	*The General Theory and After: A Supplement*
XXX	*Bibliography and Index*

About Keynes

Blaug, Mark. *John Maynard Keynes: Life, Ideas, Legacy.* London: Macmillan, 1990.

Chandavakar, Anand. *Keynes and India: A Study in Economics and Biography.* London: Macmillan, 1989.

Fetter, Frank W. "Lenin, Keynes, and Inflation." *Economica* 44 (February 1977): 77–80.

Harrod, Roy F. *The Life of John Maynard Keynes.* New York: W. W. Norton, 1982 (1st ed.: 1951).

Hession, Charles H. *John Maynard Keynes: A Personal Biography...* New York: Macmillan, 1984.

Jenkins, Roy. "Maynard Keynes." *The Times,* London, 18, 20, 21 March 1972.

Johnson, Elizabeth S. *"The Collected Writings of John Maynard Keynes:* Some Visceral Reactions." In *Essays in Modern Economics,* edited by Michael Parkin and A. R. Nobay. London: Longman, 1973.

Johnson, Elizabeth S., and Harry G. Johnson. *The Shadow of Keynes.* Chicago: University of Chicago Press, 1978.

Keynes, Florence Ada. *Gathering up the Threads: A Study in Family Biography.* Cambridge: Heffer, 1950.

Keynes, Geoffrey. *The Gates of Memory.* Oxford: Clarendon Press, 1981.

Keynes, John Maynard, and Lydia Lopokova. *The Letters of John Maynard Keynes and Lydia Lopokova,* edited by Polly Hill and Richard Keynes. New York: Charles Scribner's Sons, 1989.

Keynes, Milo, ed. *Essays on John Maynard Keynes.* Cambridge: Cambridge University Press, 1975.

Moggridge, Donald E. *Keynes.* London: Macmillan, 1980 (1st ed.: 1976).

———. "Keynes: The Economist." Mimeograph of lecture, Keynes College, University of Kent, 10 November 1972.

———. *Maynard Keynes: An Economist's Biography.* London and New York: Routledge, 1992.

Pigou, Arthur C., and Richard F. Kahn. *John Maynard Keynes, Baron Keynes of Tilton 1883–1946.* Pamphlet, proceedings of the British Academy, vol. 32. London: Geoffrey Camberlege, n.d.

Robbins, Lionel, and James Meade. *The Wartime Diaries of Lionel Robbins and James Meade,* edited by Susan Howson and Donald E. Moggridge. London: Macmillan, 1990.

Robinson, E. A. G. *John Maynard Keynes: Economist-Author-Statesman.* Pamphlet. London: Oxford University Press, 1971.

———. "John Maynard Keynes." *Economic Journal* 57 (March 1947): 1–68.

Rosenbaum, S. P. "Keynes, Lawrence and Cambridge Revisited." *The Cambridge Quarterly* 11, no. 1 (Fall 1982): 252–64.

Samuelson, Paul A. "Lord Keynes and *The General Theory.*" In Wood, ed. *John Maynard Keynes Critical Assessments,* 2: 190–202.

Skidelsky, Robert. *John Maynard Keynes,* Vol. 1: *Hopes Betrayed 1883–1920.* New York: Viking, 1986 (1st ed. 1983); Vol. 2: *The Economist as Saviour 1920–1937.* London: Macmillan, 1992.

———. "Keynes and the Reconstruction of Liberalism." *Encounter* 52 (April 1979): 29–37.

Straight, Michael. *After Long Silence.* New York: W. W. Norton, 1983.

Persons

Bell, Clive. *Civilization and Old Friends.* Chicago: University of Chicago Press, 1973.

Bell, Quentin. *Virginia Woolf: A Biography.* New York: Harcourt Brace Jovanovich, 1974.

Blaug, Mark. *Great Economists Before Keynes.* New York: Cambridge University Press, 1988 (1st ed.: 1986).

———. *Great Economists Since Keynes.* New York: Cambridge University Press, 1988 (1st ed.: 1985).

Boyle, Andrew. *Montagu Norman: A Biography.* London: Cassell, 1967.

Bullock, Alan. *The Life and Times of Ernest Bevin,* Vol. 1: *Trade Union Leader 1881–1940.* London: Heinemann, 1960.

Campbell, John. *Lloyd George: The Goat in the Wilderness 1922–1931.* London: Jonathan Cape, 1977.

Crick, Bernard. *George Orwell: A Life.* Boston: Little, Brown, 1981.

Deacon, Richard. *The Cambridge Apostles.* New York: Farrar, Straus and Giroux, 1985.

Edel, Leon. *Bloomsbury: A House of Lions.* Philadelphia: Lippincott, 1979.

Gerzina, Gretchen. *Carrington.* London: John Murray, 1989.

Henderson, Hubert D. *The Inter-War Years and Other Papers,* edited by Henry Clay. Oxford: Clarendon Press, 1955.

Holroyd, Michael. *Lytton Strachey.* 2 vols. New York: Holt, Rinehart and Winston, 1968.

Keynes, Milo, ed. *Lydia Lopokova.* London: Weidenfeld and Nicolson, 1983.

Klamer, Arjo. *Conversations with Economists.* Totowa, NJ: Rowman and Allanheld, 1984.

Levy, Paul. *G. E. Moore and the Cambridge Apostles.* London: Weidenfeld and Nicolson, 1979.

Macmillan, Harold. *Winds of Change 1914–1939.* London: Macmillan, 1966.

Macmillan, Lord (Hugh P.). *A Man of Law's Tale.* London: Macmillan, 1952.

Marquand, David. *Ramsay MacDonald.* London: Jonathan Cape, 1971.

Martin, Kingsley. *Editor "New Statesman" Years, 1931–1945.* Chicago: Henry Regnery, 1970 (1st ed.: 1968).

———. *Father Figures: A First Volume of Autobiography.* London: Hutchinson, 1966.

Mosley, Sir Oswald. *My Life.* London: Nelson, 1968.

O'Brien, Dennis P. *Lionel Robbins.* London: Macmillan, 1988.

Robbins, Lionel. *Autobiography of an Economist.* London: Macmillan-St. Martin's Press, 1971.

Robertson, Sir Dennis. *Essays in Money and Interest* (with a memoir by Sir John Hicks). London: Collins-Fontana Library, 1966.

Samuelson, Paul A. "Dennis H. Robertson 1890–1963." *Quarterly Journal of Economics* 77 (November 1963): 517–36.

Skidelsky, Robert. *Oswald Mosley.* London: Macmillan, 1975.

Spalding, Frances. *Vanessa Bell.* New York: Ticknor and Fields, 1983.

Steel, Ronald. *Walter Lippmann and the American Century.* Boston: Little, Brown, 1980.

Woolf, Leonard. *Beginning Again: An Autobiography of the Years 1911–1918.* London: Hogarth Press, 1964.

———. *Downhill All the Way: An Autobiography of the Years 1919–1939.* London: Hogarth Press, 1967.

Woolf, Virginia. *The Diary of Virginia Woolf,* 5 vols., edited by Anne Olivier Bell. London: Hogarth Press, 1977–84.

———. *The Letters of Virginia Woolf,* 6 vols., edited by Nigel Nicolson. London: Hogarth Press, 1975–80.

———. *A Room of One's Own and Three Guineas.* London: Chatto and Windus-Hogarth Press, 1984.

Theory

Ackley, Gardner. "Liquidity Preference and Loanable Funds Theories of Interest: Comment." *American Economic Review* 47 (September 1957): 662–73.

—————. *Macroeconomic Theory.* New York: Macmillan, 1969.

Amadeo, Edward J. *Keynes's Principle of Effective Demand.* Aldershot, England: Edward Elgar, 1989.

Arestis, Philip. *The Post-Keynesian Approach to Economics.* Aldershot, England: Edward Elgar, 1992.

Baldassarri, Mario, ed. *Keynes and the Economic Policies of the 1980s.* New York: St. Martin's Press, 1992.

Balogh, Thomas. *The Irrelevance of Conventional Economics.* New York: Liveright, 1982.

Barro, Robert J., and Hershel I. Grossman, *Money, Employment and Inflation.* Cambridge: Cambridge University Press, 1976.

Bateman, Bradley W. "The Elusive Logical Relation: An Essay on Change and Continuity in Keynes's Thought." In Moggridge, *Perspectives in the History of Economic Thought,* Vol. 4: *Keynes, Macroeconomics and Method,* 73–84.

—————. "G. E. Moore and J. M. Keynes: A Missing Chapter in the History of the Expected Utility Model." *American Economic Review* 78 (December 1988): 1098–1106.

—————. "Keynes's Changing Conception of Probability." *Economics and Philosophy* 3 (April 1987): 97–120.

Bateman, Bradley W., and John B. Davis, eds. *Keynes and Philosophy: Essays on the Origin of Keynes's Thought.* Aldershot, England: Edward Elgar, 1991.

Beenstock, Michael. "*The General Theory,* Secular Stagnation, and the World Economy." In John Burton, ed., *Keynes's* General Theory: *Fifty Years On,* 121–35.

Begg, David K. H. *The Rational Expectations Revolution in Economic Theory.* Baltimore: Johns Hopkins Press, 1985.

Bell, Daniel, and Irving Kristol, eds. *The Crisis in Economic Theory.* New York: Basic Books, 1981.

Berlin, Isaiah. *Russian Thinkers.* New York: Viking, 1978.

Black, Max. "Probability." *Encyclopedia of Philosophy* (1967).

Blaug, Mark. *Economic Theory in Retrospect.* Cambridge: Cambridge University Press, 1985.

Blinder, Alan S. "Distribution Effects and the Aggregate Consumption Function." *Journal of Political Economy* 83 (1975): 447–75.

Borooah, V. K., and D. R. Sharpe, "Aggregate Consumption and the Distribution of Income in the United Kingdom: An Econometric Analysis." *Economic Journal* 96 (June 1986): 449–66.

Broad, C. D. Review of *Treatise on Probability. Mind* 31 (new series: January 1922): 72–85.

Burton, John, ed. *Keynes's* General Theory: *Fifty Years On.* London: Institute of Economic Affairs, 1986.

Cain, Neville. "Cambridge and Its Revolution: A Perspective on the Multiplier and Effective Demand." *Economic Record* 55 (June 1979): 108–17.

Carabelli, Anna M. *On Keynes's Method.* London: Macmillan, 1988.

Cardim de Carvalho, Fernando J. *Mr. Keynes and the Post Keynesians.* Aldershot, England: Edward Elgar, 1992.

Chick, Victoria. *Macroeconomics After Keynes: A Reconsideration of* The General Theory. Cambridge, MA: MIT Press, 1983.

Clower, Robert W. *Money and Markets: Essays by Robert A. Clower,* edited by Donald Walker. Cambridge: Cambridge University Press, 1984.

Coddington, Alan. *Keynesian Economics: The Search for First Principles.* London: Allen & Unwin, 1983.

Davenport, H. J. *The Economics of Alfred Marshall.* New York: Augustus M. Kelley, 1965 (1st ed.: 1935).

Davidson, Paul. "Is Probability Theory Relevant for Uncertainty? A Post Keynesian Perspective." *Journal of Economic Perspectives* 5 (Winter 1991): 129–43.

———. *Money and the Real World.* London: Macmillan, 1978 (1st ed.: 1972).

Davis, J. Ronnie. *The New Economics and the Old Economists.* Ames: Iowa State University Press, 1971.

Dernburg, Thomas F., and Duncan M. McDougall. *Macroeconomics.* New York: McGraw-Hill, 1972 (1st ed.: 1960).

Deutscher, Patrick. *R. G. Hawtrey and the Development of Macroeconomics.* London: Macmillan, 1990.

Dillard, Dudley. *The Economics of John Maynard Keynes.* New York: Prentice Hall, 1948.

Dimand, Robert W. *The Origins of the Keynesian Revolution: The Development of Keynes' Theory of Employment and Output.* Stanford, CA: Stanford University Press, 1988.

Duesenberry, James S. *Income, Saving, and the Theory of Consumer Behavior.* Cambridge, MA: Harvard University Press, 1949.

Dutt, A. K., and E. J. Amadeo. *Keynes's Third Alternative? The Neo-Ricardian Keynesians and the Post Keynesians.* Aldershot, England: Edward Elgar, 1990.

Eatwell, John, and Murray Milgate, eds. *Keynes's Economics and the Theory of Value and Distribution.* New York: Oxford University Press, 1983.

Eichner, Alfred S., ed. *A Guide to Post-Keynesian Economics.* White Plains, NY: M. E. Sharpe, 1979.

Eshag, Eprime. *From Marshall to Keynes: An Essay on the Monetary Theory of the Cambridge School.* London: Basil Blackwell, 1963.

Ferber, Robert. "Research on Household Behavior." *American Economic Review* 52 (March 1962): 19–63.

Fisher, Irving. *The Money Illusion.* New York: Adelphi, 1928.

Fitzgibbons, Athol. *Keynes's Vision: A New Political Economy.* Oxford: Clarendon Press, 1988.

Fletcher, Gordon A. *The Keynesian Revolution and Its Critics: Issues of Theory and Policy for the Monetary Production Economy.* London: Macmillan, 1987.

Fouraker, Lawrence E. "The Cambridge Didactic Style." *Journal of Political Economy* 46 (February 1958): 65–73.

Foxwell, H. S. Review of *Indian Currency and Finance. Economic Journal* 23 (December 1913): 561–72.

Fusfeld, Daniel R. *Economics.* Lexington, MA: D. C. Heath, 1971.

Gali, Jordi. "How Well Does the IS–LM Model Fit Postwar U. S. Data?" *Quarterly Journal of Economics* 107 (May 1992): 709–38.

Garraty, John A. *Unemployment in History: Economic Thought and Public Policy.* New York: Harper & Row, 1978.

Garrison, Roger W. "Keynesian Splenetics: From Social Philosophy to Macroeconomics." *Critical Review* 6 (Fall 1992): 471–92.

Geiringer, Hilda. "Probability: Objective Theory." *Dictionary of the History of Ideas* (1973).

Gerrard, Bill, and John Hillard, eds. *The Philosophy and Economics of J. M. Keynes.* Aldershot, England: Edward Elgar, 1992.

Glahe, Fred R. *Keynes's* General Theory...: *A Concordance.* Savage, MD: Bowman & Littlefield, 1991.

Golloday, Fredrick L. *Macroeconomics.* Menlo Park, CA: Benjamin-Cummings, 1978.

Gordon, Robert J. *Milton Friedman's Monetary Framework.* Chicago: University of Chicago Press, 1974.

Gregory, Paul R. *Essentials of Economics.* Glenview, IL: Scott Foresman-Little Brown, 1990.

Hacking, Ian. *The Emergence of Probability.* Cambridge: Cambridge University Press, 1975.

Hansen, Alvin H. *Economic Policy and Full Employment.* New York: McGraw-Hill, 1947.

— — —. "Economic Progress and Declining Population Growth." *American Economic Review* 29 (March 1939): 1–15.

— — —. *Federal Fiscal Policy Required for Full Employment.* Pamphlet. New York: New York University, 1946.

— — —. *Fiscal Policy and Business Cycles.* New York: Norton, 1941.

— — —. *Full Recovery or Stagnation.* New York: Norton, 1938.

— — —. *A Guide to Keynes.* New York: McGraw-Hill, 1953.

Harcourt, G. C. *Controversies in Political Economy.* New York: New York University Press, 1986.

— — —. *On Political Economists and Modern Political Economy,* edited by Claudio Sardoni. London and New York: Routledge, 1992.

— — —, ed. *Keynes and His Contemporaries.* New York: St. Martin's, 1985.

Hardy, Charles O. Review of *Treatise on Money. American Economic Review* 21 (March 1931): 150–55.

Harris, Seymour E. *John Maynard Keynes: Economist and Policy Maker.* New York: Scribner's Sons, 1955.

— — —, ed. *The New Economics: Keynes' Influence on Theory and Public Policy.* New York: Augustus M. Kelley, 1965 (reprint with additional articles; 1st ed.: 1947).

Hawtrey, Ralph G. *The Art of Central Banking.* London: Frank Cass, 1962 (1st ed.: 1932).

— — —. *Capital and Employment.* London: Longmans, Green, 1937.

Hayek, Friedrich A. *New Studies in Philosophy, Politics, Economics, and the History of Ideas.* Chicago: University of Chicago Press, 1978.

―――. *Prices and Production.* London: George Routledge, 1935 (2d revised and enlarged edition).

―――."Reflections on the Pure Theory of Money of Mr. J. M. Keynes," parts 1, 2. *Economica* 11 (old series: August 1931): 270-95; 12 (old series: February 1932): 22-44.

―――. *A Tiger by the Tail: The Keynesian Legacy of Inflation.* San Francisco: Cato Institute, 1979.

Hazlitt, Henry. *The Failure of the "New Economics."* Lanham, MD: University Press of America, 1983 (1st ed.: 1959).

―――, ed. *The Critics of Keynesian Economics.* New Rochelle, NY: Arlington House, 1977.

Helburn, Suzanne W., and David F. Bramhall, eds. *Marx, Schumpeter, Keynes.* Armonk, NY: M. E. Sharpe, 1986.

Hicks, John R. *Collected Essays on Economic Theory.* 3 vols. Cambridge, MA: Harvard University Press, 1981-83.

―――. *The Crisis in Keynesian Economics.* New York: Basic Books, 1974.

―――. *Critical Essays in Monetary Theory.* Oxford: Clarendon Press, 1967.

―――. "Recollections and Documents." *Economica* 40 (February 1973): 2-11.

―――. "A Rehabilitation of 'Classical' Economics?" *Economic Journal* 67 (June 1957): 278-89.

―――. *Value and Capital.* Oxford: Clarendon Press, 1939.

Hill, Roger, ed. *Keynes, Money and Monetarism.* London: Macmillan, 1989.

Hilliard, John, ed. *J. M. Keynes in Retrospect: The Legacy of the Keynesian Revolution.* Aldershot, England: Edward Elgar, 1988.

Hutchinson, T. W. *The Politics and Philosophy of Economics: Marxians, Keynesians and Austrians.* New York: New York University Press, 1984.

Hutt, W. H. *Keynesianism—Retrospect and Prospect.* Chicago: Regnery, 1963.

Johnson, Harry G. "The General Theory after 25 Years." In Natalie Marshall, ed., *Keynes: Updated or Outdated,* 39-49.

―――. "Monetary Theory and Policy." *American Economic Review* 52 (June 1962): 335-78.

————. *On Economics and Society.* Chicago: University of Chicago Press, 1978.

————. "Some Cambridge Controversies in Monetary Theory." *Review of Economic Studies* 19 (1951–52): 90–104.

Kahn, Richard F. *The Economics of the Short Period.* London: Macmillan, 1989.

————. *The Making of Keynes' General Theory.* Cambridge: Cambridge University Press, 1984.

————. "The Relation of Home Investment to Unemployment." *Economic Journal* 41 (June 1931): 173–98.

Keynes, John Neville. *The Scope and Method of Political Economy.* New York: Kelley & Millman, 1955 (1st ed.: 1891).

————. *Studies and Exercises in Formal Logic.* London: Macmillan, 1906 (1st ed.: 1884).

Kindleberger, Charles P. *Keynesianism and Monetarism.* London: George Allen & Unwin, 1986.

Klein, Lawrence R. *The Keynesian Revolution.* New York: Macmillan, 1947.

Knight, Frank H. *Risk, Uncertainty and Profit.* Chicago: University of Chicago Press, 1985.

————. "Unemployment: And Mr. Keynes's Revolution in Economic Theory." In Hazlitt, ed., *The Critics of Keynesian Economics,* 67–95.

Kruger, Lorenz, Lorraine J. Daston, and Michael Heidelberger. *The Probabilistic Revolution.* 2 vols. Cambridge, MA: Bradford–MIT Press, 1987.

Kyburg, Henry E., Jr. *Epistemology and Inference.* Minneapolis: University of Minnesota Press, 1983.

Laidler, David. *The Demand for Money: Theories and Evidence.* Scranton, PA: International Textbook Co., 1969.

————. *The Golden Age of the Quantity Theory: The Development of Neoclassical Monetary Economics 1870–1914.* London: Philip Allan, 1991.

Lambert, Paul. "The Evolution of Keynes's Thought from the *Treatise on Money* to the *General Theory.*" *Annals of Public and Co-operative Economy* 40 (July–September 1969): 243–63.

Lavington, Frederick. "Uncertainty in Its Relation to the Net Rate of Interest." *Economic Journal* 22 (September 1912): 398–409.

Lawson, Tony, and Hashem Pesaran, eds. *Keynes' Economics: Methodological Issues.* Canberra and London: Croom Helm, 1985.

Leijonhufvud, Axel. *Keynes and the Classics.* Pamphlet. London: Institute of Economic Affairs, 1969.

———. *On Keynesian Economics and the Economics of Keynes.* New York: Oxford University Press, 1968.

Lekachman, Robert *The Age of Keynes.* New York: Random House, 1966.

———, ed. *Keynes's* General Theory: *Reports of Three Decades.* New York: St. Martin's Press, 1964.

Leontief, Wassily W. "The Fundamental Assumption of Mr. Keynes's Monetary Theory of Unemployment." *Quarterly Journal of Economics* 51 (November 1936): 192–97.

Littleboy, Bruce. *On Interpreting Keynes: A Study in Reconciliation.* London and New York: Routledge, 1990.

Lubell, Harold. "Effects of Redistribution of Income on Consumers' Expenditure." *American Economic Review* 37 (March 1947): 157–70.

McConnell, Campbell R. *Economics: Principles, Problems, and Policies.* 6th ed. New York: McGraw-Hill, 1975.

Maclachlan, Fiona C. *Keynes's General Theory of Interest: A Reconsideration.* London and New York: Routledge, 1993.

Malinvaud, Edmond. *The Theory of Unemployment Reconsidered.* Oxford: Basil Blackwell, 1977.

Mankiw, N. Gregory, ed. "Symposium: Keynesian Economics Today," *Journal of Economic Perspectives* 7 (Winter 1993): 3–82.

Mankiw, N. Gregory, and David Romer, eds. *New Keynesian Economics.* 2 vols. Cambridge, MA: MIT Press, 1991.

Marshall, Alfred. *Principles of Economics,* 2 vols., edited by C. W. Guillebaud. London: Macmillan, 1961 (9th variorum ed.; 1st ed.: 1890).

Marshall, Natalie, ed. *Keynes: Updated or Outdated?* Lexington, MA: D. C. Heath, 1970.

Meltzer, Allan H. *Keynes's Monetary Theory: A Different Interpretation.* Cambridge: Cambridge University Press, 1985.

Milgate, Murray. *Capital and Employment: A Study of Keynes's Economics.* New York: Academic Press, 1982.

Miller, Roger Leroy. *Economics Today.* San Francisco: Canfield Press, 1972.

Mini, Piero V. *Keynes, Bloomsbury and* The General Theory. London: Macmillan, 1991.

Minsky, Hyman P. "The Financial Instability Hypothesis." In Wood, ed. *JMK: Critical Assessments,* 4: 282–92.

————. *John Maynard Keynes.* New York: Columbia University Press, 1975.

Mises, Ludwig von. *Epistemological Problems of Economics.* New York: New York University Press, 1981.

Mises, Richard von. *Probability, Statistics and Truth.* New York: Dover, 1981 (1st German ed.: 1928).

Mitchell, B. R. *European Historical Statistics, 1750–1970.* Abridged edition. New York: Columbia University Press, 1978.

Moggridge, Donald E. *Perspectives in the History of Economic Thought, Vol. 4: Keynes, Macroeconomics and Method.* Aldershot, England: Edward Elgar, 1990.

Moore, G. E. *Principia Ethica.* Cambridge: Cambridge University Press, 1962 (1st ed.: 1903).

Mueller, M. G., ed. *Readings in Macroeconomics.* London: Holt, Rinehart & Winston, 1969.

O'Donnell, R. M. *Keynes: Philosophy, Economics and Politics.* New York: St. Martin's Press, 1989.

————. "The Unwritten Books and Papers of J. M. Keynes." *History of Political Economy* 24 (Winter 1992): 769–817.

————, ed. *Keynes as Philosopher-Economist.* New York: St. Martin's Press, 1991.

Ohlin, Bertil. "Some Notes on the Stockholm Theory of Savings and Interest." *Economic Journal* 47, part 1 (March 1937): 53–69; part 2 (June 1937): 221–40.

Patinkin, Don. *Anticipations of the* General Theory? *And Other Essays on Keynes.* Chicago: University of Chicago Press, 1984.

————. "John Maynard Keynes." *The New Palgrave* (1987 edition).

————. "Keynes and Economics Today." Papers and Proceedings. *American Economic Review* 74 (May 1984): 97–101.

————. "Keynesian Economics Rehabilitated: A Rejoinder to Professor Hicks." *Economic Journal* 69 (September 1959): 582–87.

————. *Keynes' Monetary Thought.* Durham, NC: Duke University Press, 1976.

————. *Money, Interest, and Prices: An Integration of Monetary and Value Theory.* Evanston, IL: Row, Peterson, 1956.

————. "On Different Interpretations of the *General Theory.*" *Journal of Monetary Economics* 26 (1990): 203–43.

Patinkin, Don, and J. Clark Keith, eds. *Keynes, Cambridge and the* General Theory. Toronto: Toronto University Press, 1978.

Pigou, Arthur C. *Industrial Fluctuations*. London: Macmillan, 1929.

———. *Keynes's* General Theory. London: Macmillan, 1950.

———. "Mr. J. M. Keynes' *General Theory....*" In Wood, ed. *JMK: Critical Assessments*, 2: 18-31.

———. *Unemployment*. London: Williams & Norgate, 1913.

Presley, J. R. *Robertsonian Economics*. London: Macmillan, 1978.

Ramsey, Frank P. *The Foundations of Mathematics and Other Logical Essays*. London: Kegan Paul, Trench, Trubner, 1931.

Robertson, Dennis H. *Banking Policy and the Price Level*. London: P. S. King, 1926.

———. *Essays in Monetary Theory*. London: P. S. King, 1940.

———. *Money*. Chicago: University of Chicago Press, 1959 (1st ed.: 1922).

———. "Mr Keynes's Theory of Money." *Economic Journal* 41 (September 1931): 395-411.

———. Review of *The Economic Consequences of the Peace*. *Economic Journal* 30 (March 1920): 77-84.

———. "Some Notes on Mr Keynes's General Theory of Employment." *Quarterly Journal of Economics* 51 (November 1936): 168-91.

Robinson, Joan. *Collected Economic Papers*. 5 vols. Oxford: Basil Blackwell, 1951-79.

———. *Contributions to Modern Economics*. Oxford: Basil Blackwell, 1978.

———. *The Economics of Imperfect Competition*. London: Macmillan, 1933.

———. *An Essay on Marxian Economics*. London: Macmillan, 1942.

———. *Further Contributions to Modern Economics*. Oxford: Basil Blackwell, 1980.

———. "A Parable on Savings and Investment." *Economica* 13 (old series: February 1932): 75-84.

———. *The Rate of Interest and Other Essays*. London: Macmillan, 1952.

———. "What are the Questions?" *Journal of Economic Literature* 15 (December 1977): 318-39.

Rousseas, Stephen. *Post Keynesian Economics*. Armonk, NY: M. E. Sharpe, 1986.

Ruffin, Roy J., and Paul R. Gregory. *Principles of Macroeconomics*. Glenview, IL: Scott, Foresman–Little, Brown. 1990.

Russell, Bertrand. *Human Knowledge: Its Scope and Limits.* London: George Allen & Unwin, 1948.

———. Review of *Treatise on Probability. Mathematical Gazette* 11 (July 1922): 119-25.

Rymes, Thomas K. *Keynes's Lectures Notes of a Representative Student.* London: Macmillan, 1989.

Samuelson, Paul A. *Economics.* 9th, 10th eds. New York: McGraw-Hill, 1973, 1976.

———. "Economists and the History of Ideas." *American Economic Review* 52 (March 1962): 1-17.

———. "Lord Keynes and *The General Theory.*" In Wood, ed., *JMK: Critical Assessments,* 2: 190-202.

Samuelson, Paul A., and William D. Nordhaus. *Economics.* 13th, 14th eds. New York: McGraw-Hill, 1989, 1992.

Sawyer, Malcolm C. *The Economics of Michal Kalecki.* Armonk, NY: M. E. Sharpe, 1985.

———, ed. *Post-Keynesian Economics.* Aldershot, England: Edward Elgar, 1988.

Schumpeter, Joseph A. *Capitalism, Socialism and Democracy.* New York: Harper Colophon, 1975.

———. *Essays of J. A. Schumpeter,* edited by R. V. Clemence. Cambridge, MA: Addison-Wesley Press, 1951.

———. *History of Economic Analysis.* New York: Oxford University Press, 1986.

———. "Science and Ideology." *American Economic Review* 39 (March 1949): 345-59.

———. *Ten Great Economists.* London: Allen & Unwin, 1952.

Seligman, Ben B. *Main Currents in Modern Economics.* 3 vols. Chicago: Quadrangle, 1971.

Shackle, G. L. S. *Imagination and the Nature of Choice.* Edinburgh: Edinburgh University Press, 1979.

———. *The Nature of Economic Thought.* Selected Papers 1955-64. Cambridge: Cambridge University Press, 1966.

———. *The Years of High Theory: Invention and Tradition in Economic Thought 1926-1939.* Cambridge: Cambridge University Press, 1983 (1st ed.: 1967).

Shaw, E. S. "False Issues in the Interest-Theory Controversy." *Journal of Political Economy* 46 (December 1938): 838-56.

Shaw, G. K. *Keynesian Economics: The Permanent Revolution.* Aldershot, England: Edward Elgar, 1988.

———. *The Keynesian Heritage.* 2 vols. Aldershot, England: Edward Elgar, 1983.

———. *Rational Expectations.* New York: St. Martins's Press, 1984.

Silk, Leonard. *Contemporary Economics: Principles and Issues.* New York: McGraw-Hill, 1975.

Skousen, Mark, ed. *Dissent on Keynes: A Critical Appraisal of Keynesian Economics.* New York: Praeger, 1992.

Smith, Warren L. "Monetary Theories of the Rate of Interest: A Dynamic Analysis." *Review of Economics and Statistics* 40 (1958): 15–21.

Sraffa, Piero. "Dr. Hayek on Money and Capital." *Economic Journal* 42 (March 1932): 42–53.

Stigler, George J. *The Intellectual and the Marketplace.* Cambridge, MA: Harvard University Press, 1984.

Tarshis, Lorie. "Post-Keynesian Economics: A Promise that Bounced?" Papers and Proceedings. *American Economic Review* 70 (May 1980): 10–14.

Taussig, Frank W. "Consumption and the National Dividend." *Quarterly Journal of Economics* 51 (November 1936): 198–203.

Thurow, Lester C. *Dangerous Currents: The State of Economics.* New York: Random House, 1984.

Trevithick, J. A. *Involuntary Unemployment.* New York and London: Harvester Wheatsheaf, 1992.

Tsiang, S. C. "Liquidity Preference and Loanable Funds Theories, Multiplier and Velocity Analyses: A Synthesis." *American Economic Review* 46 (September 1956): 539–64.

Turner, Marjorie S. *Joan Robinson and the Americans.* Armonk, NY: M. E. Sharpe, 1989.

Vicarelli, Fausto. *Keynes: The Instability of Capitalism.* Philadelphia: University of Pennsylvania Press, 1984.

Viner, Jacob. "Mr. Keynes on the Causes of Unemployment." *Quarterly Journal of Economics* 51 (November 1936): 147–67.

Warming, Jens. "International Difficulties Arising Out of the Financing of Public Works During Depression." *Economic Journal* 42 (June 1932): 211–24.

Weintraub, Sidney. *Keynes, Keynesians and Monetarists*. Philadelphia: University of Pennsylvania Press, 1978.

——, ed. *Modern Economic Thought*. Philadelphia: University of Pennsylvania Press, 1977.

Wicksell, Knut. *Interest and Prices*. Translated by R. F. Kahn. London: Macmillan, 1936 (German ed.: 1898).

Williams, J. H. "The Monetary Doctrines of J. M. Keynes." *Quarterly Journal of Economics* 45 (August 1931): 547–87.

Wood, John Cunningham, ed. *John Maynard Keynes: Critical Assessments*. 4 vols. Canberra and London: Croom Helm, 1983.

Worswick, David, and James Trevithick, eds. *Keynes and the Modern World*. Cambridge: Cambridge University Press, 1983.

Wright, David McCord. *The Keynesian System*. New York: Fordham University Press, 1962.

Yellen, Janet L. "On Keynesian Economics and the Economics of the Post-Keynesians." Papers and Proceedings. *American Economic Review* 70 (May 1980): 15–19.

Young, Warren. *Interpreting Mr. Keynes: The IS–LM Enigma*. Cambridge: Polity Press, 1987.

Policy and Events

Aldcroft, Derek H. *From Versailles to Wall Street 1919–1929*. Berkeley: University of California Press, 1981.

Bagchi, Amiya K. *The Presidency Banks and the Indian Economy*. Published on Behalf of the State Bank of India. Calcutta: Oxford University Press, 1989.

Beveridge, Sir William H. "An Economic General Staff," parts 1, 2. *The Nation* 34 (29 December 1923; 5 January 1924): 485–86, 509–10.

Buchanan, James M., and Richard E. Wagner. *Democracy in Deficit: The Political Legacy of Lord Keynes*. New York: Academic Press, 1977.

Cairncross, Alec, and Barry Eichengreen. *Sterling in Decline: The Devaluations of 1931, 1949 and 1967*. Oxford: Blackwell, 1983.

Cecco, Marcello de. *Money and Empire: The International Gold Standard 1890–1914*. Totowa, NJ: Rowan & Littlefield, 1975.

Clarke, Peter. *The Keynesian Revolution in the Making, 1924–1936*. Oxford: Clarendon Press, 1988.

Collins, Robert M. *The Business Response to Keynes, 1929–1964.* New York: Columbia University Press, 1981.

Committee on Finance and Industry. *Report.* (Cmd. 3897). London: H. M. Stationery Office, 1969 (reprint).

———. *Minutes of Evidence Taken before the Committee on Finance and Industry.* 2 vols. London: H. M. Stationery Office, 1931.

Cutler, Tony, Karel Williams, and John Williams. *Keynes, Beveridge and Beyond.* London: Routledge & Kegan Paul, 1986.

Donaldson, Frances. *The Marconi Scandal.* London: Rupert Hart-Davis, 1962.

Dow, J. C. R. *The Management of the British Economy 1945–60.* Cambridge: Cambridge University Press, 1970.

Eyck, Erich. *A History of the Weimar Republic.* 2 vols. New York: John Wiley, 1967.

Felix, David. *Walther Rathenau and the Weimar Republic: The Politics of Reparations.* Baltimore: Johns Hopkins Press, 1971.

Fink, Carole. *The Genoa Conference.* Chapel Hill: University of North Carolina Press, 1984.

Galbraith, John Kenneth. "How Keynes Came to America." In *A Contemporary Guide to Economics Peace and Laughter,* 43–59. Boston: Houghton Mifflin, 1971.

———. *A Life in Our Times.* Boston: Houghton Mifflin, 1981.

Garraty, John A. *The Great Depression.* New York: Harcourt Brace Jovanovich, 1986.

Germany. Statistisches Amt. *Statistisches Jahrbuch für das Deutsche Reich,* 1937.

Grigg, P. J. *Prejudice and Judgment.* London: Jonathan Cape, 1948.

Hall, Peter A., ed. *The Political Power of Economic Ideas: Keynesianism Across Nations.* Princeton: Princeton University Press, 1989.

Howson, Susan. "'A Dear Money Man'?: Keynes on Monetary Policy, 1920." *Economic Journal* 83 (June 1973): 456–64.

———. *Domestic Monetary Management in Britain 1919–38.* Cambridge: Cambridge University Press, 1975.

Howson, Susan, and Donald Winch. *The Economic Advisory Council 1930–1939.* Cambridge: Cambridge University Press, 1977.

Jenkins, Roy. *Asquith.* New York: Chilmark Press, 1965.

Kaminsky, Arnold P. *The India Office 1880–1910.* Westport, CT: Greenwood, 1986.

Kent, Bruce. *The Spoils of War: The Politics, Economics, and Diplomacy of Reparations 1918–1932.* Oxford: Clarendon Press, 1987.

Kindleberger, Charles P. *A Financial History of Western Europe.* London: George Allen & Unwin, 1985.

———. *The World in Depression.* Berkeley: University of California Press, 1973.

Lentin, Antony. *Lloyd George, Woodrow Wilson, and the Guilt of Germany: An Essay on the Pre-History of Appeasement.* Leicester, England: Leicester University Press, 1984.

Liberal Industrial Inquiry. *Britain's Industrial Future.* London: Ernest Benn, 1928.

Marx, Karl, and Friedrich Engels. *The Marx–Engels Reader,* 2d ed., edited by Robert C. Tucker. New York: Norton, 1978.

Medlicott, W. N. *Contemporary England 1914–1964.* London: Longman, 1976.

Moggridge, Donald E. *British Monetary Policy 1924–1931: The Norman Conquest of $4.86.* Cambridge: Cambridge University Press, 1972.

Morgan, E. Victor. *Studies in British Financial Policy, 1914–25.* London: Macmillan, 1952.

Peden, G. C. "Sir Richard Hopkins and the 'Keynesian Revolution' in Economic Policy, 1929–1945." *Economic History Review* 36 (second series: May 1983): 281–96.

Perkins, Frances. *The Roosevelt I Knew.* New York: Viking, 1946.

Rowse, A. L. *Mr. Keynes and the Labour Movement.* London: Macmillan, 1936.

Sayers, R. S. *The Bank of England 1891–1944.* 3 vols. Cambridge: Cambridge University Press, 1976.

Stein, Herbert. *The Fiscal Revolution in America.* Chicago: University of Chicago Press, 1969.

Index*

* The major economic factors and conceptions, e.g., employment, liquidity preference, etc., can also be found under the entry for *The General Theory*.